# PSYCHOTHERAPY
## *The Purchase of Friendship*

# PSYCHOTHERAPY

## *The Purchase of Friendship*

### WILLIAM SCHOFIELD

*With a New Introduction by the Author*

Transaction Books
New Brunswick (U.S.A.) and Oxford (U.K.)

Library of Congress Catalog Number: 86–1355
ISBN: 0–88738–659–8
Printed in the United States of America

**Library of Congress Cataloging in Publication Data**

Schofield, William
   Psychotherapy: the purchase of friendship.

   Reprint. Originally published: Englewood Cliffs,
N.J.: Prentice-Hall, © 1964.
   Bibliography:p.
   1. Psychotherapy.   I. Title.   [DNLM: 1. Psychotherapy.
WM 420 S367p 1964a]
RC480.S25 1986      616.89′ 14      86-1355
ISBN 0–88738–659–8

*To*
*William M. Grimshaw*
*and the late*
*Albert Z. Mann*
*warm friends, wise counselors*

# Acknowledgments (1964)

No book is truly written by one man. Rather, each author has inherited something of the wisdom, something of the inspiration, and something of the dedication of his teachers—to this may be added the seasoning of his particular perspectives—and his writing is an effort to test his own understanding and to fulfill in part his obligations to his teachers. I am pleased to dedicate this volume to two of my earliest teachers, with deepest gratitude for their sensitive counsel and vital encouragement.

I acknowledge my great debt to those psychologists with whom it has been my good fortune to study and my special pleasure to be professionally associated. Foremost among these are the late Donald G. Paterson, and Professors Starke R. Hathaway and Paul E. Meehl.

It will be obvious that this work could be produced only in a climate of psychology that encourages students to "think otherwise" and to respect evidence, or the lack of it. In this sense, I am indebted to all of my former preceptors and present colleagues of the Department of Psychology at the University of Minnesota.

A special word of acknowledgment is due to Dr. Donald W. Hastings, Head of the Department of Psychiatry of the University of Minnesota Medical School—the setting in which I have spent the major portion of my professional time during the past seventeen years. His ready willingness to provide a hospitable and rewarding environment for *all* mental health workers, and his consistent orientation toward meeting the demands of the future in preference to maintaining an already outmoded *status quo*, have been a source of important stimulation. I am grateful, too, for the informal help given by many of my colleagues in the Department of Psychiatry.

Acknowledgment is gratefully made to those publishers who have graciously consented to reproductions from their works: American Orthopsychiatric Association; American Psychiatric Association;

viii

American Psychological Association; American Public Health Association; Grune and Stratton, Inc.; Harper & Row, Publishers, Inc.; Harvard University Press; Johns Hopkins Press; McGraw-Hill Book Co., Inc.; Milbank Memorial Fund; Nation Company, Inc.; W. W. Norton and Company, Inc.; and W. B. Saunders Company. Special acknowledgment is made to Basic Books, Inc., Publishers for their permission to draw extensively from their publications of the monographs of the Joint Commission on Mental Illness and Health, and to John Wiley & Sons, Inc. for permission to quote from August B. Hollingshead and Frederick C. Redlich's, *Social Class and Mental Illness.*

I am grateful also for the permissions to quote that were kindly granted by Professor Hans Jurgen Eysenck, Dr. Benjamin Malzberg, Dr. Nathan K. Rickles, Professor Saul Rosenzweig, and Dr. Lewis R. Wolberg.

I am indebted to Mrs. Colleen J. Vergin for her excellent assistance in preparation of the manuscript.

Finally, I am most grateful to my wife, Geraldine Bryan Schofield, who in a very rich variety of ways has made it impossible for me not to write, and whose unpurchasable friendship has been a continuous inspiration.

W. S.

# Acknowledgments (1986)

I am indebted to those colleagues, students, clients, and friends who, over the last twenty years, have directly stimulated my continuing study of psychotherapy, both as a clinical field and a social phenomenon. I am particularly indebted to those colleagues and students who, especially since the work went out of print in 1974, expressed a continuing wish to have it once more available. I am especially very indebted to Irving Louis Horowitz for his interest and encouragement, and for the compliment of having the work included in a series of "classics." I am very grateful to Katherine Sarkanen for the cheerful patience and care with which she prepared the several drafts of the manuscript.

# Introduction to the Transaction Edition

## William Schofield

Two decades have passed since the first publication of this work. In reflecting on recent history one is inclined to view the period as unusually tumultuous and marked by more rapid change than has characterized earlier periods. Whether such perception is valid or distorted by the continuing reverberations of the most recent developments, there must be recognition that the last two decades have been marked by some events that have continuing impact on our lives. There have been others that may be viewed best as marking one extreme of particular social pendulums that will revert, possibly briefly, to middle ground before rising to the opposite vertex.

In the past twenty years we have witnessed social, political, economic, and cultural evolution—marked by achievements to be applauded and by decadence to be decried. We are all washed by the waves of history that may carry us ashore to safe footing or tow us toward an ocean of hopelessness.

> You can drum on immense drums
> the monotonous daily motions of the people
> taking from earth and air
> their morsels of bread and love,
> a carryover from yesterday into tomorrow.
> You can blow on great brass horns
> the awful clamors of war and revolution
> when swarming anonymous shadowshapes
> obliterate the old names,
> Big names and cross out what was
> and offer what is on a fresh new page.

> —Carl Sandburg

As humans in the last years of the twentieth century the communication media make us daily and immediate witness to events in every sector of our planet. We witness a culmination of human aspiration when man walks on the moon. We witness a frustration of humanity when hordes of our fellow beings starve to death. What we see and hear of our world can empower our capacity for inspiration or fuel the engines of our despondency.

Can it be, in the words of Wordsworth (1806), that "the world is too much with us, late and soon"? Can it be that a significant portion of those persons who are entered in our social ledgers as emotionally disturbed, or mentally ill, are in fact suffering at core from a pernicious demoralization (Frank, 1982)? Can it be that our mental health professionals are inadequately attuned, if aware at all, of the need to distinguish when it is best to support repression in the service of the ego and when it is better to stimulate inspiration in the service of the will (Schofield, 1979)? Can it be that we are training a cadre of professionals who are especially adept at curing fears of snakes and spiders and peculiarly inept at treating conditions of demoralization after they have been carelessly diagnosed as affective disorders?

In the last two decades we have seen signs of hope and signals of despair. An American black, Martin Luther King, Jr., received the Nobel Peace Prize, and later fell to an assassin's bullet. The assassination of President John F. Kennedy inspired his followers to carry on the dream of a Great Society with the goals of equality of opportunity and justice. Our progressive enmirement in Vietnam fostered the omnipresent "guns or butter" debate and led to economic derangements that are now experienced in a deficit economy and to a conflict of impaired civility between the "haves" and "have nots," marked in the extreme by urban riots. As political power has passed from the liberals to the conservatives, the economic pressure of the national deficit has provided a rationale for budgetary assaults on social service programs generally, and particularly on those that provide care to the emotionally and mentally distressed.

The political-economic pressure to reduce funds for social programs has been rationalized also by the needs of "national defense." As our international relations, especially with the U.S.S.R., have moved from cold war to detente to cold war, we are constantly reminded of the threat of nuclear war, with efforts to persuade us that our only safeguard against our "enemy" is our potential to threaten inescapable retaliation in kind. It is impossible to calibrate the degree to which the threat of nuclear annihilation is increasingly perceived as real and imminent, and thus contributes as a silent factor in the complex of more immediate stressors that produce demoralization, alienation, anomie, or depression. It is reasonable to surmise that it may be a contributing factor in the disenchantment of our youth who, having no faith in a long-range future, settle for the immediate satisfaction afforded by drugs, or end their uncertainty and powerlessness by the total withdrawal of suicide, a tragedy that has quadrupled in frequency among teenagers since 1960.

Counselor-therapists who might be able to combat the "nothing really matters" syndrome of the client who knows that eventually the sun will burn out are faced with a more difficult challenge by the client who is convinced that his or her children have no future.

There are significant developments with promise for a better social environment. Notable among these is the women's movement, dramatically exemplified in the effort to achieve passage of the Equal Rights Amendment to the Constitution. In a variety of other ways, women have expressed successfully their demand for equality of recognition, respect, and role parity in our culture. Their self-directed efforts at consciousness raising have had spin-off benefits for males who have appreciated the stimulus to escape the fetters of their "macho" role assignments. As women have "come out" of the kitchen, homosexuals have in increasing numbers come out of the "closet." The Gay Liberation and the women's movement have moved us to a freer, less repressive culture. As with all such movements, there must be concern that the goal of equality of opportunity is neither subverted nor distorted by demands for special treatment. With upheaval in cultural norms, many individuals experience both personal and interpersonal conflicts. They may benefit from psychological counseling if their counselors are not constrained by role stereotypes of their own, conscious or unconscious. It is stereotypic thinking and counter to the spirit of these movements to argue that, e.g., only a female therapist truly can understand a female client, and vice versa (not withstanding Freud's famous puzzlement!).

Of no lesser importance than the women's movement and the liberation of homosexuals is the movement to bring recognition, concern, and correction to the neglect and repression of a very large segment of our population—the elderly. This movement, exemplified nationally by the Gray Panthers, has sharpened public awareness that the percentage of our population over age 65 is nearly 12 percent and growing steadily. Our senior citizens require and deserve not only to be physically and economically secure, but to be provided also with challenge and opportunity to continue an active, productive investment of interest and energy in the world about them. There are probably no diseases of aging to which the elderly are more susceptible than those of psychological isolation and depression. Mental health professionals have been alerted to the broad public health challenge of our graying population and are addressing the problems of "geropsychology" with renewed research interest and programs of clinical intervention (Poon, 1980).

Of equal promise is the growing recognition that our natural resources are finite and endangered. With the battle of the conservators and the exploiters joined, there has been a raising of consciousness and opportunities to join the effort to preserve our inheritance and protect our resources. An element in much neurotic maladjustment is an over-investment in self and some degree of isolation from or indifference to concerns of the community. Environmentalism is but one of many social causes with which an individual can find the support of comrades-in-arms. The therapist-counselor must be aware of a patient's deficiency of perspective. What's the value of "success" if we end up with water that is not potable and air that is unbreathable?

Science and technology have brought discovery and invention that have increased tremendously our capacities to control, correct, and communicate. Among the more "silent" advances is the perfection of the laser, with application to retinal repair as one example among many. In contrast, touching nearly everyone's life has been the development and widespread application of computer technology. Within this technological advance, the dispersion of the so-called personal computer has been of such magnitude as to create a new subculture. And an interesting paradox is presented, since the personal computer can mediate very impersonal communication!

Research to develop computer programs that could "treat" distressed individuals (via computer-mediated "conversation") is a rather fringe effort. However, in recent years there has been extensive development of computer-based methods of "assessment," including extensive history-taking (Reynolds et al., 1985). In essence, a client can be interrogated (*not* interviewed!), can record responses, have those responses tabulated, scored, profiled, and interpreted (diagnosed) without the distracting (?) sight and sound of another human. In the worst case scenario (not necessarily an imaginative fiction) the client of the impersonal computer can receive a diagnosis and possibly even a prescription for action without personal interaction with a professional! Every technological advance has the potential for abuse; we rarely fail to exercise that potential. In the application of computers to the field of mental health, the greatest risk of abuse rests with those professionals who, lacking sensitivity to the issues of validity, reliability, and errors of measurement, may be seduced by the appearance of machine objectivity and cost-benefit arguments.

Advances in medical science have included discoveries that promise greater control over our lives, together with the need for difficult ethical decisions. The successes of organ transplant surgery have brought hard questions of how to select recipients when demand for organs exceeds supply, and how to finance the high costs of these procedures. The question of the wishes and the psychological needs of both donor and recipient have been relatively neglected in the implicit assumption that we must always do whatever is doable. These hard questions have been brought to a critical focus with the recent demonstrations of the artificial heart (Starzl, 1985; Annas, 1985).

The implications for mental health (and mental illness) are even more pressing as a result of achievements in the biology of reproduction and gene identification. Making it possible for childless couples to know the joy of their own natural children through in vitro conception and artificial insemination is an unmixed blessing. As procedures to enable couples to predetermine the sex of their children become more reliable, the certainty of the "blessing" is less clear. The use of "surrogate wombs" has already revealed the potential for psychological distress in both "donors" and recipients. Finally, we see the power of medical technology called to the service of self-realization or self-actualization by women who demand the right to bear and raise children without the encumbrances of wifehood and traditional family, responding to a psychological need that can be satisfied by proper access to a nameless sperm bank (Walters, 1979). It is doable; should it be done (Sarason, 1984)? Do mental health professionals have the knowledge and concern to prepare for a generation whose hunger for identity may be expressed by a paraphrase of the old hymn, "I feel like a fatherless child"?

In the past twenty years the collaboration of physical and biological scientists has provided medicine with instrumentation for increasingly precise examination of the functioning of the human at anatomic, cellular, molecular, and submolecular levels. Such methods as computerized axial tomography (CAT-scan), magnetic resonance imaging, and positron emission tomography (PET) require very expensive instrumentation; the cost of establishing a PET laboratory is estimated at $2,000,000. The cost to the front-line medical center of such powerful instruments for research and diagnosis cannot be regained simply by direct charges to the patients for whom their use is indicated, but must be amortized by increases in base fees to all clients of the center. This is but one example of many in which the advances of science have led to the increasing cost of medical care. In recent years the cost of health care has increased steadily until it now exceeds 10 percent of our gross national product. Finding mechanisms to contain these rising costs while making the benefits of our scientific advances available to our citizens has been in the forefront of social challenges in the 1980s. Both the federal government and private insurers have developed plans to contain the rising costs of medical care. Most notable has been the development, supported by federal start-up grants, of health maintenance organizations (HMOs). These are essentially prepaid, per capita programs of health insurance for large groups in which participating physicians are rewarded for efficiency and cost containment, most clearly by practicing good preventive medicine, reducing the need for hospitalization, and shortening the length of expensive hospitalization for the patient. It is a concern of all mental health professionals that most HMOs, and private insurance plans for individuals, provide extremely limited coverage for mental health disorders, a typical example limiting payment of outpatient mental health services to $750 per year. This sparse coverage may reflect a general perception of the imprecision of both diagnosis and treatment of emotional illness, and the potential for abuse. However, it is a counterproductive strategy for the containment of costs in the face of growing evidence that patients who utilize mental health services show a significant reduction in hospitalization and other more expensive medical interventions (Mumford et al., 1984).

A parallel development of at least equal and possibly greater import than the advances in medical diagnosis and treatment has been the rise of the "health movement," the attraction of a significant segment of the populace toward behaviors, especially in regard to diet and exercise, whose goal is the achievement and maintenance of "wellness." Part of the impetus to the movement has arisen from research establishing the relationship between certain behaviors and illness (e.g., smoking and cancer, obesity and heart disease), and part from the increasing public awareness that our major killers are no longer infectious agents, but rather failures of organ systems that can be attributed in significant measure to unhealthy lifestyles. We have been alerted to the changes in the nature of our major health problems, and to the importance for the health status of individuals that they adopt behaviors that are both disease preventing and health promoting. (*Healthy People: Surgeon General's Report,* 1979).

Wellness promotions (diet programs, antismoking clinics) have been extensively researched by behavioral scientists. Psychologists in particular have had a major role in the design of such programs and their evaluation. Dropouts and relapsers present a particular challenge. There is a need to recognize that efforts to change a personal habit that brings immediate gratification are at risk to fail when the individual's morale is deficient or impaired. In general, it appears that programs entailing group membership and group participation are more effective than individual counseling.

The experience from such programs has relevance for psychotherapy even when the goals of such therapy may be less specifically targeted in behavioral terms. A primary example of a potential for psychological intervention to reduce the risk of serious physical illness arose with recognition of the apparent relationship between so-called Type A personality and the incidence of cardiovascular disease (Matthews, 1982; Powell, 1984). Here the risk arises not in a circumscribed behavior but in a constellation of attitudes, values, and temperament such that the individual is continuously under pressure that is in large measure self-induced, albeit the rewards for "achievement" may contribute to the maintenance of the pattern (Boyd, 1984). The pattern is seemingly life-long, deeply ingrained, and resistant to change inasmuch as the surface behaviors reflect underlying elements of temperament, which may be constitutional in nature, coupled with a value structure that has been reinforced.

The call to self-determined "wellness" in the sphere of physical health has had a counterpart among professional mental health workers in increasing concern for prevention of mental illness. Here the knowledge of "causes" of mental *health* are less clearly established than our awareness of what contributes to positive physical health and what contributes to mental illness. Prevention of disorder and promotion of salubrity are interactive. Physical health and mental health are dynamically interrelated. However, there is need for mental health professionals to search out the dimensions and sources of mental well-being. We have ample philosophical literature on the good life well lived. We are lacking in support for objective study of how emotionally healthy persons stay that way.

Within the specific domain of mental illness there have been striking developments. Of greatest significance among these is the burgeoning field of psychopharmacology—the discovery, refinement, and application of a panoply of drugs for the treatment of major and minor emotional and behavioral disorders. Psychiatry is now supplied with a special pharmacopeia ranging from major antipsychotic drugs (neuroleptics) to minor tranquilizers (ataractics) (Moriarty et al., 1984). There are a host of specific drugs for relief of anxiety and for mood elevation (antidepressants). The progress in drug therapy coupled with discoveries in the neurosciences (e.g., discovery of "natural opiates"—the endorphins and enkephalins, and the dexamethasone suppression test to aid in diagnosis of major affective disorder) have contributed to a professional movement that has been noted as the "remedicalization of psychiatry." This is seen by many psychiatrists as a much desired strengthening of their previously tenuous bonds to the discipline of medicine. The progress in psychopharmacology has not been uncomplicated. None of the drugs constitutes a "cure" and only a few have as yet achieved the status of "treatment of choice." Finding the right medication and the proper dosage level for the individual patient is frequently difficult. While many of the drugs have minor side-effects, if used for long-term maintenance of symptom relief some drugs can result in late development of serious neurological syndromes, notably tardive dyskinesia.

Of great importance for the public at large has been the impact of drugs on the management of major psychiatric illness. The discovery of effective medications coincided with public policy (e.g., Community Mental Health Act, 1963) to bring the means whereby it was planned to stop the long-standing embarrassment of "warehousing" chronic patients in mental hospitals. There was hope that the incidence of hospitalization would decrease and that hospital stays would be shortened. There was in fact a 66 percent decrease in the total number of beds in state and county mental hospitals between 1970 and 1982. Actually some state-operated mental hospitals in some states were closed down. In the same period, the median length of stay in such hospitals fell from 41 to 23 days. However, in this time approximately 80 percent of admissions to state and county hospitals were readmissions, a fact that underlines the reality of chronicity and gave rise to what has been labeled the "revolving door" phenomenon. At the same time, as expected and planned, the total number of outpatient visits to psychiatric facilities more than doubled. Evaluation by statistical surveys of the net effect of the psychiatric revolution is complicated by a shift in the pattern of facility utilization. As a result both of new public facilities and the expansion of private health insurance with mental health benefits, an increasing number of patients are receiving care in the psychiatric units and clinics of general hospitals and private psychiatric hospitals (Manderscheid et al., 1985; Kiesler, 1982; Kiseling, 1983).

There are two consequences for the field of psychotherapy that have arisen from the impact of psychotropic medications. The first of these is the decreasing attention by psychiatrists (and physicians) to psychological factors as etiologic in the onset and persistence of emotional distress, especially anxiety and depression. With the availability of a medically respectable prescription that brings rather prompt symptomatic relief, many physicians are disinclined to concern themselves with the psychosocial situation of the patient, and may be inattentive to those attributes and behaviors of the patient that predispose to future episodes of distress. This neglect of the patient's need for psychological counsel may contribute in part to the problem of the noncompliant patient who does not follow the medical regimen, who terminates medication prematurely, or who abuses the prescription. While there are some psychiatrists and physicians who, recognizing their patients' need for personal counsel and their own lack of motivation for or comfort in therapeutic conversation, make appropriate referrals to qualified psychotherapists, the overall impact of the advances in chemotherapy has been to reduce the number of appropriate candidates who are receiving the psychotherapy they require and from which they would benefit.

A second and related consequence of the "remedicalization" of psychiatry occurs in the residency training programs for future psychiatrists. Many training centers are choosing to focus on "biological" psychiatry. As a result, their residency curricula are devoid of or deficient in didactic instruction and instructional supervision that would provide the psychiatrist-to-be with an understanding of and minimal competencies with basic methods of psychological intervention. The graduates of such programs are likely to be insensitive to the indicators for appropriate referrals.

Of equal breadth of influence, if less significant impact, has been the appearance of a new official nomenclature for "nervous and mental" disorders. The Diagnostic and Statistical Manual of Mental Disorders, third edition, was published in 1980 (American Psychiatric Association). DSM-III, as it is referred to, supplanting a diagnostic system that had been in place since 1968, represents the product of five years of study, drafting, and field trials under the auspices of some 15 committees of the psychiatric association, assisted by special advisors. Evaluation of the new nosology has been marked by several points of heated debate, some interprofessional, others intraprofessional. An early proposal to define mental disorders as a subclass of medical disorders was seen as egregiously political rather than scientific, was vehemently opposed by nonmedical therapists and behavioral scientists, and was not pursued (Schacht, 1985; Spitzer, 1985). Within psychiatry, there was strong opposition to the deletion of the neuroses as a major diagnositic category, a deletion successfully defended by the authors of DSM-III on the grounds that the concept of "neurosis" was too closely associated with the Freudian theory of etiology and, hence, inappropriate in a nosology that was intended to be free of conflicting etiological theorization. While clearly an advance over DSM-II by virtue of providing a multiaxial system that includes ratings of "stressors" and "previous level of adjustment," and more extended and more precise descriptors of the required symptomatic elements for most of the clinical diagnoses, it has been received with critical reservation by those mental health professionals who see it as too medically (i.e., biological, constitutional, hereditary) in its set, presenting a "disease-based" model of maladjustment (Smith & Kraft, 1983). However, DSM-III is the official dictionary for public accounting in mental health service programs, and private insurers require DSM-III diagnoses for reimbursable service by mental health professionals. Thus, some psychotherapists find themselves forced to pretend acceptance of a quasi-scientific, quasi-semantic construction that does violence to their conceptions of psychological maladjustment and forces them to ethical perversions.

The persisting problems in achieving a universally recognized definition of mental illness that would be consistent with natural fact, permit reliable application, and clearly separate such illness from those disturbances with a demonstrable organic pathology, continues to trouble researchers who seek to determine the incidence of mental illness over time and from community to community. One of the products of the President's Commission on Mental Health (1977) was a review of studies to determine the prevalence of mental illness. A review of all epidemiological studies completed after 1950 indicated a range in the reported rates of all types of psychopathology in the U.S. from as low as 0.55 percent to as high as 69 percent (Dohrenwend et al., 1980) Similar variation in findings were obtained when North American and European studies were combined (3.7 percent to 55.8 percent). Such wide variation is indicative in part of the survey-to-survey variability in the criterion (definition) of putative cases of mental illness. It was noted that beginning in the 1950s there was a trend among epidemiologists to apply increasingly broad definitions to "mental disorder." This, combined with the limited reliability of clinical judgments of interview-derived data, leaves seriously in doubt the question of how prevalent mental illness is in our society. Note must be made also of the fact that the incidence of "cases," especially of milder disorders, is influenced by therapists who have both an imprecise nosology and pecuniary motives in deciding who is a legitimate candidate for psychotherapy. An important result of the extreme range in reported rates of mental disorder is that they provide support both for those public officials who want to reduce or "hold the line" on expenditures for care and research as well as for other officials who seek to increase funding. A striking conclusion of the epidemiological overview was that "large proportions, perhaps 75 percent of individuals suffering from either a clinical psychological disorder or a significant degree of psychological distress, have never been in treatment" (Dohrenwend et al., 1980). If this is a reliable estimate there are large numbers of persons who could be studied in search of answers to vital questions: Do they lack ready access to the network of services? Do they avoid such services, and if so, why? And perhaps of greatest interest, how do they cope with their "disorders"? How are they maintained in the community and outside the rolls of mental health agencies?

Within the matrix of social developments sketched above, the last twenty years have been marked by changes in the enterprise of psychotherapy. Sources of supply of "conversation with therapeutic intent" noted in the original publication (1964) have been increased specifically and expanded generally. To the three primary mental health professions recognized earlier—psychiatry, clinical psychology, and psychiatric social work—the ensuing years have been marked by the entry of other professionals as purveyors of psychotherapy. Most visible among these have been psychiatric nurses, pastoral counselors, and, in largest numbers, individuals identified as family and marriage counselors. Each of these professionals has been trained as a specialist for a particular role; when they enter the market as "psychotherapists" they function, in large number, as generalists. Furthermore, with respect to the three primary professions of psychotherapists (i.e., medicine, psychology, and social work), there is good evidence that the processes of recruitment, education, and training end with a supply of private practitioners who are highly similar in values and attitudes (Henry, Sims, & Spray, 1971). There is no convincing evidence that their therapeutic conversation reflects the specifics of their presumably differentiated professional training. While the general increase in the supply of therapists may be a social good, it may not be assumed so, absent evidence that the overall quality of service delivery is maintained.

The national offices of the three major mental health professions have provided data on their rolls. In the last ten years, among the three primary mental health professions there has been smallest growth in the number of psychiatrists, who now number some 38,000. By contrast, clinical social workers have shown the greatest rate of growth and now total 60,000, the largest group of professional therapists. Marriage and family counselors have more than quadrupled their numbers over the last ten years and at a current total of 28,000 are nearly as numerous as clinical psychologists, at 33,000 (Golen, 1985).

With a total supply of nearly 160,000 variously qualified psychotherapists available to the public, more than double the number ten years ago, may we assume that an increased proportion of all valid candidates for therapeutic conversation are indeed receiving help? Or have the increased stresses of our economic, social, and political environments added to the numbers of our dis-eased citizens, so that perhaps even the "catch-up" point eludes us? That our total resources for management of "mental disorders" may be reaching the point of adequacy is suggested by the fact that in 1975, over 50 percent of all such cases were seen by primary care physicians as outpatients, a number more than three times that seen by mental health professionals. However, it is likely that these general physicians, availing themselves of the psychotropic pharmacopeia, are using medical prescription rather than psychological intervention and not influencing the demand (need?) for psychotherapy (Regnier et al., 1978). While the discoveries of chemotherapy have proven of great worth in the treatment of major psychiatric illness, their long-term impact on treatment of psychological dis-ease may be found to have been deleterious.

Finally, the relative impact of the growth in numbers of the several mental health professions cannot be appraised without distinguishing the supply via public agencies from the supply in the private practice sector. Individuals whose comprehensive health insurance includes mental health benefits are restricted largely to psychiatrists and licensed psychologists. Although psychologists are licensed for private practice in all 50 states, only 40 states require insurers to reimburse for services of psychologists, and a much smaller

number, only 14 states, require coverage for services of clinical social workers, although social workers are licensed for practice in 35 states (Golen,
1985).

Professional psychotherapists are embattled on two fronts. On the legislative front, as suggested by the data above, some professionals are seeking formal social sanction to purvey therapeutic conversation just as other
professionals—who may hold a bit of a corner on the market—lobby to
prevent any further intrusion on their territory (American Medical Association, American Psychiatric Association, and American Psychoanalytic Association, 1954). Any rational analysis of the essential nature of psychotherapy
should make it clear that no single existing profession can hope to establish
any quasi-official hegemony over the field, except possibly for the briefest of
periods.

On the other front, professional therapists are engaged in a struggle to
establish that one "school," theory, or technique of psychotherapy is superior
to all others. How many others? A recent exhaustive search of the literature
produced a compendium of 250 "systems and techniques," with 100 others
eliminated because they were "untried" or "in a very few cases" because of
their "flakiness"! (Herink, 1980) Again, a rational analysis of the enterprise
suggests the improbability of that number of meaningfully differentiable "systems," quite apart from the question of established differential effectiveness.
How many ostensible schools (theory and associated techniques) are there
really? Sober explication, comparison, debate, and research in recent years
have distinguished major systems: psychoanalytic-psychodynamic; cognitive
(including rational-emotive); behavioral; cognitive-behavioral; client-
centered; and a cluster of interrelated theory-methods under a general rubric
of existential-gestalt-transactional. While no single school has established a
clear superiority either of theoretical formulation or therapeutic efficacy,
each has established sufficient credibility to account for the growing tendency of experienced therapists to identify themselves as "eclectic" rather
than "pure" practitioners à la Freud, Rogers, Ellis, or other founders (Smith,
1982). The implications are clear for young persons who have decided to
pursue careers as psychotherapists. They need to be very conscious of their
motives (distinguishing the satisfaction of serving others meaningfully from
the perquisites of a particular role), they need to choose thoughtfully a particular professional entry (e.g., training in psychiatry takes much longer, costs
much more, and pays much better), and they need to choose whether they
will be educated and taught how to think about psychotherapy, or indoctri-
nated and trained to "do therapy" (Matarazzo, 1971).

The times have changed. There are more of all of us—consumers and counselors. We communicate more rapidly, and the news seems chiefly depressing.

The social drama moves into another act. But the players and plot are familiar. "Plus ça change, plus la même chose." Those specific data, numbers, offered in 1964, no longer hold. But the interrelationships of the quantified facts are unchanged. More kinds of psychotherapists are seeing more clients in a wider variety of settings. While the training of most therapists continues to be dominated by the disciplines of psychiatry, psychology, and social work in fully accredited graduate programs, training is now offered in nontraditional programs, only some of which have university affiliation (Peterson, 1985). It is not clear as yet that the preparation of professional mental health workers in these new programs is more sound, more appropriate, and more efficient than that of the established professions, although that is the expressed goal. More critical is the failure thus far to show that graduates of professional training programs are more effective than individuals with much less training (Berman & Norton, 1985).

There is better evidence than previously that psychotherapy does make a difference, that individuals achieve relief from distress and improved functioning as a result of psychological intervention (Smith et al., 1980; Landman & Dawes, 1982; Shapiro & Shapiro, 1982). We still lack a convincing accumulation of research demonstrating that a particular kind of therapy is "treatment of choice" for a particular form of psychological distress. It can be hoped that the increase in "electicism" by psychotherapists means that they are increasingly applying a rationally and selectively differentiated therapeutic approach to problems that have been carefully, differentially diagnosed (Lazarus, 1981). It may not be assumed from survey results that therapists who self-identify as "eclectics" are in fact using theory and technique selectively, as each case requires, rather than simply practicing a smorgasbord of personalized therapeutics.

With respect to the analyses, paradoxes, and theses offered by the text—it may best be said, some twenty years later—"stet." There is additional evidence that specialists in one-to-one psychotherapy, regardless of their professional identification, are more alike than different in their theoretical allegiances. This homogeneity of values extends to the realm of cultural and philosophical orientation and is reflected in a considerable homogeneity of their patients. The modal psychotherapy patient, seen in private offices, is still a YAVIS type (Henry, Sims, & Spray, 1973; Marmor, 1975).

Further surveys of the relative impact of formal, different didactic instruction versus supervised experience for each of the major mental health professions, and the agreement among them as to which experiences contribute most positively to the gaining of therapeutic skill, supports the argument for a unified program to train a new professional specialist (Henry, Sims, & Spray, 1973).

With the reissue of the unrevised work, there will be opportunity for some earlier potential readers who never got beyond the title to learn that the notion that all psychotherapy is *nothing more* than exchange of friendship for a fee is *not* the major thesis (Schofield, 1970).

If as many as one in every ten patients seen in private practice is diagnosed as "relatively healthy," there must be continuing concern for the possible overtreating of persons who are not legitimate candidates for psychotherapy (Henry, Sims & Spray, 1973). It is these applicants, and possibly a significant portion of those diagnosed as "psychoneurotic," who may need primarily a reorientation to their existing social resources for the therapy of friendship. Such reorientation (resocialization) and provision of a *therapeutic diagnosis* for such persons does not demand the intensive, long-term psychodynamic therapy required for individuals with long-standing personality disorders, nor even the program of behavioral modification indicated for the sufferer with a circumscribed impairment. It is a valid part of professional practice for the psychotherapist to recognize those few instances in which circumstances make it appropriate to accept the role of substitute friend. The role should be satisfied by the same concern, caring, and consistency brought to all thera- peutic endeavor. It is critical that the therapist not lose awareness of the role and the limits on substitution; always the "patient's" capacity for friendship, albeit initially in the safety of the substitution, must be mobilized by the therapist to move the patient toward more genuine, natural, and spontaneous relationships in the real community.

# References

Frank, J.D. In Harvey, J.H., Parks, M.M. (eds.), *Psychotherapy Research and Behavior Change* (Master Lecture Series, vol. 1). Washington, D.C., American Psychological Association, 1982.

Schofield, W. Psychology, inspiration, and faith (symposium on dealing with religious issues in counseling and psychotherapy). *Journal of Religion and Health*, 1979, *18*, 197-202.

Poon, L.W. (ed.). *Aging in the 1980s: Psychological issues.* Washington, D.C.: American Psychological Association, 1980.

Reynolds, R.V.C., McNamara, J.R., Marion, R.V., & Tobin, D.L. Computerized service delivery in clinical psychology. *Professional Psychology: Research and Practice*, 1985, *16*, 339-353.

Starzl, T.E. Will live organ donations no longer be justified? *Hastings Center Report*, 1985, *15*, 5-12.

Annas, G.J. No cheers for temporary artificial hearts. *Hastings Center Report*, 1985, *15*, 27-28.

Walters, L. Human in vitro fertilization: A review of the ethical literature. *Hastings Center Report*, 1979, *9*, 23-43.

Sarason, S.B. If it can be studied or developed, should it be? *American Psychologist*, 1984, *39*, 477-485.

Mumford, E., Schlesinger, H.J., Glass, G.V., Patrick, C., & Cuerdon, T. A new look at evidence about reduced cost of medical utilization following mental health treatment. *American Journal of Psychiatry*, 1984, *141*, 1145-1158.

*Healthy people: The Surgeon general's report on health promotion and disease prevention, 1979.* Washington, D.C., U.S. Government Printing Office.

Matthews, K.A. Psychological perspectives on the Type A behavior pattern. *Psychological Bulletin*, 1982, *91*, 292-323.

Powell, L.H. The Type A behavior pattern: An update on conceptual assessment, and intervention research. *Behavioral Medicine Update*, 1984, *6*, 7-10.

Boyd, D.P. Type A behavior, financial performance and organizational growth in small business firms. *Journal of Occupational Psychology*, 1984, *57*, 137-140.

Moriarty, K.M., Alagna, S.W., & Lake, C.R. Psychopharmacology: An historical perspective. Symposium on Clinical Psychopharmacology I. *The Psychiatric Clinics of North America.* Philadelphia: W.B. Saunders Co., 1984.

Manderscheid, R.W., Witkin, M.J., Rosenstein, M.J., Milazzo-Sayre, L.J., Bethel, H.E., & MacAskill, R.L. Specialty mental health services: System and patient characteristics—United States. Chapter 2 in *Mental Health, U.S.* Taube, C.A. and Barrett, S.A. (eds). DHHS Pub. No. ADM85-1378. Washington, D.C.: Superintendent of Documents, 1985.

Kiesler, C.A. Public and professional myths about mental hospitalization: An empirical reassessment of policy-related beliefs. *American Psychologist*, 1982, *37*, 1323-39.

Kiesling, R. Critique of Kiesler articles. (Commentary) *American Psychologist*, 1983, *38*, 1127-1128.

American Psychiatric Association. *Diagnostic and statistical manual of mental disorders* (3rd ed.) Washington, D.C.: APA, 1980.

Schacht, T.E. DSM-III and the politics of truth. *American Psychologist*, 1985, *40*, 513-521.

Spitzer, R.L. DSM-III and the politics-science dichotomy syndrome: A response to Thomas E. Schact's "DSM-III and the politics of truth." *American Psychologist*, 1985, *40*, 522-526.

Smith, D., & Kraft, W.A. DSM-III: Do psychologists really want an alternative? *American Psychologist*, 1983, *38*, 777-785.

Dohrenwend, B.P., Dohrenwend, B.S., Gould, M.S., Link, B., Neugebauer, R., & Wunsch-Hitzig, R. *Mental Illness in the United States: Epidemiological Estimates*. New York: Praeger Publishers, 1980.

Henry, W.E., Sims, J.H., & Spray, S.L. *The fifth profession: Becoming a psychotherapist*. San Francisco: Jossey-Bass, 1971.

Golen, O. "Social workers vault into a leading role in psychotherapy." *New York Times*, April 30, 1985, pp. 17-20

Regnier, D.A., Goldberg, I.D., & Taube, C.A. The de facto U.S. mental health services system. *Archives of General Psychiatry*, 1978, *35*, 685-693.

American Medical Association, American Psychiatric Association, & American Psychoanalytic Association. Resolution on relations of medicine and psychology. *American Journal of Psychiatry*, 1954, *3*, 385-386.

Herink, R. *The Psychotherapy Handbook*. New York: New American Library, 1980.

Smith, D. Trends in counseling and psychotherapy. *American Psychologist*, 1982, *37*, 802-809.

Matarazzo, R. Research on the teaching and learning of psychotherapeutic skills. Chapter 24 in *Handbook of Psychotherapy and Behavior Change: An Empirical Analysis*. Bergin, A.E. and Garfield, S.L. (eds.). New York: John Wiley and Sons, 1971.

Peterson, D.R. Twenty years of practitioner training in psychology. *American Psychologist*, 1985, *40*, 441-451.

Berman, J.S., & Norton, N.C. Does professional training make a therapist more effective? *Psychological Bulletin*, 1985, *98*, 401-407.

Smith, M.L., Glass, G.V., & Miller, T.I. *The benefits of psychotherapy*. Baltimore: Johns Hopkins University Press, 1980.

Landman, J.T., & Dawes, R.M. Psychotherapy outcome: Conclusions stand up under scrutiny. *American Psychologist*, 1982, *37*, 504-516.

Shapiro, D.A., & Shapiro, D. Meta-analysis of comparative therapy outcome studies: A replication and refinement. *Psychological Bulletin*, 1982, *92*, 581-604.

Lazarus, A.A. *The Practice of multi-modal therapy*. New York: McGraw-Hill Book Company, 1981.

Henry, W.E., Sims, J.H., & Spray, S.L. *Public and private lives of psychotherapists*. San Francisco: Jossey-Bass, 1973.

Marmor, Judd. *Psychiatrists and their patients: A national study of private office practice*. Washington, D.C.: Joint Information Service of the American Psychiatric Association and National Association for Mental Health, 1975.

Schofield, W. The psychotherapist as friend. *Humanitas*, 1970, *2*, 211-223.

# ∙§ Contents §∙

# Introduction

These pages are devoted to the subject of personal maladjustment —its nature, extent, and treatment in our nation. In particular, the following theses are proposed and examined:

In terms of social welfare and national economy, mental illness is the most serious of our public health problems.

In the decade following World War II there has been an expanding national consciousness of the problem of mental illness, and increasing energies and funds have been devoted to its control.

Professional and lay persons alike have been misled toward unrealistic goals and the perpetuation of inadequate methods in managing the national burden of psychological disorder.

Pursuit of impossible objectives and the freezing of practice into unfitting molds has resulted from

—failure to approach the problem initially with an intensive philosophical analysis of the logic of diagnosis, its role in the entire therapeutic project, and its peculiar complexities in the area of mental and emotional distress.

—failure to examine philosophically and psychologically the importance of *unhappiness,* its determinants and its role in personal maladaptation.

—failure to appraise carefully the amount and quality of the simpler disturbances of personality integration in relation to the full range of psychiatric dysfunction.

—failure to rise above those all too human reactionary and self-aggrandizing motives which are fostered by necessarily strong professional identifications.

The total case load of those who are mentally and emotionally dis-eased (*sic*) is composed primarily of persons who are neither in need of, nor responsive to, specific medication, surgery, hospitalization, or other physical regimens.

*1*

The most promising procedure which thus far has been uncovered for management, treatment, and prophylaxis of the so-called functional mental and nervous sicknesses is a conversation which has therapeutic intent and occurs in a relationship of friendship.

We have not as yet begun to devote nearly adequate time, energies, or funds to explorations in search of the unique and crucial properties, if any, of the therapeutic conversation.

The great bulk of our research to date on psychological ministration to psychological discomfort has been seriously restricted by a priori convictions that only a small number (*i.e.,* two to four) of highly specified patterns of training-and-experience can produce persons capable of establishing, directing, and maintaining therapeutic conversations.

In the area of mental illness, unrealistic goals and misinformed attitudes with respect to the character and distribution of presently incurable disorders have led to a failure to develop and apply palliative techniques with the sincerity and reasonableness with which mitigation is afforded by the physician and surgeon.

Current programs of public education in mental hygiene, in measure as they are successful, have an unavoidable side-effect that parallels some of the outcomes of successful commercial advertising!

—Persons are sensitized; they are encouraged to self-examination; they look for evidences of guilt, defect, or failure to "live up" to a personal potential and cultural ideal.
—Demand is created; sensitivity is followed by desire for relief.
—Specific expectations are fostered; certain procedures or particular products are invested with remedial potency.
—"Trade-marks" and unit-cost combine to generate a prestige hierarchy which is not necessarily correlated with effectiveness.

These "advertising outcomes" of public education have created a consumer demand, at all levels of the "therapeutic conversation" market, that far exceeds available resources.

There is a peculiar circularity of the supply–demand function in the area of mental hygiene; increases in supply increase demand rather than reducing the supply-to-demand ratio, and level of supply remains always beneath level of demand. As more therapists are trained, demand for their conversation increases.

In light of the above, in addition to limitations of our training resources, there will never be enough M.D. specialists in psychiatry, enough Ph.D. specialists in clinical psychology, or enough M.A. specialists in psychiatric social work to provide remedial services to all who may feel need of them.

Correction of this burgeoning socio-individual psychopathology demands action along two fronts: we must, at the same time, increase the number of persons who are adequately skilled and appropriately competent to converse therapeutically with the multitudes of the miserable and *also* effectively reduce the demand for and need of such professional friendship.

—We must begin a massive exploratory-experimental endeavor directed toward the demarcation of a new profession whose members can be effectively trained with sufficient rapidity and in sufficient numbers to provide the needed extension and potentiation of the critical-shortage skills of physician, psychologist, and social worker.

—We must honestly confront our citizens with those considerations which will encourage an intelligently humane social climate, a logistically reasonable structure of social services, and a restored respect for *individual* responsibility in that philosophical venture in which rests every person's greatest freedom—that searching of the unknown which is the essence of human life.

# CHAPTER ONE

# The Problem

## I. THE COUNTABLE THOUSANDS

Over one half of *all* the hospital beds in this country are occupied by mental patients. There are 600,000 psychiatric patients housed in public and private mental hospitals at any given time. There are approximately 125,000 new admissions annually to public institutions for custodial care of psychiatrically ill persons. Of the total number of patients admitted to state hospitals each year, nearly one third are patients who are entering such hospitals for at least the second time.[1]

Such facts impress upon us the size of the problem in respect to the sheer number of persons who require hospitalization. They imply to us the tremendous economic costs that are involved—in terms of the expense of the custody and care of the patients, and in terms of the loss to our economy entailed in their incapacitation as productive citizens.[2] These data state clearly the position of mental illness as our nation's paramount health problem.

These facts do not and cannot convey in themselves, to even the most sensitive and imaginative of persons, the true dimensions of hurt and loss experienced by these thousands upon thousands of psychological invalids. Statistics which are intended to bring precision to descriptive communication fail utterly when the essential subject is suffering. Human misery does not yield to quantification. One can make a census of the bodies of patients, but the psychic pain and emotional torment of one patient is not additive to that of another. When men and women are bereft of reason, tyrannized by emotion, or reduced to vegetative automatism, their suffering does not permit of numeration.

Really to know such suffering at all, short of experiencing it ourselves, we must see it directly. We must visit a mental hospital; we must see the faces of patient after patient; we must observe the daily routine of their mechanical existence; we must ask where they came from, how long they have been here, what tomorrow promises for them; and then, we must think that these are but a very few. These lives of monotonous melancholy and empty euphoria are multiplied six hundred thousandfold. Perhaps then we approach the true magnitude of the pathology. And if we succeed in capturing a full vision of the suffering stemming from mental disorder, it is for a brief instant only. Protective forgetting guards us from the distress of constant awareness of these isolated sick ones. At home again, surrounded by the small pleasures and large pursuits of our existence, we do not remind ourselves of what we saw or thought; we do not bring up painful images of the human deprivation we observed.

Newspapers, magazines, radio, and television carry programs designed to inform the public with regard to the massive enigma of mental illness and to exhort our interests and efforts in campaigns to increase funds or improve facilities. Our attention may be momentarily arrested by a statement that one out of every fifteen individuals who live to be 65 years of age will have spent some period of his life in a mental hospital, but such a statement does not nourish the persistent questioning attitude that comes through personal acquaintance with a single patient.[3]

## II. THE HIDDEN MILLIONS

The patients who may be readily counted, whose illness is of such nature as to lead to hospitalization, are not the ones under primary consideration here. Rather, it is the unnumbered mass of lesser sufferers, the partial cripples, with whom we are concerned. These are the individuals who are emotionally maladjusted and psychologically disordered but whose mental illness permits them to lead a tortuous existence outside of hospital walls. Only a very rough approximation of their total number is possible.

They are partially enumerable as those chronic visitors to physicians' offices with complaints that are vague, anatomically and physiologically irrational, and unsupported by any findings of actual organic defect. These are the recalcitrant 50 to 70 per cent of the general practitioner's case load who are sooner or later labeled "neurotic." Included also in the extramural population of psychiatric cases are those persons who are seen on an outpatient basis in public mental hygiene clinics or social agencies and by private psychiatrists and psychologists. These too are countable.

Most present-day authorities are not content to let the realm of mental illness be bounded by these recordable patients. They practice the delicate art of extrapolation and arrive at estimates of the "real sum" of mentally sick persons in the total population. In such activity they are not out of step with general practice in the field of public health which recognizes that there are multiple factors determining whether a given case of a specific disease ever comes to formal diagnosis. Thus, it is logically descriptive to speak of the person known to carry the active tubercle bacillus in his lungs as having had tuberculosis even before he was X-rayed, visited a physician, or had a formal diagnosis of his symptoms. After such a diagnosis, it is appropriate to recognize that the individual *has* been ill. The disease does not begin its existence, except in a very arbitrary and formal sense, with the occurrence of the diagnosis. Accordingly, it is not at all fictional to think of the total incidence of a disease such as tuberculosis as composed of those recorded, diagnosed cases *plus* an additional estimated number of undiagnosed cases. Biometric experts have developed methods for rather exact estimating of the number of such putative cases, utilizing among other factors data on the number of cases that come to diagnosis per period of time and the prior duration of the illness as indicated by the stage of symptoms at the time of diagnosis.

Similarly, it is appropriate to conceive of the total number of mentally ill at any given time as composed of those institutionalized and otherwise recorded cases *plus* an estimated number of individuals who carry the "germs" of mental illness and have manifest symptoms, but have not yet come to diagnosis. Recent surveys of probability samples of urban and rural populations have led to the finding that as many as *one third* of these populations presented some degree of psychiatric symptomatology and to the equally startling finding that less than 20 per cent were free of any sign of emotional distress.[4,5]

We must pause here, before we undertake any appraisal of the social import of these last figures, to question whether there are any differences between physical and mental illness that would make the estimation of the real or total incidence of psychiatric disorder in our population subject to sources of significant errors which do not occur in the estimation of physical ailment. There are such differences, and one of the most basic of them may be briefly illustrated.

## Definitions of some communicable diseases

*Influenza:* "Clinically an acute, highly communicable disease, characterized by abrupt onset with fever which lasts 1 to 6 days, chills or chilliness, aches and pains in the back and limbs, and prostration. Respiratory symptoms include coryza, sore throat and cough. Usually a self limited disease with recovery in 48 to 72 hours; influenza derives its importance from the complications that follow, especially pneumonia in those debilitated by old age, by other disease, or in young infants.

"Laboratory confirmation is by recovery of virus from throat washings or by demonstration of a significant rise in antibodies against a specific influenza virus in serums obtained during acute and convalescent stages of the disease."

*Measles:* "An acute highly communicable viral disease with a prodromal stage characterized by catarrhal symptoms and Koplik spots on the buccal mucous membranes. A morbilliform rash appears on the third or fourth day affecting face, body and extremities, and sometimes ending in branny desquamation. Leucopenia is usual."

*Acute Lobar Pneumonia:* "An acute bacterial infection characterized by sudden onset with chill followed by fever, often pain in the chest, usually a productive cough, dyspnea, and leucocytosis. Roentgen-ray examination may disclose pulmonary lesions prior to other evidence of consolidation. Not infrequently pneumococcal pneumonia is bronchial rather than lobar, especially in children, with vomiting and convulsions often the first manifestations.

"Laboratory confirmation is by bacteriological examination of sputum or discharges of the respiratory tract. A rise in antibody titer between acute-phase and convalescent-phase serums is useful in problem cases, and culture of the blood in severe infections." [6]

## Some definitions of psychological disorder

*Neurosis (Psychoneurosis):* "The psychoneuroses comprise a relatively benign group of personality disturbances which are often described as being intermediate, or as forming a connecting link, between the various adaptive devices unconsciously utilized by the average mind on the one hand and the extreme, often disorganizing, methods observed in the psychotic on the other." [7]

"The term psychoneurosis has . . . two connotations. In the first and historical connotation the meaning of psychoneurosis is purely descriptive. It is a term referring to conditions characterized by certain mental and physical symptoms and signs, occurring in various combinations. . . . None of these are dependent on the existence of any discoverable physical disease.

. . . "another connotation, more fundamental, since it is an aetiological one . . . is to the effect that the existence of a psychoneurotic reaction is an indication of mental conflict. Neurotic reactions are the commonest modes of faulty response to the stresses of life, and especially to those inner tensions that come about from confused and unsatisfactory relationships with other people. . . .

"Clinically, a psychoneurosis implies either a bodily disturbance without a structural lesion, and dependent in a way unknown to the patient on mental causes; or a mental disturbance, not the result of bodily disease, in the form usually of morbid fears of many different kinds, or episodic disturbed mental states such as losses of memory and trances, or persistent troublesome thoughts, or acts which the patient feels compelled to do—all of which the patient realizes to be abnormal and the meaning of which he is at a loss to understand." [8]

"The psychoneuroses are mild or minor mental reactions which represent attempts to find satisfaction in life situations rendered unsatisfactory by faulty attitudes or by faulty emotional developments. These attempts are manifested by various physiologic reactions, complaints of bodily discomfort, or recurrent mental trends recognized by the patient as being faulty or unusual. Practically, they are somewhat artificially divided into various etiologic entities. The etiology varies in individual cases but they all have in common the inability to meet life situations, and all of them resort to substitution efforts or symbolic gratification of urges not recognized by nor accepted by the individual." [9]

"All neurotic phenomena are based on insufficiencies of the normal control apparatus. They can be understood as involuntary emergency discharges that supplant the normal ones. The insufficiency can be brought about in two ways. One way is through an increase in the influx of stimuli: too much excitation enters the mental apparatus in a given unit of time and cannot be mastered; such experiences are called traumatic. The other way is through a previous blocking or decrease of discharge which has produced a damming up of tension within the organism so that normal excitations now operate relatively like traumatic ones. These two possible ways are not mutually exclusive. A trauma may initiate an ensuing blocking of discharge; and a primary blocking, by creating a state of being dammed up, may cause subsequent average stimuli to have a traumatic effect." [10]

"Psychopathology implies that following situations of stress, the individual manifests suffering, symptoms, impaired efficiency, lessened ability for enjoyment, lack of adequate insight. . . .
"In all neurotic manifestations, the patient's vital needs are involved as well as his evaluation of himself (self-esteem), of other individuals (security feelings), and of the situation with which he has to cope. Thus, one can say that in neurotic manifestations, the patient's whole personality and whole body are involved. . . ." [11]

"The chief characteristic of these disorders [psychoneurotic] is 'anxiety' which may be directly felt and expressed or which may be unconsciously and automatically controlled by the utilization of various psychological defense mechanisms (repression, conversion, displacement, and others). In contrast to those with psychoses, patients with psychoneurotic disorders do not exhibit gross distortion or falsification of external reality (delusions, hallucinations, illusions) and they do not present gross disorganizations of personality. . . .
" 'Anxiety' in psychoneurotic disorders is a danger signal felt and perceived by the conscious portion of the personality. It is produced by a threat from within the personality (*e.g.*, by super-charged repressed emotions, including such aggressive impulses as hostility and resentment) with or without stimulation from such external situations as loss of love, loss of prestige, or threat of injury. The various ways in which the patient attempts to hurdle this anxiety results in the various types of reactions. . . ." [12]

A single perusal of these two samples of definitions, one of physical illnesses and one of psychological illnesses, suffices to illustrate crucial differences. In essence, the differences are in the specificity of symptoms, their locus, order of presentation, precise physical appearance, and course. In these matters the definitions of physical illnesses tend to be explicit, precise, and circumscribed. By contrast, the definitions of mental illness tend to suffer from implicitness, ambiguity and nonrestrictiveness. (It is this difference in precision at the basic level of description of the phenomena which contributes heavily to separation of the so-called exact sciences from other "sciences.")

The sample definitions also suggest that the physical diseases are in some instances objectively diagnosable by the utilization of exact laboratory procedures that can confirm or refute a clinical diagnosis; such laboratory or "test" procedures have not yet been developed to an equal level of precision for psychological illness. The laboratory procedures and diagnostic tests of clinical medicine must be evaluated by expert "readers," and judgments of the pathology or normality of X rays, electrocardiograms, and other tests are not without error.[13] But quite aside from the contribution of such laboratory tests, description of the clinical symptoms of recognized physical maladies has a specificity that makes the diagnosis of most such illnesses a less arbitrary process than holds for psychological disorders.

We may return now to the matter of quantifying the prevalence of mental illness. The taking of an accurate census of mental illness involves directly the question of the reliability or accuracy of diagnosis. The accuracy of diagnosis can be viewed in the form of two queries:

1) Of the true number of cases of a given illness in a population how many are detected (assuming the complete population is surveyed with existing diagnostic techniques)?
2) Of a given sample composed of both ill and well persons respectively, how many of the total sample would be jointly diagnosed correctly (either "sick" or "well") by two or more diagnosticians?

These questions are interrelated; the level of accuracy in terms of Query 1 is a function of the degree of agreement found in Query 2. And it is important to note that Query 2 provides recognition of "false positives" (healthy persons called sick) as well as "false negatives" (sick persons called well).

In the context examined here, the most critical phase of the diagnostic process involves the differentiation between adjustment or normality and *mildest* maladjustment as defined in the conceptually abstruse terms exemplified above. This might appear to be a more difficult task than that of differentiating among the various forms of mental illness in a sample composed exclusively of patients. In the latter instance, the somewhat more detailed and specific accounts of symptomatology would appear to facilitate diagnosis by type. We might expect the reliability of "screening" diagnoses to be something less than that of differential diagnosis. Investigations of the reliability of differential psychiatric diagnoses are few; they indicate that agreement among psychiatrists making specific independent diagnoses of heterogeneous samples of psychiatric patients ranges from 20 to 55 per cent.[14,15] These figures hardly encourage great confidence in the reliability with which neurosis is detectable; our confidence is not enhanced with the further note that least agreement is obtained in differentiating among the types of milder functional disorder.

Pertinent also is the observation that the rate of "false positive" cases among hospitalized patients is negligible. It is not beyond the realm of possibility that social process could lead (and has led) to the inappropriate hospitalization of persons who in point of fact were mentally sound. But the usual procedures required for hospitalization guard against the occurrence of such misdiagnosis. In this sense, we are secure in our usual procedure of assuming the populations of our state and other mental hospitals are comprised totally of valid cases. Though this is a reasonable assumption about cases at the time of admission, a careful review of chronic patients suggests that a significant number are retained in hospitals primarily because they do not have relatives willing to provide for their return to the community.[16] Recognizing diagnosis as a two-edged sword, we should not be unmindful that in our customary approach to mental illness statistics we are assuming perfect screening diagnosis.

Now consider the problem before a diagnostic team charged with surveying an entire urban or rural community to determine the number of inhabitants suffering from any form of mental illness, including those so-called "minor" psychoneurotic disorders which are grouped under the loosely conceived and abstractly stated definitions given above. This becomes the problem of determining whether or not each individual studied has "mental conflicts," "inner tensions," "unsatisfactory relationships to other people," "faulty attitudes," "symbolic gratification of urges," or any of the other, grosser and patent evidences of major mental illness. Ideally this determination should be made through application of reasonably operational definitions or rules of description of the above concepts, so that a second survey team working independently and reviewing the same population would identify the same individuals as respectively "sick" or "healthy." In such a survey the critical problem is to avoid false negatives, to hold to a minimum the numbers of those individuals who are mislabeled "healthy." In essence, this is the problem of a reverse approach to diagnosis: we may define as mentally ill any person who does not have perfect mental health, and we may define perfect mental health in terms of such rigorous standards that it is a condition notable for its absence rather than its presence in a majority of the population at any given time.

One might ask what is wrong with a diagnostic philosophy which implies mental health as a goal for the nation. There is nothing wrong with such a philosophy or such a goal. As applied methodology in public health surveys, however, it could have the undesirable effect of generating statistics that were overwhelming or misleading or both. The hard facts concerning unarguably diagnosed and hospitalized patients are sufficient to communicate the urgency and magnitude of the problem of mental illness and to arouse the public to recognition of the need for monies to support attacks on the problem from all fronts—research, prevention, and care. These same facts are adequate to orient the professions of psychiatry, psychology and social work to the realistic challenge that exists here and now —to the job of discovery in areas of etiology, prophylaxis, and treatment that must be done before notions of an unconflicted, tensionless society can be more than utopian fantasy. There is a subtle danger in the extrapolated statistic and the premature application of "reverse diagnosis": the resulting "real" case load can generate attitudes antithetical to scientific endeavor—attitudes either of hopelessness or heroism.

### III. DIAGNOSTIC PHILOSOPHY—THE PROBLEM OF DEFINITION

All of the foregoing suggests that the definition of mental illness is arbitrary in a degree far greater than is true for physical illness. It is the discretionary quality of the definition of mental illnesses which at once poses a problem and points to an element of solution. Mental illness is a relative rather than an absolute matter. Failure fully to recognize this leads to confusion, circular reasoning, unrealistic goals, and unnecessary frustration.

We are broadly accustomed to the notion of relativity as expressed in culture-to-culture variation in determinants of normal or adjusted personality. The works of Mead [17] and Benedict[18] were among the earliest to demonstrate that ways of behaving which are considered deviant and sick in one culture represent the "normal" pattern of the typical individual in another culture. Benedict, for example, describes an orientation toward property among the Kwakiutl Indians of the Pacific Northwest leading to behavior that in our society could be seen as paranoid in nature. We can appreciate even the subcultural referents of behavior disorder. Thus, the effective well-adjusted member of a rapidly paced and technologically based acquisitive-consumptive North American metropolis would find his *modus operandi* highly maladaptive if he persisted in them in one of the Hutterite cooperative communities of the Midwest.[19] It is not so commonly recognized that, for a given culture, the extent and nature of mental illness is a function of a relativistic definition which is variable over time—being one time rigorous, conservative, and applicable to small numbers of persons, being another time loose, liberal, and appropriate to huge numbers.

These considerations generate some intriguing, albeit paradoxical, heuristic propositions, for example,

1. The total incidence of mental illness in the population is greater during those periods in the national economy which support the expense of mental health census-taking than during economic periods that do not support such surveys.
2. The greater the number of psychiatrists, psychologists, and other trained mental health experts in the population, the higher the incidence of mental illness.

The first proposition may be restated: the essential case-finding orientation of public health surveys is such as to encourage application of a *liberal* rather than a *conservative* definition of illness; and, with emphasis on the goal of finding all *cases* showing even the slightest extent of pathology, there is an accompanying increase in the number of false positives, persons erroneously labeled ill. By contrast, when the population is not surveyed, and when health statistics are based purely on cases brought to formal diagnosis by hospital, clinic, or physician, we have a gnawing awareness of the existence of a large number of false negatives, persons whose actual pathology has escaped the gross dragnet of society's diagnostic institutions.

In this light, we can think of cultures (or subcultures) as being of a "false positive" or "false negative" type or, perhaps more accurately, as having false positive or false negative periods. The liberally oriented, economically expansionist, welfare state will be a false positive culture, *i.e.,* borderline cases will tend to be systematically labeled sick. The reactionary, economically retrenching, laissez-faire society will provide a false negative culture, *i.e.,* borderline cases will tend to be systematically labeled *not* sick. In this context, "borderline" cases are by definition those that are of very mild or minor pathology, if any, and that are not reliably (unanimously) diagnosed by independent clinicians.

This view of the case-finding process suggests the joint operation of two powerful and not necessarily independent factors in the definition of mental illness: the economy of the culture and the value system of the culture, the latter variously interiorized and individualized by the personnel who conduct surveys. In recent years experts representing those of the social sciences most directly concerned with problems of mental health and social welfare have been meeting to wrestle with the issues of theory and method arising in a newly evolving area of research, the area of social psychiatry.[20] When these experts addressed themselves to the problem of "Definition of a Case for Purposes of Research in Social Psychiatry," they generated a spectrum of suggestions ranging from denial of the existence of any good, workable criteria by which to define cases, to proposal of the highly workable, but grossly restrictive criterion of persons-who-confront-psychiatrists.[21] Falling between these extremes were abstract criteria for defining mental health or measuring mental illness; they were abstract in the sense that the concrete procedures for application of the criteria were usually not specified. Here are a few examples:

a. A two-dimensional criterion in which adjustment is expressed in 1) method of problem management and 2) need-free perception. On the first dimension, maladjustment is expressed by failure to face problems, failure to consider alternative solutions, failure to select an alternative, or finally, failure to implement the decision with action. On the second dimension, maladjustment is expressed by failure of the individual to perceive accurately those aspects of his environment with respect to which he has strong needs, failure to hold his perception undistorted by his needs.

b. A tripartite criterion composed of 1) absence of the urgency to take action (felt by the individual, by society, or both) which characterizes major disorder; 2) social agreement between therapist and patient, a sharing of the same values; and 3) a goal of maximization of the patient's potential (contrasting with restoration to "reasonable adjustment" as a goal in major abnormality).

c. A criterion statement indicating that the areas of appraisal should be the person's 1) physical health or illness, and adjustment to it; 2)

intrapersonal functioning; 3) interpersonal functioning; and 4) relationship to his value system; and that the mode of appraisal should
combine 1) clinical judgment; 2) community opinion; and 3) the
person's own evaluation of his status.
  d. A symptom-based criterion in which inefficiency, nonproductivity,
     and social or moral conflict are emphasized; however, detection of
     such functional impairment in any of a variety of possibly "patho-
     genic situations" is seen as appropriately shared by physician, edu-
     cator, employer, clergyman.
  e. A criterion based on the network of the individual's interpersonal
     relationships, the kind of relationship he has to all persons im-
     portant to him.

Of course, as is almost certain to happen whenever a group di-
rects its attention to the problem of specifying what is to constitute
the unit of observation in a research into an essentially social phenomenon, there was at least one voice raised in protest, denying
that it is necessary to describe a phenomenon reliably *before* one
attempts to study the relationship it holds to other variables. To a
point, this protest is supportable; but if a circumscribed phenomenon to be studied is not defined with reasonable precision, then at
least the operations of the research process must be concretely explicated.
  The existence of various values is implicit in the above general
criteria of mental illness or maladjustment. The conference was
not without awareness of the role played by value orientations, as
illustrated in the following statement (Marie Jahoda): "The difficulty in answering it ('What is a case?') comes from the fact that
inevitably at some place there is a value judgment involved. I think
that mental health or mental sickness cannot be conceived of without reference to some basic value. We are all trained to exclude
values from our thinking; and the way we try to exclude them is
not to talk about them. A more appropriate manner of dealing with
this basic difficulty is to spell out what the values are that underlie
our particular concept of mental health or mental illness." [22]
  How do value systems relate to the problem of defining mental
illness? In answering this question, we are helped to see that the
diagnostic problem which superficially appears to be concrete and
practical has roots in issues of an highly philosophical nature. A
value system may place major worth on the individual or on society
—actions may be preferred that augment the status of the individual
at the expense of the group, or choices may be made that enhance

the strength of society to the relative disregard of the individual. Recognition of the right to "conscientious objection" during wartime is expressive of a value system in which the individual's scruples are given priority over what conceivably could be the nation's security. By contrast, laws such as the ill-fated Prohibition Act are expressive of a value orientation in which the presumed welfare of society is predominant over individual freedom.

The definition problem is only partly clarified if we know that within the pertinent value system (for example, that of North American urban culture, mid-twentieth century) the "welfare" of the individual is focal. What may be specifically valued is the absolute *productivity* of the individual, and valuing those arrangements that favor the productivity of the individual is a circular way of valuing the society which consumes his products. More consistently individual-oriented is a value system that is chiefly concerned with the optimal productivity of the individual, with provision of those circumstances that permit him to work up to capacity, to be neither an over- or under-achiever, but rather to experience full application of his capacities and abilities. In this *efficiency*-oriented value system, it is again easy to detect the circular path from personal adjustment to social gain. Finally, we can conceive of an individual-oriented value system in which the person's achievement-reward experiences are secondary in importance to the question of his happiness. In such a value system, regardless of the level of the individual's output or the efficiency of his working and social relationships, he is regarded as ill and maladjusted if he experiences subjective mental or emotional distress and if he says (or would report upon question) over any period of time, "I am unhappy."

In Figure I below, all possible combinations of the factors of productivity, efficiency, and happiness are arranged so as to suggest a scale from greatest to least severity of personal maladjustment within the range of those psychological disorders which are grouped as "minor," "mild," or "neurotic." The individual's happiness is to be understood as his emotional response to his perception of his relations to his work, to his family and friends, and to his community. The figure suggests that all but the least severe of these milder disturbances are brought to some sort of at least colloquial diagnosis by a societal radar that is particularly sensitive to failures in productivity or efficiency. The chronic absentee from the factory (who perhaps needs Monday for recuperative purposes); the accident-prone, compensated disability case; the evening and week-end worker who needs extra hours to "catch up"; the devotee of a vitamin-aspirin-barbiturate diet who gains brief respite, if any, from pains, pressures, pulsations, or pustules for which the physician can determine no certain locus or pathology; the job-hopper whose record shows no failure because he never remains with a task long enough to demonstrate achievement; the "academic tramp" who matriculates eternally and matures never—all such as these are variously caught in those institutional screens of society which are gauged to matters of output and effectiveness.

Figure I.

A Hypothetical Continuum of Personal Maladjustment

| Source of Diagnosis | Essentially Social Diagnoses (in school, factory, community) ← ⎯⎯⎯ → | | | Essentially Personal Diagnoses (self-diagnosis) | |
|---|---|---|---|---|---|
| "Clinical" Status of Individual | Non-productive Inefficient Unhappy | Non-productive Inefficient Happy | Productive Inefficient Happy | Productive Inefficient Unhappy | Productive Efficient Unhappy |
| Severity of Social Pathology | Most Severe ← ⎯⎯⎯⎯⎯⎯⎯⎯⎯⎯⎯⎯⎯⎯⎯⎯⎯ → Least Severe | | | | |

When the individual is perceived as productive and efficient in his several social roles but *feels* emotionally and mentally distressed, depressed, or unhappy, and when he reacts to this feeling with a verbal response, "I am unhappy," he has made essentially a crude self-diagnosis. This self-appraisal contributes more formally to a diagnosis if he repeats his statement to a psychiatrist.* At this point, the self-diagnosis becomes a social diagnosis. At this point, too, we may illustrate again the relativity of mental illness and the manner in which the economy and the value system of a culture determine

* "Formally," in the sense that teachers, clergymen, and social workers are not recognized generally as competent to make "psychiatric" diagnoses, although these "front-line" persons frequently do provide the earliest diagnoses of personality disturbances.

"how much" mental illness is endemic to it. The probability that an unhappy person will make public acknowledgment of his state (*i.e.*, admit it to a professional person for whom the client automatically becomes a census datum) varies directly with the number of such professional persons accessible to him (the economic factor), and with the extent to which the culture is at the time exhorting unhappy persons to express their burdens (the value factor). The greater the number of psychiatrists (or other psychotherapists) in a community the greater is the influence of subtle pressures upon frustrated and conflicted persons to step forth and announce themselves. These subtle pressures are augmented by formal programs of mental hygiene and public "education" which imply that unhappiness is a psychiatric illness for which cures are known and treatments are available.

Study of the history of psychiatry reveals that patterns of symptomatology in the functional disorders (those for which no underlying organic pathology is found) change over time. This is perhaps most clearly reflected in the case of conversion hysteria, a type of neurosis that once filled the neurological clinics of Europe, particularly those of Janet and Charcot in France, and was also common in the early years of American psychiatry. These once common disorders, characterized by neuromuscular dysfunction or autonomy of function (blindness, deafness, paralysis, or spasms, tics, and contractures) have become a rarity in the metropolitan clinic. Such hysterical conversion symptoms as we do see now tend to be much subtler in form and constitute not nearly so large a portion of the neuroses. Why? It is as if there are fashions in neurosis; the process of symptom formation is responsive to the individual's awareness of what is currently acceptable to the culture. Furthermore, the economic and value factors interact so that the "functioning" definition of a maladjusted personality is intermediate on the one hand to a criterion of "what the traffic will bear," and on the other hand to a criterion of culturally idealized "normality."

If a mental-health education program or community survey uncovers cases that are greatly in excess of the number that can be treated by existing facilities, there will be a tendency for only the more severely disturbed cases to be treated, that is, to be diagnosed as really ill. Under such circumstances of demand-exceeding-supply, essentially productive and efficient but unhappy persons tend not to be recognized as "sick enough" to require treatment. But what is the nature of an illness which requires no treatment? And is there in this social operation perhaps an implicit recognition that for such sickness no effective treatment exists?

The line may be drawn too rigorously. In a demand-exceeding-supply situation, the screening process does not uniformly select or reject applicants for treatment in terms of the severity dimension alone. Those with milder symptoms, many of those self-diagnosed unhappy persons who are not necessarily also unproductive and inept, may find sources of help if they can pay higher fees. They cannot, however, effectively compete with more disturbed persons of lesser income for publicly supported treatment in clinics. This leads to another paradoxical proposition:

> Those persons who pay the highest fees for psychotherapy will tend to have the mildest degrees of maladjustment.

The validity of this proposition involves an assumption of no relationship between socio-economic status and tendencies to certain types or degree of neurosis.* Put bluntly, unhappiness as an isolated symptom occurs in the lower as well as the upper economic classes, but the former cannot afford to pay for its treatment. Also, severe cases of failure to produce and gross inefficiency will be found among the high-fee patients but they will constitute a smaller proportion of such patients than they will of low-fee patients.

Even the apparently rigorous and operationally oriented definition of cases in terms of persons who come to treatment results in a highly relative criterion, the amount of mental illness at a given time being relative to economic and value factors as well as to the absolute number of therapists available. If the relativity of even this rather concrete definition of a mentally ill person (*i.e.,* a person in treatment for such illness) could be more generally perceived, its use as a criterion in survey studies would possibly not be so uneasily viewed by investigators who see it as "artificial" and too restrictive.

### IV. NUMEROLOGY, NOSOLOGY, AND NONSENSE

One of the participants in the conference referred to earlier resorted to some imaginative arithmetic to demonstrate the "artificial limit" imposed by the in-treatment definition of mental illness.[23]

* This assumption may be seriously questioned though not clearly refuted by data to be presented in Chapter Three.

Briefly the argument runs as follows: Assume approximately 7,000 psychiatrists in the country; of these, approximately one half are "committed" to institutions for long-term custodial care of the severely disturbed; if the remaining 3,500 psychiatrists were in full-time, private practice for 40 hours per week, each could provide a total of 2,080 hours of patient care per year; the 3,500 could "treat" a total of 7,280,000 patients per year, with the completely non-sensical assumption that each patient received (required!) only one hour of care; rejecting this condition, the upper limit on the number of mentally ill defined by the "treatment criterion" is something under 7,000,000 or approximately 4 per cent of the total population.* The author of this excursion properly labels this estimate as "artificial," but he also implies that it is artificially *low* by calling the figure a limit rather than an estimate. Also by implication, a satisfactory criterion would be one which permitted a census greater than 7,000,000. How much greater?

Let us attempt another approach to the problem of estimation that is equally imaginative but free of the artificial limiting factor of a fixed number of therapists. Suppose we ask how many mentally ill persons there are in a given year, defining such persons as all those who acknowledge that they would seek and use the services of a psychiatrist if such services were available. Operationally, this would involve surveying all adults and asking each of them with respect to themselves and to all children for whom they were responsible, "Could you and would you utilize the services of a psychiatrist if one were available to you?" It might seem that this approach would satisfy the problem of minimizing the number of "false negatives," of persons actually in need of a psychiatrist but who would not be detected by any other approach; it would seem that this approach should come closest to satisfying those who wish an accurate estimate of the "absolute" number of psychiatric cases. But——

The number of cases which would be identified by this "need" approach (in contrast to a "facility" approach) to enumeration would be determined heavily by what the interviewees understood to be the nature, function, and services of a psychiatrist, or what they understood to be the character of "needs" (symptoms or complaints) which one brings to such a specialist. Immediately it is clear

* The number of active full members of the American Psychiatric Association in 1956 was slightly over 7,000. The population of the United States then was approximately 165,000,000.

that this approach to a nonartificially limiting case-finding criterion runs smack against the problem of definition, the philosophy of diagnosis, and the principle of indeterminacy (*i.e.*, the fact, first recognized in the physical sciences, that the procedures of measurement may directly influence the behavior of the phenomena under study). This approach does not escape from limits, or for that matter from artificiality. It is only that the degree of artificiality may be less, which is to say that we value our more inclusive definition of mental illness as being relatively more useful or appropriate to our purpose than a more exclusive definition.

Let us accept a diagnostic philosophy that values primarily the minimization of "false negative" cases and accepts the risks (costs) involved in relatively high "false positive" rates. Recognizing that the number of cases is relative to our definition of mental illness, suppose we define a case as a person who acknowledges need for and willingness to accept psychiatric help. Now, further, assume that we identify the psychiatrist as a person with special training and experience in the treatment of emotional difficulties. Suppose that we further identify this physician as a person who will listen sympathetically or objectively to one's troubles, a person who will maintain the strictest confidence regarding anything revealed to him, and finally a person who commands processes of such a nature that those who leave his office generally feel better than when they entered. The level of this identification is about what would be (and is) offered in informational programs concerned with the psychiatrist as psychotherapist. It is a level appropriate to informing the public prior to an inclusive search for cases. Finally, it is probably parallel to the stereotype of the psychiatrist (psychotherapist) held by the average semi-sophisticated layman who has not had therapy.

If we were to conduct our case-finding survey within this context, how large a number of maladjusted persons would we uncover? Put another way—is there *any* person who does not at least once in the course of a year experience a struggle with conflicts or feelings of such a nature that he feels he could be helped by talking out his perplexity with an understanding, confidence-maintaining, and wise friend? Now, if a person were under the influence of social taboos that prohibited such talk from the conversation of friendship, and if he were under the further influence of a social climate that encouraged members to speak of their conflicts only to specialists (or more precisely, to expect real help only from experts)—would not such a person, would not all persons under such circumstances, respond with a vibrant "Yes!" to the query, "Could a psychiatrist help you?"

We have by switching the focus of our definition of mental illness simply altered the nature of the artificiality of our count and the social implications of the limit at which we arrive. Instead of a fixed number of therapists, we have a fixed number of patients equal to the total population. Let's apply a little arithmetic to our new approach. Assume a population of 190,000,000 persons (each an actual or potential patient). Assume that our psychiatrist works a 40-hour week and consequently offers 2,080 hours of patient care per year. How many psychiatrists will we need for our population? The answer in round numbers is 90,000! This is roughly one psychiatrist for every 2,000 of the general population.

Several highly questionable and clearly indefensible assumptions are involved in this statistic:

1) That all cases require an equal amount of psychiatric time, viz. one hour.
2) That the same ratio of cases per psychiatrist which is effective in treatment or prevention of early developing or mild cases is adequate to the treatment or management of chronic, severe cases.
3) That our psychiatrists take no vacation and further, that they need each other, that is, are included as potential patients in the total population!

Absurd assumptions, asinine arithmetic, cockeyed conclusions— but only in matter of degree. This illustration of one of the extremes of case finding (case making?) simply points up the semantic seductions which peril the mental health surveyor who must steer a course that avoids both the "false positive" shoals and the becalming "false negative" sea. Part of the difficulty lies in a cultural bias that has led epidemiologists to contaminate screening criteria of "positive" mental health or absence of mental illness with questions of availability of or need for psychiatrists. There is a generally unrecognized *non sequitur* in this. If a population is screened in terms of concepts of healthy personality and positive mental hygiene so that the mildest and earliest stages of maladjustment are detected, it is doubtful whether such cases should be blanketed under the category of "illness," and it is even more doubtful whether such maladjustment is *ipso facto* of psychiatric dimensions, requiring treatment by a psychiatrist.

If our diagnostic philosophy and definitional net is structured to catch persons in whom the basic and possibly sole symptom is a claim of unhappiness—a personal, subjective distress which may have varied, complex, and hidden origins, is it quite reasonable to classify such unhappiness as illness and, thus, to assign to it those extensive etiologic, pathologic, and therapeutic connotations identified with physical medicine? If we do call unhappiness an illness, does it accordingly, without great forcing of our concepts of sickness and health and of psychology and biology, fall into the realm of medicine and specifically into the field of psychiatry? What is unique to the training and experience of the physician-specialist in psychiatry that makes him pre-eminently prepared to minister to the disenchanted and the doubtful? These questions will be given further consideration in a later chapter.

## V. SUPPLY AND "DEMAND"

In 1946, public-health officials estimated that our nation needed 14,000 psychiatrists; this would have provided one psychiatrist to approximately every 10,000 of the general population.[24] In 1948, spokesmen for American psychiatry indicated a need for 20,000 psychiatrists, or a ratio of one psychiatrist to approximately every 8,000 of the general population.[25] According to the first estimate there was a shortage of not less than 10,000 psychiatrists. The 1948 estimate indicated an immediate need for an additional 16,000 psychiatrists. The American Psychiatric Association has recommended a minimal standard of one psychiatrist for every 200 hospitalized patients.[26]

The manner in which such estimates are made is not always stated explicitly. For the most part they have not rested upon epidemiological surveys of communities or regions that have only in the past ten years become a prominent research area. Rather, these estimates have been based on hospital and clinic statistics, indices of mental illness rates and population growth, and extrapolation from other estimates. Implicit in such estimates of the number of psychiatrists needed by our society is the assumption that maladjustment (ranging, for example, from chronic organic psychosis at one extreme to marital dissatisfaction at another extreme) is the appropriate and necessary charge of the psychiatrist, and the assumption that these wide boundaries define "mental illness." The estimates will be realistically oriented to treatment and prevention possibilities only if these assumptions are reasonable.

Fully qualified psychiatrists are certified by the American Board of Psychiatry and Neurology. They are graduate physicians who, in addition to the required one-year internship following completion of the four years of medical school, have had not less than three years of supervised training (the psychiatric residency) in an approved psychiatric setting, plus two years of appropriate experience in psychiatric practice. With this background of training and experience they become eligible for the board examinations, which are a "means of distinguishing the fully qualified specialist from the would-be specialist of inferior training and inadequate experience." [27]

A psychiatrist may be defined somewhat less strictly. Full membership in the American Psychiatric Association (APA) requires that the graduate physician will have had not less than one year of "practice" in a mental hospital and an additional three years of specialization in the practice of psychiatry.[28]

As of 1962, there were 7,100 diplomates in psychiatry of the American Board of Psychiatry and Neurology (ABPN).* This number of fully certified psychiatrists affords a ratio of one psychiatrist to approximately every 30,000 of the total general population. If we subtract from this number the approximately 3,000 required to meet the proposed minimal standards for care of the hospitalized mentally ill, a balance of about 4,000 would be left to care for the nonhospitalized population, a ratio of one diplomate psychiatrist to approximately every 60,000 of the nonhospitalized population.

In 1962, the total of active members and fellows of the American Psychiatric Association was 9,450.[29] This number provides one specialist in mental illness for approximately every 20,000 of the total general population. If 3,000 of these psychiatrists were in mental hospitals (the number which would be required by APA standards), the remaining 6,450 would provide a ratio of one psychiatrist to every 30,000 of the nonhospitalized general population.

It is clear that the number of psychiatrists, defined either in terms of full certification or of qualification for membership in the professional society, falls far short of the number that would be required to satisfy estimated "ideal" ratios of psychiatrist-to-population. And the rate at which new psychiatrists are being trained, in view of the rate of growth of our population, is insufficient to improve the existing ratios or to reduce the shortages. The average

* Personal communication from Dr. David A. Boyd, Executive Secretary-Treasurer, American Board of Psychiatry and Neurology, Inc., March, 1963.

yearly increment of the American Psychiatric Association has been less than 440 members for the past ten years. Similarly, over the past five years, the number of specialists passing the examinations in psychiatry of ABPN has averaged less than 300 annually.

Assuming a population of 190,000,000 and a "minimal standard" ratio of one psychiatrist per 8,000 of the general population, there is a present *shortage* of between 14,000 to 17,000 psychiatrists, depending upon whether the APA or ABPN definition of a psychiatrist is used. If our population were to cease growth, and if there were no change in the incidence of hospitalized and unhospitalized mental illness, it would require from 30 to 60 years to overcome the estimated current shortage of psychiatrists at our present rates of training. To meet the estimated shortage within the next ten years would require that physicians be recruited and trained for psychiatry at from three to six times the present rate.

Of the psychiatrists who complete residency training each year only about 200 enter public service of some type.[30] This is far short of the 500 per year that would be required (at the prescribed ratio of 1 to 200 resident patients) simply to care for the annual increment of 10,000 patients in the resident population of our mental hospitals.

Since psychiatrists are recruited from graduate physicians, since the proportion of medical school graduates choosing to take specialty training in psychiatry has remained very constant (approximately 10 per cent) in recent years, and since there seems little likelihood of a significant increase in the total number of physicians to be trained in our country in the near future, we are not likely to achieve an effective increase in the total number of psychiatrists available to meet our expanding mental health needs, as schools, courts, prisons, general hospitals, and community health agencies are increasingly recognizing their needs for consultation and services.[31]

Parenthetically, a brief word is in order concerning the supply of psychoanalysts and their contribution to the mental health problem. There are only slightly over 1,000 members of the American Psychoanalytic Association. New members, fully qualified analysts, are added at a rate of only 50 to 75 per year. Their training is extensive and slow; their average age upon completing all training requirements is over thirty-five. If they specialize in individual psychoanalytic therapy, as most of them do, they will treat an average of fewer than 200 patients in their lifetimes.[32] Psychoanalysts play a very significant role as teachers and, to a lesser extent, as researchers.

They have generated a truly voluminous literature on the etiology and treatment of neuroses. But their direct contribution to the care of the mentally ill has been insignificant, and will probably continue to be so.

An exhaustive analysis of the sources both of supply and of demand for professional mental health personnel ends in the conclusion that we face a future of continuing, drastic shortages of personnel in all aspects of our mental health programs.[33]

In addition to psychiatry, two other professions play major roles in meeting the demands for mental health services: clinical psychology and psychiatric social work. For both of these professions, also, demand for personnel considerably exceeds supply. (See Appendix.)

## VI. THE INFLATIONARY SPIRAL

Psychiatrists, psychologists, social workers, and public health scientists who have concerned themselves with the epidemiological aspects of mental illness and with estimation of the public's need for mental hygiene services have had several goals. At a pure research level, knowledge of the over-all incidence of mental illness in relation to a complex of socio-enonomic, ecological, biological, and cultural factors would stimulate hypotheses about and investigation of suggested determinants of the occurrence and typing of psychological breakdown. At an applied research level, such precise knowledge of the extent and distribution of cases would enhance the assignment of therapeutic resources, the application of prophylactic measures, and reasonably controlled evaluation of both. Administratively, it would facilitate estimation of the personnel needs in the mental health sciences and furnish material for educational efforts to engage the interest and resources of the public in support of such needs. Pursuit of these goals would seem to serve public interest. But knowledge does not immediately and uniformly contribute in an all-or-none manner either positively or negatively to social welfare. Discovery sometimes results in mixed blessings. Witness the history of explosives!

Investigators of the epidemiology of mental illness have not characteristically manifested awareness of the functional dependence of their findings upon their formal definitions of a case, or upon their operational biases as expressed in the training and orientation of the persons conducting surveys and identifying cases. Incidence of illness will vary as a function of what is formally defined as pathology and what is recognized as requiring a specified therapy. Failure to give due consideration to the semantic and cultural relativities has encouraged a careless disdain for certain case-finding approaches as too artificial and limited (*e.g.*, definitions of "cases" as only those persons in treatment by a psychiatrist). Such disdain is absurd in the context of a search for the "true" number of cases, when such a search implies a limit and the limit involves defining propositions that share that "artificiality" (or better, arbitrariness) that is inherent in all symbolic systems.

In addition to a failure to appreciate the significant interpretive problems stemming from the semantic slipperiness of this research phenomenon, these surveyors have not generally acknowledged the fact that their efforts at measurement may very well disturb the material being investigated. Most simply, case-finding tends frequently to result in case-making. We may conjecture that a necessary element in the condition of mental illness is some degree of introspection and an awareness of distress or dysfunction. The existence of a mental health survey or the conceptual climate (value system) in which such a survey is undertaken may provide the crucial stimulus to such introspection and to the resulting awareness of an "acceptable" complaint. Again, there is a way in which illness, or at least some aspect of the total condition of illness, comes first into existence with formal definition of the illness or the making of a diagnosis. In a very real sense, the patient suffering from cancer has a new dimension to his illness after the diagnosis is made. He is in a real sense made more ill by the diagnosis which translates his distress into a Sickness. In this way, it is possible to conceive of a process whereby a pre-existing psychological and physical state blossoms into illness when a culture instructs in self-examination and defines symptoms.

Some case-finding may be case-making. The desirable goals of determining the extent of mental illness are confounded by the fact that the survey process can contribute subtly to psychological distress. The individual who is dissatisfied with his work, unhappy in his social relationships, lacking in recreational skills, devoid of long-range goals, and without a personal philosophy is not helped by sensitization to the notion that he is "sick." Particularly is he not helped if such sensitization occurs in a situation in which professional aid is not available to him.

Following World War II there has been a great awareness of and concern about the problem of mental illness at all levels of social organization. The essential focus has been on ways of providing more and better care of patients and to a slightly lesser degree on prevention. In pursuing these aims there has been action on three fronts: 1) determination of the extent of the problem; 2) training of more psychiatrists, clinical psychologists, psychiatric social workers, and other mental health personnel; and 3) institution of additional hospital and clinic facilities. As indicated above, the number of psychiatrists that should be trained has been related to the estimates of the number required. It would seem that the research and training fronts constitute strategically related battle lines. But, there is reason in the arguments presented above to wonder if the two endeavors may have effectively canceled each other. It may well be that as we pursue both the case-finding and the training goals, we manage to furnish that number of therapists just sufficient to keep up with the expanding case load and are not effectively changing the relative availability of treatment. This possibility must be examined thoroughly by anyone who would assume that the solution to our mental health problem rests simply in the provision of more psychiatrists.

Before we are immobilized by these discouraging implications we should make a careful search for possible sources of error. We should be most critical of any implicit assumptions. Obvious sources of possible fallacy exist:

1) In estimating the extent of mental illness in the nonhospitalized population, certain basically arbitrary, relative, and uncertainly reliable diagnostic criteria must be applied. Are these criteria reasonable, explicit, and practical, or are they of such a nature as to generate an insupportably large population of false positive cases?

2) What data are available to support the contention that one psychiatrist per 200 hospitalized patients is either necessary or desirable? If there are 400 patients per specialist, will they receive half as much treatment and show half as much improvement as those having a 200 to 1 ratio? Has anyone established the functional relationship between number of patients per psychiatrist and the rate of improvement and number of discharges per period of time? Is this "minimal standard" ratio prescribed in terms of facilitating research programs or with respect to adequate administration of presently existing therapeutic procedures?

3) What precisely is the unique, crucial, or appropriate role of the psychiatrist in the nonmedical treatment of those nonmedically

involved and nonhospitalized, milder, circumscribed personality disorders? Are these cases reasonably included in his "social" case load?

4) The estimated shortages of psychiatrists are based on the assumption that in the nonhospitalized general population there is a large number of mentally ill persons who require the services of a psychiatrist. In so far as these patients are not hospitalized, it is to be inferred that their sickness is less severe and incapacitating and/or involves less threat to their physical and social well-being than is true of the hospitalized patients, or is not considered particularly amenable to those forms of medical therapy and institutional program for which hospitalization furnishes a necessary environment. If this is so, we may well ask just precisely what it is about the nature of these nonhospitalized mental illnesses and the treatment they receive that makes the services of a psychiatrist necessary. To what extent do they involve medical derangement and to what extent do they demand and respond to medical intervention? If any sizable portion of the nonhospitalized mentally ill are essentially without medical symptoms and inaccessible to medical intervention, is it intelligent to assert that their adequate treatment demands access to a specialist whose primary training is in medicine? If we understand that the essential form which treatment of these extramural cases takes is that of therapeutic conversation, to what extent is the physician-specialist appropriately trained and specifically a *sine qua non* for provision of such conversation?

In short, prediction of the total number of psychiatrists required by our population and estimates of the optimal psychiatrists-to-patients ratios constitutes a cultural mirage. Such statistics may be of some slight exhortatory and pseudo-informational value in arousing public and professional interest and increasing financial, clinical, and educational resources for the training of larger numbers of specialists. Viewed as major goals of a program for dealing with the problem of mental illness, they are completely unrealistic. The notion that the battle against mental illness is to be won simply by enrolling a sufficient number of expert combatants is a subtle delusion that seduces public and profession alike to march *à petit pied* toward that continuously receding horizon which is the nation's case load.

Demands for service grow as facilities are expanded. Expansion of facilities and increase in personnel has a direct effect on the working definition of a case, and an indirect effect on the probability with which an individual will diagnose himself as "mal-adjusted" or needing help. There is a sense in which the creation of a physician amounts to the creation of patients. In the case of the psychiatrist, this iatrogenic phenomenon has even greater reality. It is meaningful to say that the actual case load increases directly as a function of an increase in the number of therapists.[34] From such a proposition it does not follow that a "pretend they are not there and maybe they will go away" philosophy should be inculcated, or that failure-to-diagnose is prophylactic. Nevertheless, it should be clear from the preceding that the plague of mental illness will escape successful isolation, treatment, or prevention if effecting of these remedial measures is ultimately dependent on producing enough psychiatrists.

In supply of psychiatrists there appears to be a real bottleneck. If it is this bottleneck which holds up an effective attack on the entire mental illness front, the problem would appear to be without solution. But analysis suggests that to look upon the shortage of psychiatrists (or any experts) as the major problem is to propound a fiction. Just such a fiction is propounded in any forecasting that is unmindful of the excessive demands likely to result from incautious arousal of public expectation, that is unaware of the iatro-genic, suggestive effect on borderline cases of increasing amounts of therapeutic resources, that is uncritical of the case-making by-product of case-finding procedures, and that is unsophisticated with regard to the fundamental social and philosophical implications of particular ways in which a culture at a particular time defines personality disorder for purposes of formal social diagnosis.

In the foregoing, psychiatry and psychiatrists have furnished the focus for a critical analysis of our present social climate in regard to matters of diagnosing, treating, and preventing mental illness. They do not stand alone as exemplary of, or responsible for, the overly simplified, absolutistic approach. It has not been psychiatrists alone who have encouraged the assumption of such an entity as the "true" census of mentally ill. It is not they alone who encourage the unrealistic supposition that successful management of the total burden of mental illness requires only that we train more and more persons in the image of, and with the same therapeutic techniques as, our current experts. Clinical psychologists and psychiatric social workers have been equally enthusiastic about the doctrine of "more therapists per fewer persons" as the royal road to better conditions of treatment and prophylaxis. "There's nothing wrong with our people that having more of us wouldn't help." This might be the party slogan for all three professional groups. Clinical psychology and psychiatric social work have also engaged in the self-drugging activity of estimating how many of their respective kind our population really needs.

No one of these primary mental health professions has taken any obvious lead over the others in promulgating a careful review of the adequacy of the current pattern of professional training and practice in terms of present real needs or reasonable expectations for the future. All three have settled comfortably into the sedating bath of a cultural atmosphere in which the psychiatric disciplines have a "bullish" market, are invested with unquestioned salutary potency, and are encouraged from public and private sources alike to increase their reproductive capacities.

In this treatise, the term psychiatry frequently should be understood to stand generically for those disciplines identified as major recipients of the burden of mental illness: the medical specialty itself, and the closely allied basic science of clinical psychology and applied technology of social work. It is not convenience alone that dictates usage of this shorthand. Both historical accident and semantic casuistry have contributed to a general social identification of psychiatry as the ultimate agency for disposition of and dispensation to the psychologically disturbed. Psychiatry has not seen fit as a profession to be uncomfortably self-conscious about assuming a specious medical responsibility for the predominantly ambulatory and nonmedical patients inhabiting our state "hospitals," nor has it been abashed by the inheritance of the nonorganically sick person whose assignment under a rubric of mental "illness" brings him within the traditional purview of the physician. Clinical psychology and psychiatric social work are not without their imperialistic designs, but they are rather late on the scene and their tacit "island mandates" over the simpler maladjustments and family conflicts leave them relatively free of those pejorative terms to which psychiatry's place in the sun makes it naturally liable.

While all three of these professions have manifested increasingly active preoccupation with issues which bear pointedly on self-aggrandizing motives, there is no basis to question that the over-all welfare of our society is the sincere, primary concern of each of them. But, in their legalistic, sophistic endeavors to establish inter-professional boundaries guarded by sanctions and prohibitions of traffic, it is difficult, if not impossible, to detect that the psychiatrist, psychologist, and social worker really mean to map the realm of human unhappiness so that there will be both clear signposts and accessible roads guiding temporarily lost travelers back to homes in which they are secure and to pursuits in which they are satisfied. Certainly no one of these prominent and socially influential groups has evinced any effective professional leadership in stimulating either a truly searching review of the present pattern of training and service or a reasonable appraisal of the needs of the future as viewed against other realities of our social economy. The surveys of the epidemiology of mental illness which have had broad professional support suffer from implicit commitment to current conceptions of diagnosis and treatment.

It is equally true that no one of these three vital professions has provided significant stimulus to a critical examination of those parts of our current social climate composed of definitive attitudes toward mental illness, value attitudes toward individual unhappiness, and expectations of present therapeutic efficacy. The psychotherapist has insightfully recognized that his patients variously cast him in the role of father, teacher, lover, or saint, and that through these roles and recognition of them by the patients, they are helped. He has extended somewhat imaginatively the structure of psychodynamics to the realm of politics, international relations, and moral philosophy. He has not, however, generally reflected on the long-term consequences of a cultural encouragement of the offices of a professional surrogate and the indirect but consequent discouragement of emotionally deprived persons from seeking acceptance, dependence, and security in the more normal and accessible channels of friendship. With some recognition that both his expertness and his powers have been oversold, he has not, however, shown much tendency to dissuade the public from its present condition of an acceptance tending toward awe and adoration. His reluctance to introduce any temporizing influence is understandable when viewed in historical perspective. But he cannot forever escape responsibility for leading the lay population toward better understanding of the psychotherapists' role in a properly oriented society.

Recently critical examination of their respective roles and responsibilities has been generated in each of these professions primarily out of fears of encroachment or suppression by the others. These fears have led to strivings for legal prerogatives and intraprofessional investitures with status symbols. The basic profit-motive, trade union features of these activities have been very inadequately hidden by sonorous and platitudinous oaths of allegiance to the protection and welfare of the public. Psychiatric social work has been relatively less energetic in these interprofessional skirmishes, apparently less threatened and less threatening, and until recently, rather unconscious that it was subtly insured against the Oedipal jealousy of father-psychiatrist and the sibling rivalry of brother-psychologist by a semantic policy of referring to its therapeutic conversations by the disarmingly ambiguous term, "case work," rather than by the loaded, pseudo-proprietary (and equally ambiguous) "psychotherapy."

These professions which are responsible for providing social leadership as well as clinical management in the field of mental illness have been sadly lacking in the former. No one of them has shown an inclination toward a detailed inventory of its present actual contribution in the light of a sober appraisal of present needs and future demands. None has seemed inclined to a self-analysis in which its most unique and specific, actual and potential contributions to prevention and treatment of maladjustment would be analyzed in terms of the equipment and skills of the others, and jointly viewed against a reasonably projected job-and-market analysis.

## VII. THE PSYCHIATRIC TEAM AND PSYCHOTHERAPY

As a result of programs of public information, many people have some knowledge of the so-called "psychiatric team," the common staffing unit which is to be found in hospitals and clinics. The implication of the "team" designation is that the psychiatrist, psychologist, and social worker bring to bear their respective specialized knowledges and techniques in an integrated attack on the clinical problems brought before them. Such an integrated, division-of-labor approach is sound in theory and, where it is in fact consistently practiced, it can afford an efficient and economical utilization of the three disciplines, each of which does have a very real contribution to make. With negligible exception, the professions themselves are sold on the "team approach," and it is natural that they have used its appealing connotations in informing the public as to personnel needs.

In point of fact, in a great many hospitals and clinics and with respect to a great many individual cases, the psychiatric team exists primarily as a rather expensive administrative hierarchy rather than as an actually functioning integration of various roles in an over-all therapeutic plan. It is very common to find each of the "players" engaged in exactly the same activities with the same kind of patient; that is, they all engage in therapeutic conversation. It would be possible to audit sizable random samples of treatment interviews of psychiatrists, psychologists, and social workers with their respective patients; it would not be possible to tell which was which from their psychotherapeutic activity alone. Although each of these professional workers has received an extensive, very different, and assumedly appropriate training, the differences in training are neither clearly nor frequently manifested in their "psychotherapy," "counseling," or "case work" interviews with patients they treat. The sources of this basic homogeneity of practice and its theoretical, professional, and social implications will be examined later.

The "core" psychiatric team has been commonly stereotyped as composed of psychiatrist, psychologist and social worker, even when the locus of team activity is an in-patient hospital service. It is most unfortunate that there has not been a more explicit statement of the role of the nurse as a team member and recognition that her potential contribution far exceeds her typical use as a combination clerk-watchdog, inasmuch as she has more extensive and varied contact with the patient than anyone else. To some degree there is recent evidence of efforts to broaden and add meaning to the team concept. Recognition of the potential contributions of occupational therapists, recreational leaders, and others to the effecting of an integrated, total program of psychological management of the patient is a necessary first step. Development of efficiency and imagination in accomplishing an actual integration of such resources is a difficult challenge.[35]

The fact that all three members of the psychiatric team spend a sizable portion of their time in non-team, individualized but nondifferentiable psychotherapeutic activities results from at least two obvious forces. First, the extent of the demand for psychological treatment constituted by the case load of patients for which psychotherapy is either the treatment of choice or required in addition to strictly medical procedures is so great that no one of the professions, least of all psychiatry, or all combined, exists in sufficient numbers to meet the demand for personal interview therapy. Second, members of each of these professions have a strong drive to "do psychotherapy," a drive that is related in part to interests and values that lead them into social service occupations and in part to convictions that their particular form of training equips them at least as well as, if not better than, the other professions for this work.

*It is to the everlasting credit of large numbers of psychiatrists, holding final clinical and legal authority, that they have not only permitted but have encouraged the so-called ancillary workers to join with them in the common job of psychotherapy.* Responsive to the realities of the clinic and the ward, sensitive to their basic commitments to the welfare of the patients, sensible of the limited specificity of treatment by conversation, these psychiatrists have exercised a generosity and reasonableness in their interprofessional relations that are sorely belied by the small-spirited and meanly reasoned attitudes of many of their colleagues (particularly when in convention assembled). It may be, also, that their liberality is expressive of an awareness that the outcomes of therapeutic conversation are not certainly different when conducted by one rather than another of their colleagues.

That there is a sizable amount of professionally condoned if not officially sanctioned sharing of responsibility for psychotherapy rather than actual reservation of this activity to any one specialist-expert might seem to relegate the restrictive efforts and interprofessional tensions that have developed notably in the last decade to the realm of natural, temporary outcomes of rapid growth of all three groups. It should not be overlooked that outside of the smoke and fire of arguments generated by self-interest there is an important question that bears on the welfare of the patient. How may each of the experts *best* contribute to the maximum therapeutic benefit for the largest number of patients? In seeking to answer this fundamental question, it must be recognized that when each is engaged in the process of therapeutic conversation, he is not during such periods making application of his most unique skills. When the physician-specialist is engaged in direct psychotherapy, his extensive and expensive medical knowledge is not being applied to medical treatment of patients, nor to teaching and supervision of other therapists (including students), nor to research aimed at development or evaluation of such therapies. When the psychologist is doing personal interview therapy, he is not applying his specific observational-analytic tools and procedures to clarification of the diagnoses of patients nor is he contributing his *unique* research sophistication to the vital areas of personality diagnosis, etiology of psychological disorder, prognosis, and outcomes, nor is he teaching others. When the psychiatric social worker is affording therapeutic conversation she is not applying her special skills to the collection and collation of data that delineate the life space of the patient, nor is she using her special knowledge in appraising and integrating those resources of family and community that fit the needs of the patient, nor is she contributing to research into the nature of family patterns, group roles, community structure, and social attitudes as they relate to mental illness.

There are two serious implications from the observation that the psychiatric team, as presently constituted and as presently disposed with respect to psychotherapy, manifests a sharing instead of a division of labor. There is an implication that the crucial clinical task of diagnosis, treatment, and disposition is being pursued with less than maximal efficiency. There is the even more serious implication that the scientific endeavor, on which all progress toward understanding and eradication of illness is based, is receiving less attention and effort than is necessary and possible.

# References

1. *Patients in Mental Institutions, 1958;* Part II. *Public Hospitals for the Mentally Ill;* Part III. *Private Hospitals for the Mentally Ill and General Hospitals with Psychiatric Facilities* (Washington, D.C.: U.S. Department of Health, Education and Welfare, Public Health Service, 1960).

2. Rashi Fein, *Economics of Mental Illness.* Monograph Series No. 2. Joint Commission on Mental Illness and Health (New York: Basic Books, Inc., 1958).

3. Herbert Goldhamer and Andrew Marshall, *Psychosis and Civilization. Two Studies in the Frequency of Mental Disorders* (Glencoe, Illinois: The Free Press, 1953), p. 116.

4. Dorothea C. Leighton, "The Distribution of Psychiatric Symptoms in a Small Town," *Amer. J. Psychiat.*, 112 (1956), pp. 716-23.

5. Leo Srole, Thomas S. Lagner, Stanley T. Michael, Marvin K. Opler, and Thomas A. C. Rennie, *Mental Health in the Metropolis: The Midtown Manhattan Study* (New York: McGraw-Hill Book Company, Inc., 1962), p. 138f.

6. An official report of the American Public Health Association, *The Control of Communicable Diseases in Man*, 8th Edition (New York: American Public Health Association, 1955), pp. 90, 106, 130.

7. Arthur P. Noyes and Lawrence C. Kolb, *Modern Clinical Psychiatry*, 5th Edition (Philadelphia: W. B. Saunders Company, 1958), p. 490.

8. Henderson and Gillespie's *Textbook of Psychiatry*, 9th Edition, revised by Sir David Henderson and Ivor R. C. Batchelor (London: Oxford University Press, 1962), pp. 129-31.

9. Edward A. Strecker, Franklin G. Ebaugh, and Jack R. Ewalt, *Practical Clinical Psychiatry*, 7th Edition (New York: The Blakiston Company, 1951), p. 371.

10. Otto Fenichel, *The Psychoanalytic Theory of Neurosis* (Copyright 1945 by W. W. Norton and Co., Inc., New York, N.Y. By permission of the publisher), p. 19.

11. A. H. Maslow and Bela Mittelmann, *Principles of Abnormal Psychology: The Dynamics of Psychic Illness* (New York: Harper & Row, Publishers, Inc., 1941), pp. 108-109.

12. Committee on Nomenclature and Statistics of the American Psychiatric Association, *Diagnostic and Statistical Manual—Mental Disorders* (Washington, D.C.: American Psychiatric Association Mental Hospital Service, 1952), p. 31.

13. G. S. Kilpatrick, "Observer Error in Medicine," *J. Med. Educ.*, 38, No. 1 (1963), pp. 38-43.

14. Philip Ash, "The Reliability of Psychiatric Diagnoses," *J. Abn. Soc. Psychol.*, 44, No. 2 (1949), pp. 272-77.

15. Hermann O. Schmidt and Charles P. Fonda, "The Reliability of Psychiatric Diagnoses: A New Look," *J. Abn. Soc. Psychol.*, 52, No. 2 (1956), pp. 262-67.

16. Stanton P. Fjeld, *et al.*, "A Behavioral Census of a State Hospital Population," *Psychol. Monog.*, General and Applied, 71, No. 12, Whole No. 441 (1957), p. 31.

17. Margaret Mead, *Coming of Age in Samoa*, From the South Seas: Studies of Adolescence and Sex in Primitive Societies (New York: William Morrow and Company, 1928).

18. Ruth Benedict, *Patterns of Culture* (New York: Houghton Mifflin Co., 1934).

19. Joseph W. Eaton and Robert J. Weil, *Culture and Mental Disorders* (Glencoe, Illinois: The Free Press, 1955).

20. H. Warren Dunham, "The Field of Social Psychiatry," *Amer. Sociol. Rev.*, 13 (1948), pp. 183-97.

21. "Definition of a Case for Purposes of Research in Social Psychiatry," In *Interrelations between the Social Environment and Psychiatric Disorders*, Annual Conference of the Milbank Memorial Fund (New York: Milbank Memorial Fund, 1953).

22. *Ibid.*, p. 142.

23. *Ibid.*, pp. 124-25.

24. Robert H. Felix, "The National Mental Health Act, How It Can Operate to Meet a National Problem," *Mental Hygiene*, 31 (1947), pp. 363-74.

25. Group for the Advancement of Psychiatry. Report No. 5. *Public Psychiatric Hospitals* (Topeka: April, 1948).

26. *Standards for Hospitals and Clinics*. American Psychiatric Association, 1956.

27. American Board of Psychiatry and Neurology, Inc. *General Requirements for Applicants in Directory of Medical Specialists.* Vol. 10 (Chicago: Marquis Publications, Inc., 1961).

28. Constitution and By-Laws of the American Psychiatric Association. In *Biographical Directory of the American Psychiatric Association* (New York: R. R. Bowker Company, 1958).

29. *List of Fellows and Members of the American Psychiatric Association,* 1961-62 (Washington, D.C.: American Psychiatric Association, 1962).

30. M. Gorman, *Every Other Bed* (Cleveland: The World Publishing Company, 1956).

31. George W. Albee, *Mental Health Manpower Trends,* Monograph Series No. 3. Joint Commission on Mental Illness and Health (New York: Basic Books, Inc., 1959).

32. Lawrence S. Kubie, "A Pilot Study of Psychoanalytic Practice in the United States," *Psychiatry,* 13 (1950), 227-45.

33. George W. Albee, *op. cit.,* pp. 241-43.

34. ———, *op. cit.,* p. 29.

35. Milton Greenblatt, Richard H. York, Esther Lucile Brown, in collaboration with Robert W. Hyde, *From Custodial to Therapeutic Patient Care in Mental Hospitals. Explorations in Social Treatment* (New York: Russell Sage Foundation, 1955).

# CHAPTER TWO

# A Perspective

## I. THE VALUE OF HISTORY

People vary greatly in their interest in history. There are some persons who find everything about the lives and circumstances of people in times past to be of very great interest. There are others whose concern for history is almost entirely circumscribed to a particular subject or era. Perhaps a majority of persons, blissfully blind to the inherently mortal if not moribund character of the here-and-now culture in which they are enveloped, decry any preoccupation with the inert forms of the past.

The professional historian may evince an attitude of quiet assurance that the study of history is an acceptable end in itself, a scholarly pursuit which has the justification of all searches after knowledge for knowledge's sake. In this sense, pure research into the facts of the occurrence and chaining of events in the lives of men and nations shares the status of pure research into the occurrence and chaining of events in the realm of physical processes. If, as happens with some frequency, the historian finds himself in a period of utilitarian retrenchment in which he is asked to prove his immediate worth, he may argue that history is essentially an account of man's problem-solving activities and that, as such, it has practical value in guiding us toward the solution of present conflicts. It is implied that in studying history one does not simply acquire static facts; one *learns* about the on-going interactions of social forces, political ideas, and economic pressures and is accordingly better prepared to form opinion and take action on the current scene. In brief, it is argued that study of history teaches how to avoid errors and how to accomplish goals.

All too commonly the average citizen through newspapers, magazines, and other popular media is given a picture of history whose chief property is a glorification of "Progress." He is led to view the technological marvels of today against a backdrop that depicts the crude and cumbersome procedures, the gross and grotesque tools, the extreme and naïve conceptions of our predecessors. He examines the prototypes of the automobile, the airplane, and the high-fidelity radio and looks back upon the owners of these antiques with a mixture of amused superiority and wonderment at their frustration tolerance.

The sophisticate and the professional are not free of the self-glorifying effect of looking backward, the narcissism of historical study whereby one sees clearly the faults of forerunners but perceives only dimly, if at all, the persistence of these very mistakes in today's program. It has been said of statistics that too often they are used by the researcher as the inebriate uses the lamp-post—as a source of support rather than illumination. It might be said that history too often is used as the nobleman uses his title—as a balm to apathy rather than a spur to achievement. History may be brought to the defense of arrogance or to the service of humility. One should not ask, "Has there been progress?" Rather, one must ask, "How much progress has there been?"

For the question of mental illness and mental health, neglect or distortion of history serves us badly. On the one hand, we have the oft-stated generalization that mental illness is increasing, and that such increase is a function of certain facets of modern society. And again, we are told that we have gained much knowledge and possess increasingly potent means for treatment and prevention of emotional disorders. A careful historical analysis which aims at factual perspective, rather than at either social exhortation or social reassurance, will test the validity of these popular assertions.

In this chapter, a brief review shall be made of the concept and treatment of mental illness over the ages, so that a critical evaluation of our current state may be made against the perspective afforded by history.

## II. THE PREVALENCE OF MENTAL ILLNESS

We do not know about the psychology of primitive man in prehistoric time. Paleontology has reconstructed for us something of the physical circumstances of his existence. We know that he inhabited a harsh, uncertain and uncontrollable world. We know that his puny physical capacities, unimplemented except for the crudest of tools and weapons, were arrayed against the violent powers of wind and water and against the brutish hostility of huge predators. Knowing these few, simple facts about prehistoric man and his environment, we can conjecture that he was totally occupied in a daily, all-engaging pursuit of security of limb and maintenance of life. In his earliest and certainly in any precommunal states, he had little time for introspective revery and for the diagnostic question, "Am I unhappy?"

Many primitive men were certainly confronted by environments that demanded constant hard work and continued vigilance. Perhaps there is a psychological "zero point" at which a physically uncontrolled environment demands so much immediate and direct coping behavior as to prohibit the development of a neurosis. And perhaps there are life situations in which the persistent threat of real danger to life militates against consideration of those possible and lesser fears which are the core of much neurotic anxiety. We know, for example, that during the period of the blitzkrieg assault upon London in World War II, and in the days of England's greatest danger, there was a trend toward decreased frequency of visits to the neuropsychiatric clinics.[1]

To the degree that neuroses as we know them require some opportunity for self-sensitization it is unlikely that our prelinguistic ancestors had the time to develop them. It requires only the assumptions of individual differences in stress tolerance and of extreme and frequent stress, however, to presume that primitive man was subject to severe mental breakdowns. These probably were disruptions of his adjustive integration that occurred in circumstances which repeatedly aroused violent fear or presented extreme deprivations.

We have no basis on which to estimate with what frequency our most primitive forebears fell victim to mental illness. There are those who like to think that over the centuries there has been an increase in the incidence of personality disorder which is related to the growing complexity and speed of modern life. These persons are inclined perhaps to think that primitive man was relatively free from psychic stress because his needs were simple and his problems few. But his needs and problems were severe and recurrent, and permitted only temporary solution, and his resources were negligible.

It may be that true neurosis (as distinguished from "total insanity") requires the nourishment of introspection and self-consciousness. Perhaps it is only when man can both look within himself and toward a future beyond the next moment, only when he can think of other people and how they perceive and evaluate him, that neurotic conflict can arise. Such weighing of self and others requires both time and the freedom from immediate tasks which are a common luxury (?) of technologically advanced cultures.

We may surmise that man's thought has evolved from exclusive preoccupation with the immediate physical environment, from concern with food, clothing, shelter, and safety from the elements and from attack, then to concern with those extended environmental phenomena of sunrises and snowfalls, of moon and stars and seasons, and then finally to his relationship to the universe and to his fellow man.

If essential control over the immediate physical environment and a degree of civilization sufficient to free man for self-preoccupation and worry about possible future threats to his security or presently imagined threats to his integrity is a basic requirement for the generation of neurotic anxiety, then man has had these prerequisites for a very long time. And the basic psychophysiological equipment required for the overlearning of danger signals and the anxiety response to stress seems not to be a very recent biological development.

In this perspective, the presumed greater prevalence of neurotic breakdown in present-day man must be attributed to the greater stresses under which he lives. But is modern man in fact subjected to greater stress than his historical predecessors? Contemporary Western civilization is complex and the tempo of life seems ever faster. We are subjected to a wide variety of pressing demands (largely of our own creation), but we have an increasing armamentarium of efficient tools with which easily to provide much of our daily demands. Is it not probable that a thoughtful and penetrating numeration of the pressures, problems, and uncertainties that confronted people 100 (or 1,000) years ago and that confront his modern counterpart would reveal chiefly a difference in content, not a difference in number or seriousness? The problems of life have changed in their nature, but not in their number or severity. We suffer an inability to project ourselves empathically into the psychological stresses of older generations. Through inadequate historical perspective (and perhaps out of need to be heroic in our own eyes) we see lives of earlier times as simpler, slower, and less stressful— while we see ourselves as immersed in a morass of economic, ethical, political, moral, and social problems which cannot be solved because there is "too much pressure" and everything moves "too rapidly"— forgetting the tremendous technological advances that have both speeded communication and essentially freed us from concern with the mundane problems of sheer existence, so that we are in fact able, if we will, to concentrate in a way never before possible on the solution of our special problems.

Has there been a significant increase in the rate of occurrence of *major* forms of mental disorder? When the severity of disturbance is such that the total functioning of personality is disrupted and the individual can no longer be safely tolerated in his community, when his symptoms are sufficiently gross to permit of easy, objective description, and when the sick individual is removed to a hospital, we have a base line that permits of valid historical comparison and that, with careful attention to adequate case histories, permits comparison of clinical diagnoses. Such comparative historical analyses, with attention to refined statistical corrections for population growth and changes in the age characteristics of our population, have rarely been attempted. In one of the best studies so far reported the authors conclude that *the rate (frequency of first admissions to hospitals per specified age groups of the general population) of the major forms of functional psychoses has been essentially the same since 1870.*[2]

Even though the best available evidence suggests that psychotic breakdown is not increasing in frequency in modern times, it may be argued that the total amount of mental illness is on the increase by virtue of the prevalence of milder, nonhospitalized forms of psychiatric disability, *e.g.*, the neuroses. In this argument we are confronted by a cultural relativity that makes analysis of documentary evidence almost impossible. Today we recognize and have diagnostic labels for varieties of personality defect which were not provided for by the social machinery of pre-1900 cultures. Failure of recognition of an illness and formal provision for its treatment does not, of course, constitute evidence of its absence. Disorders do not begin their phenomenal existence with their first recognition, description, and labeling.

Neurosis is not peculiar to modern man. Problems and pressures, the threat of large-scale disaster and the torment of doubt about ultimate values are not a special heritage of twentieth-century man. The biological capacity to experience anxiety is not a particular evolution of the post-1900 generations. If this is the "Age of Anxiety" it is because we have chosen to focus on this phenomenon and to give it a meaning and importance which it has never been previously accorded. Anxiety and hope have been experienced in various measures by men throughout the ages; there are absolutely unavoidable eventualities and insoluble uncertainties that give rise to both. Anxiety in its essential nature is no more pathological than hope—but our present culture has chosen to be anxious about anxiety.

As we struggle individually with our personal anxieties and as we daily hear the tocsin of nuclear threat it is natural that we think ourselves to be the most psychologically tormented of all generations. Sober meditation upon the fact that all men in all ages have faced danger, deprivation, and the inevitable uncertainties of existence supports the conception that the sum total of mental misery in the world has not grown or diminished greatly over the passage of time. What has changed is man's relative freedom to think about his condition, to be anxious about his anxiety, and to live in a cultural epoch which entertains the thesis that personal frustration of any sort is abnormal, that avoidance of anxiety should be a primary personal goal, and that society can provide both the knowledge and the experts for the successful prevention of unhappiness.

### III. PRIMITIVE MAN AND PSYCHIC DISORDER

Earliest history suggests that mental illness has probably been coexistent with mental life. Man's capacity to perceive, to discriminate, to create symbols for the communication of his perceptions has always entailed the possibility of error—the possibility of misperception, of poor discrimination, of inadequate communication. Such errors throughout all time have had potential to interfere with man's efforts to adapt, to live securely in his environment. There is reason to believe that earliest man had emotional equipment, that he could experience pain, and learn to fear its source and to be anxious in the presence of reminders of previous hurts. There is reason to believe that primitive man was no more a standard unit than his modern brother. Then as now there were probably wide individual differences—differences in susceptibility to pain, differences in the capacity to learn from experience so as to avoid repeated injury or failure, differences in the physiological reactivity to real and symbolic stresses.

Some men of early history showed marked disturbances in their behavior—they exhibited uncontrolled and unremitting fear in the absence of real threat, they engaged in maladaptive, inadequate protective measures, they had sudden fits and fainting spells, and they became violently rageful. Their peers could readily see that these men were disordered but could see such disorder only as a further manifestation of the threatening and unpredictable world. The same powerful agents that brought thunder and lightning must be responsible, it must have seemed, for these wild storms in men. The malevolent spirits responsible for man's general misery and hardships must be particularly abusive toward the "disordered."

While no meaningful appraisal can be made of the frequency of severe mental dysfunction in earliest man, it is reasonable to conjecture how insanity may have been perceived and treated. Prehistoric man's life space was compounded of danger and ignorance, and these are the generators of fear—in a reversible equation. In an atmosphere oppressive with fear, it would be probable that the wild outbursts of a demented person would seem fearsome, and those exposed to his violent, strange acts would be moved to self-protection rather than to treatment.

With the insight into conceptions of disordered behavior and its management revealed by the earliest historical records, we can reasonably project backwards and assume that the nature and treatment of insanity did not suddenly assume new forms with the advent of language.

Anthropomorphism is possibly the most primitive and universal of all forms of psychological thought. Primitive man's talent for projecting his personal qualities into the world about him perhaps exceeded that of his modern cousin only through freedom from self-consciousness. The ancient had need to appease and, later, desire to control the wildness which each day filled his existence with uncertainty. What could be more natural, and more promising of a successful petition, than to cast an image of man-likeness into each of nature's threatening forms? What could hold greater hope for the attainment of truce, safe passage, and successful endeavor than the possibility that the sun and the moon, the earth and the waters, and the plants and animals were but variously disguised forms of man-stuff? If this were so, the human creature could plead with his signs, hope to be comprehended, and expect sympathetic response.

> "Before medicine there was magic. Primitive man peoples the world about him with gods and demons. He sees spirits in the trees, in the winds and the moving clouds, in storms and lightning, in the running rivers, in sun and moon, in the very stones he treads upon. These spirits, benevolent and malevolent, control his destiny for good or ill. They are particularly responsible for his misfortunes. The primitive

mind does not regard sickness, disease, or even death as the consequence of natural phenomena. Rather are they looked upon as the results of supernatural intervention on the part of the spirits which fill his world. In his naïveté primitive man feels confident that by learning certain secrets and mysteries, certain rituals and incantations, he can in turn gain control of the supernatural spirits and manipulate them to his own purposes and desires, or at least to neutralize them—to ward off illness, for instance. His efforts to manipulate external forces through super- natural means or knowledge constitute the kernel of magic." [3]

So it may have been that man projected into his cosmos a stage of actors, a *dramatis personae* of anthropomorphic spirits, and sought by pantomime to convey his prayer and by prayer to achieve his security. This was *animism*, the investment of physical phe- nomena, organic and inorganic, with qualities of intention, direc- tion, and force like those perceived within himself and among his brethren. [4]

It was natural for primitive man to explain the unpredictable and uncontrolled in his own behavior with the explanation he had for wider phenomena. The disturbed person was "possessed" by an evil force, and he could be relieved by efforts to drive out the evil which was in him, to appease it, or to ease its exit from his body. Thus, in the earliest period in the history of mental illness and its treatment, we find a crude ideology of powerful, malignant forces which required strong countermeasures to cause "them" to relin- quish their grip on the sick person. In this time, holes were bored into the skulls of the "possessed" so as to relieve pressure and per- mit exit of the evil spirit. Whipping and scourging were inflicted on the sick person, but were directed at the evil within him. Primi- tive psychology, from which even the most sophisticated modern man must continually struggle to free himself, would generate the thought that evil spirits seek out sympathetic hosts—the possessed person is in his own right evil—and that therefore the exorcism of the evil spirit could appropriately include some punishment of its host.

History suggests, and modern knowledge of psychopathology makes it plausible, that some of the violent treatments which were inflicted during the period of primitive animism were effective. In this earliest period of psychiatric history, we have a probable first expression of a repeated paradox—theories of etiology or pathology which are inaccurate or inadequate, or both, may give rise to thera- pies that prove efficacious, and the very potency of the treatment, unfortunately, may prevent or delay correction of the erroneous theory. (See Chapter Four.)

How short a step was it from animism to *demonism?* How soon did our ultimate progenitors detect that there was good and bad in their spirit world? How soon did they discriminate the hostile force from the hospitable circumstance? The fact of preponderant harshness in their surroundings coupled with appreciation for their frail resources would favor a rapid focusing on the enemies among their anthropomorphic creations. The prevalence of environmental catastrophe led to the growth of demonology, the identification of evil spirits and of techniques for appeasing them or escaping their malevolent influence.[5]

Even primitive man revealed cognizance of the touchstone to social progress—division of labor and its refined expression as based on particularization of talent. There evolved gradually the role of *shaman,* specialist in the haranguing of demons, singer of incantations and purveyor of potions. His was the task of providing amnesty with the supernatural, protecting the community through group ritual, and treating the afflicted individual with a pharmacopoeia of exorcism.

## IV. NATURALISM, HUMANISM, AND PSYCHIATRY

With man's gradual increments of knowledge of the regularities of his world—of lunar cycles, the seasons, the migration of birds, and other periodic phenomena, he was able to develop an awareness of his environment as "natural." Though his world remained harsh, threatening, and in measure unpredictable, man was slowly able to free himself from fear of the supernatural. As part of this freedom, he came slowly to recognize that his own bodily ills were an expression of natural forces. In this context, mental and emotional disturbances could be seen as eruptions from within the sick person rather than the violent visitations of an evil force.[6] The priest gradually surrendered to the physician.

But for a time, the scourgings and other violences which had evolved in the struggle to cleanse man of "foreign powers" were continued when the naturalistic understanding of disordered behavior was under way. In the spirit of the new understanding of deranged behavior as natural phenomena, the same physically violent treatments could be administered in an atmosphere of humane acceptance of the victim and sympathy for him.[7] Again, we see the start of a paradox which has marked much of the history of psychiatry—faulty theory or neglect of theory, coupled with humane motive, permits the efficiency of symptom reduction to justify violence to the individual—from the minimal assault of incarceration to the extreme of brain mutilation.

There have been three great stages of enlightenment in the history of man's struggles with mental illness. The first of these came when derangements of the mind were seen as natural phenomena, not as expressions of supernatural assaults. The second came with the recognition that a humane approach, gentle care coupled with physical hygiene in a calm and sympathetic environment, brought amelioration of symptoms.

The third enlightenment, most recent and still only partially realized in consistent and large-scale application, came with the gradual appreciation of the indissoluble bonding of the mental and emotional life of the individual with his physical functioning, and brought the first real understanding of the psychological origins of physiological disorders. The healing touch was replaced with the healing word, physical symptoms were seen to respond to nonphysical treatment, and the potency of thought both to produce and to alleviate distress was revealed. The power of suggestion was appreciated and effectively utilized long before there was any understanding of the psychological laws governing it; even today, as crystallized in the specific phenomena of hypnosis, we are without a generally accepted unifying theory. From knowledge of the power of words to relieve painful physical and mental disorder, there came finally in the discoveries of Freud a recognition of the potency of ideas and their associated emotions to give rise to malfunction and failure.

In our accumulated wisdom, we now recognize that gross pathological disruption or destruction of the brain can produce disorders of behavior, and that similar disorders can be instigated by stress, frustration, and emotional trauma in the absence of any observable alteration of the gross structure or function of the central nervous system. On the side of therapy, we recognize that a painful, recurrent symptom can be relieved by ingestion of a drug, but may be also with equal effectiveness diminished or removed as a result of conversation with a perceptive counselor. It seems relatively easier to explain those disorders in which we can point to a physical agent as cause, and it seems relatively more efficient to use a physical treatment for a symptom which is responsive to it. Because of these apparent utilities and their associated practical efficiencies, we con-

tinue to labor with a dualistic approach to mental illness. We fail
to establish and maintain an integrated view of man as a unified
organism who functions holistically in adapting to the ocean of
stimuli in which he is immersed.

## V. THE CURRENT SCENE

Earlier attempts to train experts in neuropsychiatry have largely
failed. Medical education is still struggling, without notable success,
to produce physicians who can understand not only the peculiarities
and limitations of the biological apparatus with which man has to
effect his adaptations, but who can appreciate the problems of man
in making the psychosocial adaptations demanded by modern culture. Neuropsychiatry has been replaced in recent time by the separate specialties of psychiatry and neurology. And within psychiatry
there is growing evidence of a "working" schism—on the one hand,
there are psychiatrists who treat almost exclusively by the administration of drugs, electroshock, or other physical means, and on the
other hand, there are psychiatrists who almost exclusively treat by
conversation.[8]

In his own nature, man is not a complex of dissociated parts and
functions. He is a unity. A proper pill will lift his spirits, so will a
proper word. It is probable that an appropriately integrated application of medicine and conversation will accomplish more thorough
and lasting therapeutic benefit than will either alone. We do not
now understand all that we must in order to be able to prescribe
and administer optimally integrated therapy to the emotionally ill,
but even if we had such knowledge there are strong forces that
would continue to work toward fractioned, one-sided treatment.

A very provocative study points up not only the marked dualism
in the therapeutic activities of psychiatrists, but also indicates that
the selection of physical or psychological treatment is determined
less by the nature of the illness than it is by the social class of the
patient. In brief, members of the higher social class (defined by education, occupation, and residence) are much more likely to receive
psychotherapy than are members of the lower social class who typically receive electroshock therapy or custodial hospitalization.[9]

With this comparison we can once again look at the treatment of
mental illness in historical perspective. Today we recognize three
major forms of treatment: chemotherapy (the tranquilizers, antidepressants, and other drugs), shock therapies (electroshock, insulin
coma therapy, and variants of these), and psychotherapy. The use of

drugs in the treatment of emotionally disturbed persons has a long history. The current upsurge of interest and enthusiasm with the advent of the ataractic (tranquilizing) medications is responsive to a technological advance in drug chemistry rather than to any basically new idea. The ancient physicians of Greece had their pharmacopoeia; though their medications were selected with less knowledge both of chemistry and physiology, they allowed for the ubiquitous and potent effect of suggestion which is almost inextricably associated with any clinical use of medication. The Greeks were not without enthusiasm for their prescriptions. While electroshock therapy represents a highly refined and nicely controlled administration of a physical agent to produce sudden unconsciousness, the general notion of severe stimulation and violent psychological shock was a stock-in-trade of early physicians, *e.g.,* immersion to the point of drowning, the "surprise bath," and comparable procedures. The physical and chemical treatments of the early physicians are better recorded than are their prescriptions for psychological counseling, but we do know that the ancients were not totally ignorant of psychogenic factors in hysteria and melancholy and it is likely that therapeutic conversation was effectively engaged in, although the forerunner of our modern psychotherapist may not have been aware that his words were having positive impact.

If we look to ancillary treatments such as music therapy, recreational therapy, and milieu therapy, we readily find their counterparts in the descriptions of the Aesculapian sanitaria.[10]

In short, objective observation of distinctive avenues of therapeutic approach to the psychiatric patient would suggest that time has brought chiefly refinement and extension rather than basic innovation. Psychotherapy is practiced on a broader scale than ever before in history and with a greatly increased knowledge of psychopathology. When seen in full perspective this historical development constitutes less progress than suggested at first glance. As noted above, the availability of therapeutic conversation, which many authorities would hold to be the most thorough and effective of psychiatric therapies, is largely restricted by social class membership. It has been true throughout history that the treatment of the emotionally ill person has been determined less by the nature of his illness, less by his need, less by what promised cure than by his ability to pay. Sedation, seclusion, recreation, and extended personal access to the physician for support, reassurance, and exhortation (and possibly insight), have been the prescription for the wealthy. Institutionalization, restraint, and shock therapy have been the prescription for the indigent psychiatric patient. In summary, neither the essential content and nature of psychiatric treatment nor its distribution have really changed markedly over the centuries. A comparison of primitive and modern psychiatry is summarized in Figure II.

Figure II

Comparison of Primitive and Modern Approaches to Mental Illness *

| Period | Philosophy or "Theory" | Therapy | Social Attitude |
|---|---|---|---|
| | *Dualism* Good versus evil | *Exorcism* "Shock," cudgeling, trephining Drugs | Fear (from ignorance) |
| Primitive | *Etiology* "Possession" Humors (bile, blood, phlegm) "Constitution" | *"Humanism"* Music, massage, exercise, drama | Avoidance or abuse |
| | | Shaman; priest-physician | Attitudes and approaches determined by patient's status |
| | *Dualism* Psyche versus soma (psychosomatic medicine) | *Empiricism* Electroshock Psychosurgery (lobotomy) Tranquilizers | Anxiety (from a little knowledge) |
| Modern | *Etiology* Id versus Superego Biochemistry (*e.g.*, serotonin) Heredity | *Milieu Therapy* Occupational, recreational, and group therapy Psychodrama | Avoidance or institutionalization |
| | Psychodynamics | Psychoanalyst | Attitudes and approaches determined by patient's status |

* An enhanced appreciation of this comparative analysis will be facilitated by the material in Chapters Four and Five.

With the development of dynamic psychiatry based upon the more fundamental and durable of psychoanalytic insights, with the modern developments in chemotherapy, and with the growing availability of community mental health centers, it is possible for an enlightened public with the help of the pertinent professions to develop now a truly integrated and logistically feasible program for the treatment of mental illness, with treatment optimally prescribed in accord with the needs of the individual rather than dictated by irrelevant economic factors or denied by an artificially limited supply of personnel.

# References

1. Aubrey Lewis, "Incidence of Neurosis in England Under War Conditions," *Lancet*, 243 (1942), pp. 175-83.

2. Herbert Goldhamer and Andrew Marshall, *Psychosis and Civilization: Two Studies in the Frequency of Mental Illness* (Glencoe, Illinois: The Free Press, 1949).

3. Albert Deutsch, *The Mentally Ill in America. A History of Their Care and Treatment from Colonial Times,* 2nd Edition (New York: Columbia University Press, 1949), p. 1.

4. Gregory Zilboorg, *A History of Medical Psychology* (New York: W. W. Norton and Company, Inc., 1941) Chapter 2, pp. 27-35.

5. Walter Bromberg, *The Mind of Man. The Story of Man's Conquest of Mental Illness* (New York: Harper & Row, Publishers, 1937), Chapter 2, pp. 9-27.

6. Gregory Zilboorg, *op. cit.,* Chapter 3, pp. 36-92; Chapter 7, pp. 175-244.

7. Albert Deutsch, *op. cit.,* Chapter V., pp. 72-87.

8. August B. Hollingshead and Frederick C. Redlich, *Social Class and Mental Illness. A Community Study* (New York: John Wiley and Sons, Inc., 1958), pp. 155-61.

9. *Ibid.,* Chapter 9, pp. 253-303.

10. Walter Bromberg, *op. cit.,* p. 17.

# CHAPTER THREE

# The Psychotherapy Patient

## I. INTRODUCTION

Who are the consumers of psychotherapy? Who are the patients who create the demand for more sources of expert therapeutic conversation? What are the problems, complaints, and symptoms for which they seek aid? How and to what extent has their discomfort or distress interfered with their total functioning in meeting their responsibilities? What is the natural history of their dis-ease? What characterizes the onset, duration, and intensity of the disorder prior to treatment? What previous avenues of help have been tried, if any, before these patients come to the psychotherapist? What is known of the demographic characteristics of the psychiatric outpatient: how do they distribute themselves with respect to sex, religion, age, education, marital status, occupation, income, size of family, place of residence?

In light of the apparently unreserved conviction with which many mental health authorities have voiced a need for the recruitment and training of more expert psychotherapists, it is to be expected that we have something more than simple knowledge about the number of actual and potential candidates for such treatment. Especially as programs are outlined for the ideal training of the psychotherapist it is to be expected that considerable is known about the psychotherapy patient. Certainly it would seem likely that the above questions would find documented answers in the research literature of psychiatry and psychology. They do not.

While much is recorded as to the basic identifying characteristics, presenting symptomatology, and official diagnosis of the hospitalized psychiatric patient, the patient whose problems are treated exclusively on an outpatient basis has so far not been a regular subject for comprehensive census taking.

This is not to say that we do not know the forms that psychoneurosis may take so far as symptom patterns are concerned, or something of the particular problems associated with treatment of the discriminably diagnosable outpatient syndromes, and something of the rate of response to psychotherapy. Much of this information is discursive and clinical, and even when it represents statistical accumulation of the experience of a particular clinic it rarely goes beyond the diagnostic grouping of patients.

We do not have a truly comprehensive and representative picture of the broadly identifying characteristics of the consumers of psychotherapy, including the content of their problems, that goes beyond specification of such ubiquitous presenting complaints as depression and anxiety. In the absence of more information about these persons it is difficult to imagine that we can provide either specifically or adequately for their needs. Unless, of course, in our approach to mental health education we are managing to create a consumer demand for the particular product we feel they need!

Let us consider what is known about the actual and potential candidates for psychotherapy. Our information is primarily general description of those persons who manifest the type of psychiatric disorder for which psychotherapy is thought to be a primary treatment—the psychoneurotics.

It would be well at this point for the reader to turn back to Chapter One to read again the sample of formal definitions of neurotic disturbance. It was noted there that a scientifically based medical attack upon the neuroses as medical problems is hampered by the nonobjectivity, ambiguity, and inclusiveness of the diagnoses. A corollary of this fact is the absence of explicit statements of exclusion: When organic illness is not a factor, when psychic disturbance of psychotic proportion is ruled out, what patterns of disturbance or discomfort (or degrees of these) may be encountered that do *not* qualify for the label "neurosis"? Put another way, does the presence of mental conflict or the experience of anxiety or the condition of emotional depression constitute *ipso facto* a neurosis? Or, must the proper diagnosis of a neurosis entail consideration of the arousing circumstances, the duration, and the severity of these conditions? There is no clear consensus on these questions among psychiatric authorities. Note again that the formal definitions emphasize the character of the person's response and subjective experience and generally ignore the situational matrix to which the person is responding. In practice this means that a patient, without the presenting symptoms and history which would support some other diagnosis, who presents himself to an appropriate "mental health expert" with complaints of depression, conflict, or anxiety is likely to be diagnosed as psychoneurotic—even though any "hallmark" symptoms such as hysterical conversions, phobias, obsessions or compulsions may be absent. In a sense, these are "self-diagnosed" patients who are accepted by the therapist without much concern for whether they technically qualify as psychoneurotics. All of these factors contribute to the nonspecificity of a diagnosis of psychoneurosis and this nonspecificity must be kept in mind when considering the following data.

## II. PATIENTS IN TREATMENT

While the great majority of neurotics are treated exclusively on an outpatient basis, there are some whose illness is of such severity or whose life situation is so devoid of support that hospitalization is necessary. In a comprehensive statistical analysis of all psychoneurotics admitted to the public and private psychiatric hospitals of New York State between 1949-1951 (a total of 3,576), the following findings were reported:[1]

> The average neurotic patient was 38 years old at the time of hospital admission. Two thirds of the neurotics were in the 20-44 age range at admission.
> At all ages, the admission rates were higher for females than males.
> "Psychoneuroses are relatively more prevalent among the higher economic classes."
> With sex and age controlled for a standard population having a base age of 25 and over, the rate of first admissions with diagnosed psychoneuroses was *at a minimum among those with little or no formal education and increased progressively to a maximum among patients who attended college.*
> Among the hospitalized neurotics, there was a clear preponderance of single, widowed, and divorced patients over married patients. The excess of single patients was greatest among those over age 35.

In one of the very rare reports on the clientele of private psychiatrists, descriptions are given of the general characteristics of 100 unselected, consecutive cases seen in office practice.[2] Sixty percent of these patients were between the ages of 20 and 40. Slightly more than half (54 percent) were men, and slightly more than half were married (52 percent). Eighty percent were of Protestant faith. One third of these patients were office workers or skilled laborers; only 12 percent held professional jobs. One third of them had been referred to the psychiatrists by other patients; nearly one fourth were self-referrals. The major complaints presented by these patients were nervousness, tension, and depression; other complaints included insecurity, self-consciousness, and shame or confusion regarding sex. Only half of these patients were diagnosed as psychoneurotic, but psychotherapy was recommended for 70 percent of them. Forty percent of this sample made but a single visit. Of those who undertook outpatient treatment the average cost of the treatment was $240 per year.

There are some suggestive findings in a study by this writer of the characteristics of patients seen for individual psychotherapy by a representative sample of therapists representing the professions of psychiatry, psychology, and social work.* Specific diagnoses were not under investigation but it is a reasonable presumption that the majority of these patients were neurotics. The following generalizations may be proposed from this study:

The typical psychiatrist sees preponderantly more female than male patients. By contrast, psychologists and social workers tend to have clients of both sexes in equal numbers.

The complete age range is represented in the clients of the three professions. However, the number of psychiatrists who specialize in patients under age 15 is very small, while one out of five psychologists concentrates on this age group. In contrast to the social workers and psychologists, many more psychiatrists have a clientele in which persons over age 40 predominate.

The complete range of educational achievement is represented in the patients seen by all three professions. Psychiatrists are relatively inexperienced with patients having less than an eighth-grade education, while social workers very rarely carry on individual therapy with college graduates or persons with postgraduate education.

All occupational levels are represented in the psychotherapy cases of the three professional groups as are all income levels. Certain occupational groups (e.g., domestic and personal service, and agriculture, forestry, and fishing) have very little representation in the case loads of these psychotherapists. Other occupational groups (e.g., professional and managerial-office jobs) have a high frequency among the patients.

* This study will be reported in detail in Chapter Six.

## III. PATIENTS—PAST AND POTENTIAL

The only systematic cross-sectional information which we have on candidates for psychotherapy—actual and potential—is provided by a survey which was conducted under the auspices of the Joint Commission on Mental Health and Illness.[3] The information was collected by personal interview from a sample of 2,460 persons selected by standard sampling techniques so as to be representative of adults, twenty-one years of age or over, occupying private households in the United States. This survey was not directed at determination of the frequency of psychoneurosis in the general population. Rather, it was conceived as an overview of what our citizens consider to be their problems, how they view those problems, and what they do about their problems, particularly as this relates to their use of resources outside of the family. Because of the inclusiveness of the current definitions of neurosis, information of this sort about personal problems and their management is most relevant to our analysis. Here are some selected findings from this survey:

### Prevalence of Maladjustment

Over one third of the sample when queried about previous sources of *unhappiness* made reference to economic or material considerations, including their jobs.

Two out of every five respondents indicated their primary source of *worry* to be in the economic or material sphere.

Nearly one out of every five persons sampled reported that they had at some time in their past felt an "impending nervous breakdown." Less than half of these persons felt that their problem was relevant for outside help. Nearly 40 percent of these persons reported their problems as external, *e.g.*, death, illness, work tension, finances.

### Factors Related to Maladjustment

While the sexes did not differ in the frequency with which they reported unhappiness, the women more frequently reported worry, fear of breakdown, and need for help.

In general, women reported suffering from more symptoms, both physical and psychological, than did the men of the sample.

With increasing amounts of education, there is an increase in symptoms which express immobilization, inertia, and an attitude of passivity. This syndrome of immobilization is more prevalent among the younger persons than the older.

Greater distress is reported by women than by men in all adjustment areas—they are more disturbed in general adjustment, in their self-percepts, in their marital and parental functioning. This sex difference is most marked at the younger age intervals.

"Psychological anxiety" symptoms are found most frequently at the two extremes of the income distributions. Occupational status is less related to over-all adjustment than are education and income.

The unmarried (whether single, separated, divorced, or widowed) have a greater potential for psychological distress than do the married.

A feeling of impending breakdown is reported more frequently by the divorced and separated females than by any other group of either sex.

In general, single women experience less psychological discomfort than do single men.

### Factors Related to Seeking of Help

With respect to readiness to seek help for personal distress, the more highly educated persons surpass all other groups. "The highly educated are more introspective, orient themselves toward life in terms of self-questioning rather than unhappiness or dissatisfaction, express concern over the personal and inter-personal aspects of their lives, predominate in psychological rather than physical symptoms. . . . *It is of particular interest to note that the highly educated people more often go for help despite the fact that they express more happiness and satisfaction on the adjustment indices than do the less educated people.*" [Italics ours.]

Of those persons who actually sought help, over half reported problems in the area of personal relationships. Most commonly the problem was with a spouse and was less frequently ascribed to the *relationship* than to a defect in either the respondent (23 percent) or the spouse (25 percent).

### IV. STATUS AND SYNDROMES

From a major research investigation into the relationship between social class membership and mental illness, we have some information as to how the forms of neurotic disturbance under active treatment by psychiatrists are distributed in terms of social classification.[4] Every thoughtful person with a serious interest in mental illness and its treatment should have direct and thorough knowledge of the major report of this study. For our purposes here, it is necessary to know that the investigators developed an objective index for determining the social class membership of any individual. This index is based on a summation of weighted ratings of education, occupation, and place of residence, and provides a five-step hierarchy of social class. Class I, the highest social class, is composed of individuals who have had post-graduate professional education, who are executives of large concerns or engaged in one of the major professions, and whose home is located in the very finest residential area of their community. By contrast, members of the lowest social class, Class V, have had less than seven years of formal schooling, are unskilled workers, and occupy the poorest residential area of the community. While the population sampled was restricted to the greater New Haven (Connecticut) community, there is no reason to believe that the findings would not hold true for comparable metropolitan areas.

This study resulted in three major findings: 1) there is a significant relationship between the over-all prevalence or rate of mental illness and social class; 2) the types of mental illness are significantly related to social class; and 3) for a given type of illness, *e.g.*, neuroses, the form of treatment received by patients is significantly related to their social class. The latter two findings are most pertinent to the present essay.

It is of interest that the last two diagnostic categories of Table 1 together account for the largest portion of the patients in each of the social classes; except for Class IV, they account for more than half of the patients in each class. These two diagnoses (antisocial and immaturity reactions, and character neuroses) are not among the historically recognized, classical psychoneurotic diagnoses which are reflected in the first five listings of the table. The authors of this study make the following statements about these diagnoses:

"This group [antisocial and immaturity reactions] of illnesses is characterized by unapproved and intolerable behavior *with minimal or no overt sense of distress to the patient*. . . . It is a moot point whether antisocial reactions should be grouped with the neuroses. [Italics ours.]

"This diagnostic label [character neurosis] is used to describe patients

Table 1

Percentage of Patients in Each Social Class
with Specific Neurotic Diagnoses*

| | Class | | | |
|---|---|---|---|---|
| *Neurotic Diagnosis* | *I-II*** | *III* | *IV* | *V* |
| | Percentage | | | |
| Phobic-anxiety reactions | 16 | 18 | 30 | 16 |
| Depressive reactions | 12 | 12 | 10 | 8 |
| Obsessive-compulsive reactions | 7 | 5 | 5 | 0 |
| Psychosomatic reactions | 7 | 9 | 13 | 11 |
| Hysterical reactions | 1 | 1 | 6 | 12 |
| Antisocial and immaturity reactions | 21 | 32 | 23 | 37 |
| Character neuroses | 36 | 23 | 13 | 16 |

* Adapted from Table 13, p. 226, of August B. Hollingshead and Frederick C. Redlich, *Social Class and Mental Illness. A Community Study* (New York: John Wiley and Sons, Inc., 1958). Reprinted with permission of the publisher.

** Classes I and II are combined for this analysis because of the small number of cases in each of them.

who do not belong in one of the specific reaction types classified in the Veterans Administration scheme* . . . They exhibit mixed symptoms as well as relatively mild character and, to a lesser extent, some behavior disturbances."

It is notable that the "borderline" and vague diagnosis of antisocial and immaturity reaction does not reveal an orderly difference in frequency in the different social classes. The middle and lowest classes (III and V) show many more diagnoses of antisocial reaction than do the highest classes (I-II). By contrast, the nonstandard diagnosis of character neurosis is the most frequent diagnosis of patients from the two highest social classes, has progressively smaller frequency in successively lower social classes, with its frequency in the lowest class (V) being less than half that in the two highest classes (I-II). It is important to recognize that these variations in diagnostic frequency probably reflect the attitudes of the diagnostician (arising from ways of perceiving himself and others that are a function of

* The official diagnostic classification of psychiatric illnesses used by the Veterans Administration is essentially identical with the *Diagnostic and Statistical Manual* of the American Psychiatric Association.

his own social class membership) as much as the objective facts of the patients' behaviors. "We take the position that a neurosis is a state of mind not only of the sufferer, but also of the therapist, and it appears likewise to be connected to the class positions of the therapist and the patient." [5]

Within the more orthodox neurotic diagnoses of Table 1, only two, namely obsessive-compulsive reactions and hysterical reactions, show a distinctly different, nonoverlapping frequency of occurrence in the highest and lowest social classes. The differences among the social classes in the distribution of the various neurotic diagnoses are certainly less striking than the differences between the frequency of neurosis versus psychosis in the five levels of social stratification.[6] Only in the two highest social classes does the base rate of neurosis exceed that of psychosis. For all lower social classes there is an excess rate of psychoses over neuroses, and the excess is progressively larger for each consecutively lower social class. Thus, for a member of the lowest social class of whom nothing else is determined except that he is in need of psychiatric treatment, the probability that he will be diagnosed as psychotic is essentially seven times as great as the probability of a neurotic diagnosis. For a psychiatric "candidate" from the highest social class, the odds are 2 to 1 that he will be given a neurotic diagnosis.

But the psychological equipment required for the development of a neurosis is a biologically common property of most persons.* Stress, while it may vary in content or source, is not limited by class boundaries nor can it be readily established that it is greater at one social class level than another. Anxiety is experienced by most persons on occasion regardless of their class membership. This raises a serious question as to whether the class differences in diagnostic frequencies are directly reflective of differences in basic symptomatology or may not be more reflective of differences in the "diagnostic habits" of the clinician. One of the most ubiquitous of such habits is his more ready identification with and acceptance of the individual of his own class, the less understanding and more ready rejection of the person from a lower class matrix. In this regard, psychotherapists are members of the upper social classes. (See Chapter Six.)

---

\* The same assertion might be made with respect to psychosis. However, there are studies that suggest that certain forms of psychosis, notably schizophrenia, have a special genetic factor as a necessary (but not sufficient) etiologic contributor to the illness; such a factor appears, fortunately, not to be general in the population.

62

The person from an upper social class, regardless of symptomatology, tends in general to manifest many features which make him a more attractive candidate for psychotherapy. These positive attributes for therapy include good education, superior general intelligence (including the ability to communicate effectively at a level of discourse which is natural and comfortable for the therapist), and an ability to pay well for his treatment. Add to this the fact that psychotherapy is generally considered to be the therapy of choice for neurosis. Then, when confronted by a prospective patient from the upper social classes, the potential psychotherapist is subtly constrained to see the patient's illness as neurotic rather than psychotic, even if this requires forcing the diagnosis into an ambiguous category of "character neurosis."

## V. PSEUDO-NEUROSES

There is another aspect of the diagnostic problem that contributes to the great heterogeneity of psychotherapy patients and makes even more frustrating our almost complete lack of specific information as to what kinds of persons they are, what manner of conflict they experience, what symptoms they suffer, and what assets and abilities they manifest. We have noted above the ambiguities of formal diagnoses and certain subtle operations of social class membership which impair the consistency of neurotic diagnoses. These very ambiguities plus the effects of spontaneous intraclass empathy create a situation in which a large number of patients in therapy are self-diagnosed "neurotics."

Heterogeneity of patients in psychotherapy is increased by the absence of any adequate explicit treatment of the problem of identifying the individual who is not an appropriate candidate. This is not simply a question of prognostic differentiation. We do know some indicators from which we can predict whether psychotherapy is more or less likely to be effective with a particular neurotic. But there is a general absence in our psychiatric and psychological texts and other professional literature of description of the quasi-neurotic, the person whose very real problem is nonetheless *not* neurotic and for whom psychotherapy *as we ordinarily define it* is not an answer. In brief, we must ask if there are persons who are in some way psychologically uncomfortable and maladjusted (or maladapted), who are neither psychotic nor neurotic, who would be likely to seek psychotherapeutic help, and for whom intensive psychotherapy is *not* indicated.

The social worker knows better than the psychiatrist and psychologist the extremes of misery that the underprivileged members of our society must experience in the face of sheer physical deprivations and situational stresses. The mother who has inadequate clothing for her school-age children has a right to complain and to be depressed, but neither the fact of her complaint nor her depression makes her neurotic. The person with an alcoholic spouse is faced with a variety of torments and stresses; she deserves sympathy and counsel, but her need to evolve an adjustment to the very real problem of her chronically ill husband does not per se make her a neurotic.

The individual who has suffered through death the irremediable loss of a cherished companion has a painful emotional adjustment to make; it may require time and during that time he may show "symptoms" of despondency; he may need and seek emotional support, but neither his needing nor seeking is necessarily neurotic. The normal parents of a mentally retarded child will have emotional problems in their relations to each other and to their child; they may experience conflicts, insecurities, and frustrations; they will benefit from information and guidance, but they need not necessarily be candidates for intensive psychotherapy.

These are but a few examples of very common situational stresses, with marked potential for *normal* emotional response and psychological discomfort. The persons suffering such stresses are very likely to respond to wise and restricted counsel. But it is in the nature of the human personality to accept rather than reject offers of continued emotional support. If the counselor is more impressed with the symptoms of these unhappy persons than with the situations of stress which precipitate them he can be induced to an inappropriately extended effort at psychotherapy of pseudoneuroses. Apart from the probable dissipation of time and skill needed in treatment of truly neurotic disorders, failure to give adequate attention to the circumstances underlying reactive emotional symptoms may result in failure to take steps to correct those reality factors.

Are there persons who suffer essentially from a failure to have learned "how to live" (without having learned necessarily a pattern of neurotic adjustment)? And, for such persons is the professional psychotherapist the best teacher? The answers to these two questions are respectively "Yes" and "No." But psychotherapists are generally not taught to recognize their own limitations or the possible existence of individuals who would seek their help without suffering a disturbance for which orthodox psychotherapy is in fact therapeutic.

We lack detailed, thorough knowledge of what the persons who present themselves for psychotherapy are really like. We know best the more common symptoms for which they ask help. We do not know in any comprehensive way the patterning of the unsolved problems which generate their symptoms. We do not have basic information on the nature of the frustrated aspirations, the conflicts of impulse and inhibition, the particular stresses of daily reality, the confusion of goals or values, the particular frictions of their personal relationships that constitute the seedbed from which their symptoms flower.

We do know that susceptibility to neurotic ruptures of personality is not limited by age, by sex, or by class membership. The apparent greater incidence of neuroses in the upper social classes is not likely to prove to stem from a greater constitutional susceptibility to anxiety, to conflict, or to depression. Rather, the social class differential in rate of neuroses appears directly related to the differences in extent and nature of education. The members of the upper social classes are more prone to self-examination, are more ready to label symptoms as "psychological," are more accepting of the possibility of being "emotionally ill," and are quicker to seek specialized professional help.[7]

As a *symptom,* the depression of the upper-class executive is not clinically different from the depression of the lower-class housewife. Feelings of hopelessness, loss of interest, a general slowing up of mental processes and physical activity, and tendencies to withdraw from social commerce are common to the depressions of both. And if the depressive symptoms are sufficiently severe, it may happen that both the executive and the housewife will receive comparable somatic treatment (drugs, or electroconvulsive therapy) aimed at alleviation of the depression.

But, the problem is not depression. The problem is whatever has *caused* the depression, and the causes of depression in the executive are likely to be very different from the factors that have generated the same symptoms in the housewife.

It was suggested in Chapter Two, that there is little concrete evidence to support either the notion that anxiety is more prevalent in contemporary culture than in earlier periods of man's history or the idea that there are more powerful, more widespread, and more omnipresent sources of anxiety in modern life. If it appears that anxiety is "too much with us, late and soon," this is largely an artifact of a culture which has 1) given a name to the phenomenon, 2) defined its presence as the equivalent of deep-seated psychopathology, and 3) suggested that it is a public health menace which can and must be eradicated.

## VI. SELF-DIAGNOSIS AND SELF-REFERRAL

The problem is not anxiety. The problem is what causes the person to experience anxiety and what determines the pattern of his reaction to the experience of anxiety. We do not presently possess a broadly based and reasonably detailed classification of the anxiety-generating problems of twentieth-century man which cuts across all dimensions of our society. We know that the problems of the very young man are different from those of the very old, but this is hardly a sufficient differentiation on which to base selective approaches to problem solution. Among adolescents, there are some who experience acute anxiety because of problems of school achievement. There are others who are greatly distressed by the complexities of heterosexual maturation. There are others who suffer from conflicts and frustrations in both of these areas. All of them may show comparable amounts and patterns of anxiety. But the anxiety is not the problem, and no single, uniform approach to the counseling of these youths is likely to prove equally effective with all.

Experts in the mental health field generally accept the professional platitude that one must not "treat the symptom," but rather one must attack the cause. There is also general acceptance of the notion that anxiety is only a symptom of an underlying pathology. But the overwhelmingly predominant approach to the current psychotherapy of the neuroses is based on a theory in which anxiety plays a most central role and in which the basic source of anxiety is traced to the circumscribed sphere of psychosexual development. Furthermore, that theory evolved basically from clinical observations of a handful of upper-class patients from Freud's late nineteenth-century Vienna. Elaborations and revisions of the basic Freudian theory while to some extent correcting for the differences between the culture of nineteenth-century Europe and twentieth-century U.S.A.

have not significantly broadened the clinical observations on which the theory and the technique of treatment are based. It is still an orientation to etiology and treatment based on experience with middle-class and upper-class patients.

In the absence of detailed information about the nature, frequency, and patterning of psychological problems across the complete range of those major demographic variables that we know are related to personality functioning, we cannot know what manner of psychological approach is most likely to prove effective. In turn, we cannot know what program of training is best adapted to the production of therapists who will be maximally effective either with the complete spectrum of psychoneurosis, if this is a reasonable goal, or with the dynamics of special forms of personality disruption which very well may prove to be particular to the members of certain subcultures.

We have mentioned the peculiar ambiguities of diagnosis of mental illness. These ambiguities are especially troublesome in the diagnosis of the psychoneuroses, those forms of emotional disturbance for which psychological treatment is indicated. We have mentioned the prevailing system of diagnosis by symptom pattern rather than by underlying problem. And we have indicated the extreme paucity of information about the psychological problems of people who represent the complete range of our population in regard to defining characteristics of major psychosocial classes—age, sex, and so on. Finally, we have commented on the absence of agreed upon "rules of exclusion." All of these factors conjoin to create a situation in which the person who presents himself as a candidate for therapeutic conversation has made a self-diagnosis—and, significantly, he is most generally accepted on the basis of that diagnosis. This fact presents the possibility that our limited resources for psychotherapy may be overburdened in part by the presence of individuals who in fact are not proper candidates for that type of therapeutic conversation which the major therapists of our present professional culture are equipped to give.

This likelihood is enhanced by still other considerations. There is good reason to believe that the major impact of the mental hygiene movement has been on the members of the upper social classes. It is these persons whose education has made them psychologically sensitive and whose sophistication has made them socially receptive who, while not the prime target of the mental hygienists any more than any other social class, have the greatest readiness for self-referral. It is a corollary of the readiness for self-referral that the problems which the psychological sophisticate takes to the psychotherapist may be not only of lesser severity but may in fact be not focally psychoneurotic. Thus, any reasonably critical and honest therapist of long experience will have to confess that he has been confronted by some supplicants who have suffered not from anxiety nor from depression but rather from a loss of meaning in their lives, an absence of purpose, a failure of faith. Some of these persons suffer what has been termed "alienation." Their condition has been characterized by one thoughtful clinician as a very special disturbance, the nöogenetic neurosis.[8,9] Frequently they are successful, effective, productive people.

These individuals, together with many others who lack the customary symptomatic hallmarks of anxiety, depression, obsession, or compulsion yet who present themselves to the psychotherapist for help, might be uniformly described as unhappy. Their lives may be rewarding in a variety of ways and generally comfortable but nonetheless joyless. They are responsive to certain implicit messages of the mental hygiene movement—namely, that unhappiness is a form of mental illness and that the psychiatrist or psychologist is an expert in treating unhappiness.

It would be well for those who are responsible for programs of public mental health education to consider carefully whether or not there are any conditions of man's psychic life which, while painful or distressing, do not constitute neurosis and are not in their essential nature responsive to the techniques of the psychotherapist.

Our Declaration of Independence claimed as one of the rights of our citizens the "pursuit of Happiness." But freedom for this pursuit, like any other search, entails the possibility of failure. This possibility need be threatening only in an atmosphere which suggests that an absence of happy emotion is a sign of illness.

Our capacity for introspection and our inwardly directed sensitivity to our own feelings can be major sources of satisfaction and of pleasure. From these same sources spring much of our most painful experiences. We cannot have the luxury of introspective sensitivity without the cost of self-questioning and doubt.

When sensitive persons become stuck in an introspective rut of uncertainty, when they become immobilized by doubt, or when they are struggling against surrender to a conviction in an area in which all final convictions must necessarily be acts of faith, then they can be helped in their struggle by the challenge of perspectives elicited in the questions and suggestions of wise men. But the wisdom needed to elicit such perspectives is hardly the exclusive possession of any existing professional group. Neither the psychiatrist nor the psychologist is trained to be wise. They should be trained to recognize those cases that call not for psychotherapy but for exposure to wise counsel.

# References

1. Benjamin A. Malzberg, "Statistical Study of First Admissions with Psychoneuroses in New York State, 1949-1951," *Amer. J. Psychiat.*, 116 (1959), pp. 152-57.

2. Nathan K. Rickles, J. J. Klein, and M. E. Bassan, "Who Goes to a Psychiatrist? A Report on 100 Unselected, Consecutive Cases," *Amer. J. Psychiat.*, 106 (1950), pp. 845-50.

3. Gerald Gurin, Joseph Veroff, and Sheila Feld, *Americans View Their Mental Health, A Nationwide Interview Survey.* Monograph Series No. 4, Joint Commission on Mental Illness and Health (New York: Basic Books, Inc., 1960).

4. August B. Hollingshead and Frederick C. Redlich, *Social Class and Mental Illness. A Community Study* (New York: John Wiley and Sons, Inc., 1958), Chapter 8, pp. 220-50.

5. *Ibid.*, p. 237.

6. *Ibid.*, pp. 222-23.

7. Gerald Gurin, *et al.*, *op. cit.*, pp. 65-81; 187-203; 275-85.

8. Viktor Frankl, *Theorie und Therapie der Neurosen in Logotherapie und Existenzanalyse* (Vienna: Urban & Schwarzenberg, 1956), pp. 115-17.

9. ———, *Man's Search for Meaning. An Introduction to Logotherapy* (Boston: Beacon Press, 1962).

# CHAPTER FOUR

# The Physical Approach

While this essay is concerned with the problems of contemporary psychotherapy, an over-all perspective will be enhanced by some attention to the current physical methods of treatment of mental illness.

## I. INTRODUCTION

The discovery of strictly medical therapies for psychiatric patients had a period of concentrated development in the 1930's. The procedures introduced in that decade included a variety of therapeutic media: the injection of coma-producing drugs, the application of convulsion-producing electric currents, and the surgical destruction of major nerve pathways of the brain. Each of these procedures represented the modernization of a form of attack upon mental illness which had a hoary past. From the time of the earliest healer, whether shaman, witch doctor or priest-physician, the person who showed gross disturbances of his behavior became a subject at one time for drugs, at another for violent stimulation, and at still another for invasion of the bony envelope of the brain, if not of the brain itself. The earliest medical writings indicate that each of these procedures had a rationale of sorts—an explanation either in terms of presumed causal agents of the behavioral disorder, or of the avenue of therapeutic effect, which today's experts look back upon with mixed horror and amusement.

We no longer accept a visitation by evil spirits as an explanation of wild behavior. We no longer see sharp changes in personality as caused by "shock" for which the appropriate treatment is "counter-shock." We give at least some acknowledgment to the life history of the patient and to his learned patterns of adaptation (or maladaptation) as accounting for his symptomatology, even when prescribing physical treatments for his "psychological" symptoms. How will the mental health expert of A.D. 2060 look back upon the medical ministrations of today's psychiatrists? How will he view in particular the existing rationales for their physical procedures? With the advantage of his perspectives will his mixture of horror and amusement be less than that with which we now examine the history of the prescribers of emetics, the proponents of violent exorcism, and the drillers of trephine holes?

## II. MODERN MEDICAL THERAPEUTICS

The history of modern medical treatments of psychiatric disturbance may be reviewed briefly. In 1934, Meduna, a Hungarian psychiatrist, reported on the treatment of schizophrenia by the intramuscular injection of camphor in oil. He was led to this treatment by his observation that epilepsy appeared to be rare among schizophrenics. Meduna postulated a biological antagonism between epilepsy and schizophrenia and hypothesized that induction of an epileptiform seizure in schizophrenic patients might ameliorate their symptomatology. Problems of control of the timing and violence of the chemically induced seizures led Meduna later to substitute cardiozol (a very powerful stimulant sometimes used in cases of heart failure) for camphor, but problems of control of the seizures remained together with the disturbing side-effect that this form of treatment aroused massive anxiety in patients. Use of chemicals for induction of convulsions essentially disappeared with the introduction of electricity as the seizure-inducing agent. It is noteworthy that Meduna's notion that epilepsy is significantly rare among schizophrenics has not been confirmed, and his rationale of a natural antogonism between the two illnesses is not acceptable to account for whatever therapeutic effects the induced seizures may have in schizophrenia. As a matter of fact, the convulsive therapies have been found to be considerably more ameliorative of the symptoms of the affective disturbances (depressions) than of schizophrenia.

Manfred Sakel, a Viennese physician, suggested in 1935 that an hypoglycemic coma might alleviate some of the symptomatology of schizophrenia. This suggestion was based on his experience in the treatment of the withdrawal symptoms of morphine addicts by the injection of insulin. He hypothesized that the acute withdrawal symptoms were related to an hypersecretion of adrenaline and that an adrenaline antagonist, such as insulin, should be therapeutic. On the notion that certain schizophrenic symptomatology was akin to that of morphine withdrawal, Sakel experimented with insulin-induced hypoglycemic comas in schizophrenics and reported positive results. Only within the last five years has there been a carefully controlled study of the specific therapeutic action of insulin per se apart from the effects of the resulting coma.[1] In matched groups of schizophrenic patients, one of which received 35 to 40 insulin comas and one of which experienced an equal number of periods of deep sleep induced by barbiturates, approximately 40 percent of both groups recovered at the end of six months. The investigators summarized: "No conclusions can be drawn about the therapeutic value of the coma regime, but the results suggest that insulin is not the specific therapeutic agent." More clinically oriented evaluations of insulin coma therapy and comparisions of its effectiveness with that of electroconvulsive therapy have led largely to its abandonment. But sensitive, sophisticated psychiatrists have appraised the meaning of its apparent contribution to therapy:[2]

> "Insulin coma therapy brought hope to the schizophrenic, individual attention, therapeutic enthusiasm and a constructive group experience. Many patients were benefited by it. . . . Therefore, if insulin coma can now be abandoned as a treatment of schizophrenia, *the things that went with it must not be.* It probably had its most striking results in units where previously schizophrenic patients had had too little care and attention; and the history of its transient success and reputation indicates some of the ways in which the schizophrenic will continue to need *understanding,* nursing attention, and *therapeutic stimulus.*" [Italics ours.]

Psychosurgery is the general term applied to a variety of procedures which entail direct physical assault on the brain of the seriously disturbed mental patient. Its modern history dates to 1935 when a Portugese neurologist, Egas Moniz, pursuaded his colleague, Almeida Lima, a neurosurgeon, to operate on severely disturbed, chronically psychotic patients with a procedure which has come to be known as prefrontal lobotomy or leucotomy. It is a nondisfiguring but "blind" operation in which a blunt cutting instrument is introduced into the frontal region of the brain through a small trephine hole in the skull. The leucotome is then moved in a small arc so as to sever the pathways connecting the frontal lobe of the brain from the thalamus. The procedure is carried out bilaterally.

Moniz was encouraged as to the therapeutic potential and general safety of this technique partly on the basis of clinical reports on brain-injured adults, but most directly by hearing reports of the effects of this procedure on changes in temperament with retention of learned habits in operated chimpanzees.[3] The exact neurophysiological effects of this operation as they relate to the symptomatology of the patient are conjectural but it is generally accepted that the cutting of the fronto-thalamic pathways in some manner reduces the emotional "steam" of the patient's mental conflict. Thus, the patient may retain some of his preoccupations and delusions but his anxiety and apprehension are reduced. In the immediate post-surgical period he requires extensive nursing care and habit retraining (incontinence is a frequent post-operative finding). The contribution of this intensive, personal attention to the over-all response rate associated with this procedure must not be overlooked. While originally proposed as a last and drastic measure for severely disturbed patients who had failed to respond to all other treatments, within 15 years it had been performed on over 20,000 patients and its indiscriminate application has elicited a formal condemnation.[4]

In 1937, the use of electric current across the frontal pole of the brain to achieve a controlled epileptiform seizure in psychiatric patients was introduced by Ugo Cerletti of Italy.* Because of its ease of administration and its freedom from medical complications electroconvulsive therapy (ECT) became the treatment of choice for those illnesses for which its effectiveness was most readily demonstrated; these were the neurotic depressions and involutional psychoses. The dramatic freeing of patients from immobilizing depressions has given hope that ECT would be equally effective with other syndromes, but this hope has been largely surrendered in the face of negative results. The development of control over the onset, duration, and strength of convulsion afforded by ECT led to the displacement of the earlier chemical methods of seizure induction. No general rationale for the therapeutic mechanisms of ECT has been developed. Several rather different explanations have been offered for its mode of action: 1) it presents a massive, life-threatening attack upon the patient's total integrative system which responds by total mobilization and a resulting improved functioning, cere-

---

* The invention of electroconvulsive therapy is generally credited jointly to Cerletti and his colleague, Bini. The latter was responsible for the design of the current controlling and timing machine. The basic idea, and the earlier animal experimentation and neuropathological studies, were the work of Cerletti.[7]

brally and in general metabolism; 2) it disrupts the on-going patterns of cerebral functioning which sustain the depressive mental content, hence making new reaction patterns both necessary and possible; 3) by inducing a largely reversible memory defect it reduces the patient's awareness of those stresses and conflicts that precipitated his emotional reaction, thus permitting the establishment of new reaction patterns; 4) it satisfies the patient's unconscious need for punishment and affords an at least symbolic (since the procedure is itself painless) expiation of his deep-seated guilt; 5) it renders him temporarily totally helpless and dependent (in the immediate post-treatment period) in a situation that accepts and supports his dependency; this in turn potentiates or hastens a transference relationship to the therapist and may speed the total psychotherapeutic process. Little research has been done to establish which, if any, of these rationales is valid.

### III. COMMON FACTORS IN MEDICAL TREATMENTS

Before turning to the most recent development in the medical treatment of psychiatric illness, the tranquilizing drugs, let us consider some of the common features of these discoveries of the 1930's. The theory which led to each of these innovations was based on a crude combination of clinical observations concerning symptom patterns, inelegant notions about cerebral physiology and drug effects, and in some instances, limited animal experimentation. In general, the rationales put forth for these treatments were weak or conflicting and sometimes proved erroneous by later, careful research. In the absence of any generally agreed upon rationale to justify the procedures they have continued in use on the basis of their empirically established effectiveness as *symptomatic* treatments.

All of these treatments have a direct and rather immediate effect on the central nervous system and most of them put the patient into a coma.* Since personality is a function of the higher brain centers, and inasmuch as behavior is mediated by the complex stimulus–response integrating system of the brain, it is a reasonable expectation that any procedure that grossly alters brain function, even temporarily, will have some effect on behavior. It is unclear

* An exception is psychosurgical procedure which is commonly carried out under local anesthesia, with the patient remaining conscious and responsive throughout.

whether the period of coma associated with these treatments is simply a physiological side-effect that makes no particular contribution to the therapeutic mechanism, whether it is an important aspect of the total treatment, or whether it is essentially responsible for the therapeutic effect apart from the particular agent used to produce the coma.

In the comparison of patients treated by insulin versus those rendered comatose by other drugs, it was concluded that the improvement with the two drugs was comparable and that the insulin was not a specific therapeutic agent. By contrast, when electrotonic procedures simply render the patient briefly unconscious without developing the typical seizure or convulsion associated with standard electroshock therapy the therapeutic results appear to be not so good.[5] Apparently in this instance the convulsion and its underlying physiological upheavals have a therapeutic contribution in addition to the effects of coma.

It is undoubtedly significant that the patient is rendered unconscious. To be suddenly bereft of all of one's senses and to pass through an unnatural period of total out-of-touchness with one's environment is a most *dramatic* event. It is no less dramatic if it recurs repeatedly and at the control of others in a complex of healing symbols: hospital, doctors, nurses, "treatment." This is indeed "powerful medicine." It is no small act of faith to place oneself in the hands of a medical authority, to give that authoritative figure permission to render oneself repeatedly unconscious and helpless.* Such faith need not be simply a passive surrender to authority; it is likely to entail active expectations—expectation that the "treatment," with its dramatic aura of preparation of the patient, the presence of "equipment," and the numerous personnel in attendance, will result in some immediately felt changes and, furthermore, that these changes will accumulate to a total beneficial effect. In short, apart from any specific physio-chemical-anatomical effects, these medical treatments carry a strong factor of *positive suggestion* that works to influence changes in the patient. These dramatic medical treatments produce the best results when, by the deliberate thoughtfulness of the physician in his instruction and preparation

---

* Treatments such as ECT are occasionally administered to nonvoluntary patients. Frequently such patients are at best reluctant or at worst resistant to accede to the procedures. It is a clinical observation that the skeptical and resistant patients frequently experience an atypically small amount of benefit from them.

of the patient, there is an active recruitment and enhancement of all of the positively therapeutic suggestion inherent in the situation. Proper attention to the psychological features of the treatment entails considerably more than simple efforts to allay the patient's anxiety.

Still another factor common to these earlier medical treatments of psychiatric illness is of an historical nature. Three elements are involved: 1) each innovation was introduced by its discoverer with an enthusiasm and conviction that rested in large measure on the good results obtained in the initial application of the treatment to a clinical sample; 2) the percentages of patients described as responding to the treatment with "full recovery" or with "social recovery, or marked improvement" were very high; in some instances these response rates in the initial clinical reports of the innovator were higher than any ever subsequently obtained; 3) as the treatment was dispersed throughout the medical world and as it became an established, accepted procedure with certain types of patients, evaluative studies of its effectiveness showed progressively lower rates of positive response; in some instances, notably that of insulin coma therapy, it began to appear that the treatment did not produce positive results much in excess of the rate of spontaneous remission or of the response to other less complicated procedures, and the treatment was eventually discarded.

Why is it that these medical treatments have this particular historical similarity? Several forces were operative to account for this phenomenon of decay of effectiveness. In brief, a number of factors conjoined in the earliest clinical experiments with each therapy to make effective then a degree and spread of positive psychological *suggestion,* accompanying the medical specifics of the treatment, not subsequently maintained (maintainable?) when the procedure became routine.

When these new treatments were first introduced it was recognized by the experimenters that there were both certain and uncertain risks involved. Patients to be exposed to the experimental procedure were selected carefully and in accordance with general principles of medical conservatism. Accordingly, the earliest treatments were administered to patients who had been seriously psychotic for a very long time. They had not responded to a variety of other therapeutic procedures. The probability of spontaneous recovery was quite small. Most of these patients had been untreated for a long period; that is, they were essentially custodial cases not receiving particular therapeutic regimens. It is probably not an exaggeration to say that these inactive, untreated cases were, prior to the experiment, adapted to an environment and atmosphere in which they received minimal personal attention.

With their selection for the experimental procedure there were marked changes in the amount of attention they received. They were carefully examined, perhaps by several of the hospital staff. Some of them may have received a rare visit from a relative, occasioned by the need for the latter's permission for the new treatment. For a period prior to the actual treatments, they may have been more regularly and closely observed than had been true for many months. In brief, they became the objects of a sudden intensification of interest and manipulation. It is most probable that these historic patients were affected by the dramatic change in the amount of personal attention they received. We have much evidence from less "risky" experiments that the effect of increases in sheer amount of personal contact with patients is beneficial and results in improved behavior.[6]

Turning to the situation of the treatment proper, it is likely that again there was a special atmosphere of anxious concern that permeated all of the personnel present, affecting their attitudes and their approaches to the patient. Certainly in the figure of the prime mover, the medical innovator who was about to become responsible for inflicting a new, possibly dangerous, and clearly uncertain procedure upon the patient, there must have been an attitude of *heroic hopefulness*. The patient was the focus for the impact of all of this concentrated *positive suggestion* of expected *change*. Cerletti gives a delightful picture of just such a drama.[7]

Naturally in such experimental atmosphere the initial treatments were followed by a period of very careful observation of the patient. He continued to receive, in addition to the specific medical procedures, extraordinary attention. While the innovator and investigator was administering a specific physical therapy, the patient was in fact the recipient of a complex of stimuli (change of environment, increased attention, special interest) all of which carried a probable beneficial effect, in addition to the specific medical agent. Since the earliest experimental treatments were of a purely clinical nature and carried out without the usual controls necessary for rigorous evaluation, it is not possible to separate the contribution made by the suggestive psychological atmosphere from that made by the specific medical procedure to the generally positive results reported by the investigators for their earliest clinical trials.

The following brief excerpt is a contemporary illustration of the potential impact of significant psychological factors on the total response of a patient to an experimental surgical procedure:

> "In our research project it was not feasible to set up controls to evaluate the possible therapeutic effects that the enthusiasm of the participants might have on the patients. . . .
>
> "Within the first 24 hours after operation the therapist usually made an attempt to gain rapport by offering the patient something from which he could derive immediate pleasure. For instance, the therapist would find out the patient's favorite food or reading matter and on the first postoperative contact would present this to the patient. It was generally gratifying to observe the emotional response to this maneuver." [8]

These investigators are to be commended for providing an explicit and detailed account of the psychological atmosphere of their experiment. It is notable that they acknowledge the possible contribution of their extra-experimental provisions to the response of the patient.

The very high rate of recovery or of other very positive response to the therapeutic procedure led to its rapid dissemination to other clinics and hospitals. With increasing clinical application, procedures of the treatment became standardized, the nature and extent of associated risks (usually small) were established, the element of uncertainty and danger was greatly reduced if not eliminated —in brief the procedure evolved from a dangerous experiment to a routine treatment.

As these medical treatments of mental illness became established and accepted as "therapy of choice" for specific disorders, they underwent subtle but probably highly significant change. The essence of this change was that the *routine* treatment no longer occurred in a psychological atmosphere at all comparable to that of the experimental period. Increasingly, the treatment became insulin coma, or ECT, or psychosurgery *without* those special, additional factors of special activation and attention which were focused on the experimental subject. Whatever therapy was in the procedure became increasingly that of the specific action of the physical agent. It is safe to say that no patient has ever received electroconvulsive treatment in precisely the manner and especially with the surrounding psychological atmosphere created for Cerletti's first patients. As these physical treatments became routine there was increasing failure to reproduce the *total* experimental procedure. The treatments no longer were administered in an atmosphere of heroic hopefulness, but increasingly in one of passive expectation that the patient probably would respond as well as the actuarial statistics indicate he should.

It is a most reasonable hypothesis that the phenomenon of a progressive decay over time in the reported effectiveness of the physical treatments of mental illness, a phenomenon which has occurred with respect to all of the older medical procedures, is a reflection primarily of the progressive loss of attention to the psychological aspects of the treatment, to failure to capitalize consistently on all the possibilities for positive psychological suggestion which the medical procedure affords.

## IV. THE IDEAL OF INTEGRATED THERAPY

There is yet another factor common to the medical treatments of psychiatric illness. It has two facets: 1) the gradual reduction of aspirations of the therapist that the medical procedure is basically curative of the illness to a restrained acceptance that it is a procedure which yields some amelioration of symptoms; 2) the tendency for the medical treatments to be justified and their effectiveness attributed in part, by some experts, to the fact that they make the patient more accessible to psychological approaches and specifically to psychotherapy, which may be the only avenue of real cure.*

Despite the argument for using the physical treatments to ameliorate symptomatology and enhance the psychotherapeutic effort, with this argument serving as the only general rationale for the empirically established utility of the physical procedures, the patient at any given time is generally treated *either* with a medical procedure or with intensive therapeutic conversation. Consequently, the medical treatment is likely to be administered in an atmos-

---

* The fact that the hospitalized patient receiving ECT may also participate in social activities of the ward, in occupational therapy, and even in some version of group therapy in no way changes the fact that the treatment process is focused on the medical procedure and during its course attempts to establish an effective, therapeutic relationship with the patient may be largely neglected.

phere which does not capitalize on the possibilities for positive psychological impact inherent in the focal treatment, and the nature of the attendant dependency and increasing accessibility of the patient to therapeutic conversation are not grasped and maximized from the beginning. Even in the instance where medical and psychological treatment are jointly prescribed, it is frequently the case that each is the responsibility of a different person and the patient's expectations as to the direction of help are fractionated.

It is not simply a perversely regressive tendency of man to fall back into archaic ways of thinking and fallaciously oversimplified analyses of natural phenomena that accounts for our persisting dualism in the treatment of mental illness. It is not an inability to escape the seductive entrapments of "either-or" thinking, but rather the concrete difficulties of practicing a holistic approach to therapy that accounts for the frequent failures to achieve integrated therapy.

We seek a cure for mental illness. In our seeking, we are mindful of the presently overwhelming numbers of persons in need of help. In our seeking, we are hopeful. It is only natural that we should hope to discover treatments which are concrete, simple, safe, direct and that lead to rapid recovery. Whenever we chance upon a method of treatment that holds any promise and that, apart from its promise, has the encouraging properties of concreteness, directness, and rapidity, we are most naturally inclined to use it to exclusion, at least initially, of those procedures that are impalpable, indirect, and slow. And we are naturally inclined to continue its use in an exclusive way even after we are mindful that it is at best a palliative.

Most modern physicians accept at least tacitly a holistic view of man's essential nature. They see man as not simply a collection of parts, and furthermore they do not seek to resolve the anatomy of his being into two kinds of parts—body-parts and mind-parts. Rather, they eschew the body–mind dualism of older philosophies and seek a conception of man as an organismic unity. They are committed to seek an explanation of all the phenomena of man's functioning—healthy and diseased, at the level of organ pathology or of personality disruption—in terms of a simple set of concepts and laws. They expect the ultimate causal explanation of pathology as apparently diverse as that of cancer and that of psychological depression to be discovered by the sedulous application of scientific method, and they believe that the ultimate explanations will be in the terms of the physical sciences. If directly confronted with a demonstration that a particular patient's blood pressure could (and it can!) be altered in the same direction and amount by the utterance in his presence of certain words or by the administration to him of a specific quantity of a specific drug, they would insist that there were not two different *kinds* of explanation but rather that the mechanism of blood pressure control was sensitive to the impact of certain physical stimuli operating through certain physical pathways, and that the apparently "symbolic" quality of the spoken word in no way altered the fact that it impinged upon the patient as a physical stimulus (sound waves). The tacit philosophical matrix of medical training is one of physical monism. Although the graduate physician may not formally acknowledge or even consciously be *aware* of his philosophical allegiance, when confronted with functional illness of a type in which the patient's life style, attitudes, and frustrations have been demonstrated to play at least an exacerbating role, the physician does not behave as if nonphysical forces and nonphysical laws were at work. Knowing the anatomical relationships of the brain and the heart, the physician knows that the functioning of the one must have relationships to the functioning of the other. It should follow that the physician will *know* in an effectively appreciative sense that man's thinking can influence his heart rate and his blood pressure.

It is one of the paradoxes of modern medical education that, given the advantage of a unifying philosophy of science and a holistic view of man as an organismic unity, many physicians are unable to achieve or maintain a consistently unified approach to the diagnosis and treatment of man's ills. While they may be philosophical monists to whatever extent they have a premeditated philosophy of medical science, they practice as dualists—and their practical dualism most commonly takes the form of neglecting both the etiologic, contributory, and precipitating impact of the less obviously physical agents of illness—man's mental life, his worries, anxieties, conflicts, convictions, and expectations.

The psychiatrist, given the apperceptive mass of his concretely medical knowledge of man's anatomy and physiology onto which is superimposed an awareness of the vagaries of mental life and the impact of life experiences in the development of sick personalities, should excel among all physicians in bringing a holistic approach to the diagnosis and treatment of the patient as a thinking-feeling organism. Again, paradoxically, we find that only a minority of psychiatrists appear able or motivated to see their patients as psychologic wholes in need of and potentially responsive to physical-chemical-psychological treatment.

It is a fact of contemporary psychiatry that the medical specialists in mental disorder tend to align themselves in a dichotomy. On the one hand, we have those who become experts in outpatient psychotherapy and, on the other, those who specialize in the physical-chemical treatment of the hospitalized patient.[9] We need experts in both of these very different kinds of therapy, and specialization would not be bad if it did not tend to deteriorate into schismatic therapeutics, with the patient becoming a candidate now for drugs, another time for ECT, and still another time for therapeutic conversation—but never benefiting from a deliberate, integrated, and focused program of total therapy.

While the physicians and psychiatrists have the possibility of escape from the pitfalls of a philosophical dualism, in practice they are generally not able to achieve a meaningfully monistic approach to illness. Psychologists do not have the immersion in the physical sciences of the medic as a basic underpinning for their approach to a unified view of man. However, they typically have a directed education in the philosophy of science which should serve to dissuade them from an either-or explanation of behavior. Like the physician, the psychologist is typically enlightened in his sophisticated disparagement of dualism. But, like the physician, he is captive to a set of prejudices determined in no small measure by the nature of the *techniques* which are his special domain. Like the physician, he becomes a practicing dualist. As the physician neglects those not obviously physical determinants of illness and contributors to health so does the psychologist generally ignore or disparage possible physical avenues of amelioration. As psychotherapist he is prone to be inappropriately content to delay or deny therapeutic conversation to the patient while any specifically medical regimen is in force.

## V. PROSPECTS

It appears to be the natural history of the dramatic methods of physical treatment of mental disorders that they progressively lose their effectiveness with successive generations of patients. Perhaps it is that they lose their dramatic qualities as they become established. Perhaps there is a progressive erosion of the psychological atmosphere that afforded a critical part of their original dramatic impact in reducing the distress of certain symptoms; even that restricted but important impact can be optimized by conscientious devotion to holistic treatment of the unity of the patient.

In the past ten years, the drama of psychiatry has been focused on the discovery of new and potent drugs. The introduction of the ataractic medications (tranquilizers) was met with robust enthusiasm. The advent of these drugs was envisaged by some to mean that we could dispense with the construction of any further hospital facilities. Initially, the new drugs did make possible the discharge of many hospitalized patients and a marked shortening of the period of hospitalization for others. It is still too early to evaluate the basic and permanent level of contribution of this new approach in medical treatment of mental illness.

The psychotropic drugs have had primary impact on the severely disturbed patient requiring hospitalization. With hospitalized patients it has been easiest to see clinically the remarkable improvement in the management of symptoms of acute anxiety and agitation afforded by the tranquilizers, and to demonstrate statistically their effect in reducing the resident population of our state hospitals by several thousand patients each year. It is more difficult to appraise their impact in the treatment of the out-patient psychoneurotic. This difficulty is partly a function of the variation in standards for appraisal and description of out-patient symptomatology among independent clinicians. It is also a function of the rapid proliferation in the number and forms of psychotropic medication, so that careful accumulation of detailed clinical studies of any one drug, with adequate controls, has been slow.

The medical literature has many clinical reports (testimonials frequently, rather than research studies) on the effects of ataractic drugs in the treatment of out-patient neurotics. There is no doubt that acutely anxious neurotics have experienced significant amelioration of some of their distressing symptoms. They have benefited from increased physical comfortableness and, to varying degrees, from a "tranquil" attitude toward their conflicts. Like ECT, the tranquilizers provide symptomatic therapy. The patient's conflicts are not chemically dissolved and their neuroses have not been cured by medication. A major potential effect of the new chemotherapy has been to make the patient more accessible to psychotherapy, better able to think and learn about the meaning, causes, and ultimate resolution of his neurosis. But, as has been noticed previously with respect to other "physical" therapies, this enhanced accessibility to psychological approaches is not regularly capitalized on by the busy psychiatrist. There is an unfortunate tendency to let the drug be *the* treatment.

The non-curative aspect of the psychotropic medications is illustrated in one aspect of the medical rationale for their use. It is argued that some patients may suffer a chronic neuro-chemical imbalance or dysfunction (like the insulin pathology of the diabetic), that is basic to their anxiety-proneness and that, like the diabetic, they must accept a life-long program of medication.* If the medical prescription of insulin for the diabetic were not accompanied by careful instruction (even exhortation) toward appropriate diet, his illness would be poorly controlled. It is equally necessary to help the "tranquilized" neurotic to learn to cope more effectively with anxiety producing stresses of his life situation.

The attitudes of the neurotic patient toward medication deserve more careful appraisal, and integration into a total therapeutic program, than they frequently receive. Many patients reveal a strong resistance to taking medication, especially if it appears that they must continue medication over a long period. Such resistance is sometimes a mixture of a rather primitive, general suspiciousness of "drugs" coupled with a fear of becoming "dependent" upon pills. The latter attitude with regard to dependency on a medical crutch can sometimes be effectively used to enhance the patient's motivation for psychotherapy. Other neurotic patients reveal an over-readiness to receive a prescription; this may be because they share a still strong general bias that pills constitute proper *medical* treatment for a *real illness,* while they would be embarrassed by the implication that there was "nothing wrong" with them if all they needed was some "talking to." More seriously detrimental to full treatment is the subtle attitude of the neurotic that the drug prescription is an implicit confirmation of a *physical* cause of his symptoms, with consequent reduction of his willingness to submit to psychological treatment of his psychological symptoms.

It is not too early to realize that the tranquilizers do not afford a cure and they do not eliminate the need for psychological treatment. One of the greatest contributions of this early era of the tranquilizers and energizers has been to stimulate a large number of carefully designed studies that have demonstrated anew the ancient medical lore of the placebo effect: 1) many patients who are *properly administered* an inert substance will experience the same effects

* I am indebted to my colleague, Dr. Burtrum C. Schiele, for this analogy.

and manifest the same changes to be expected from a specific medi-cation;[10] 2) the psychological preparation of a patient can serve either to reduce or enhance the normal physiological response to an active chemical agent;[11] 3) patients who are psychologically re-sistant to medication and reluctant to take it do not show the same response or derive the same benefit as do those who have a positive attitude toward it.[12]

Can we anticipate the future? A generation, a half-century, sev-enty-five years from now will there still be a medical specialty of psychiatry? And, if so, how will the psychiatrist of A.D. 2000 look back upon current practices? Will he be impressed with the variety and elegant technical quality of the machines with which we presently in various forms administer electric currents of exquisitely calibrated strength and duration to the frontal cortices of our acutely disturbed patients in order to induce in them a controlled convulsion, or a period of insensibility? Will he be impressed with the abrupt mitigation of the more severe symptoms that we are able to accomplish? Will he be impressed with the myriad forms of pharmacological remedies that are now concocted and with the innovation of experimental devices and statistical analyses designed to determine precisely how much of a given alteration in patients is a function of a chemical formula and how much is a response to the psychological impact of the "giving and receiving" contract in the patient–physician relationship?

Authorities are divided by basic convictions as to what will prove in final analysis to be the ultimately necessary and sufficient factors for the development of aberrant behavior, excessive emotion, and sick thinking. They are also divided as to what shall prove in final analysis to be the absolutely irreducible minimum factor for ef-fective cure of psychological illness.

Historical perspective suggests that in some future epoch of a still more enlightened culture we shall have accepted finally and unreservedly the inescapable need to treat by teaching, the inescapa-ble truth that deprivations of love are not remediable by offers of capsules. We shall have learned that faulty logic is not the result solely of chemical imbalance and that a long history of maladaptive behavior requires a protracted period of instruction in hygienic thinking coupled with *personal* reward for that thinking and its attendant changes in behavior.

# References

1. B. Acknew, A. Harris, and A. J. Oldham, "Insulin Treatment of Schizophrenia, A Controlled Study," *Lancet,* Vol. 272 (1957), pp. 607-11.

2. Henderson and Gillespie's *Textbook of Psychiatry,* 9th Edition, revised by Sir David Henderson and Ivor R. C. Batchelor (London: Oxford University Press, 1962), pp. 347-48.

3. J. F. Fulton and Carlyle Jacobsen, "The Functions of the Frontal Lobes, A Comparative Study in Monkeys, Chimpanzees, and Man," *Abstr. Second Internat. Neurol. Congress* (London, 1935), pp. 70-71.

4. Group for the Advancement of Psychiatry, *Research in Prefrontal Lobotomy.* Report No. 6 (Topeka: June, 1948).

5. Henderson and Gillespie, *op. cit.,* p. 337.

6. Gordon Kamman, Rubel J. Lucero, Bill T. Meyer, and Allan Rechtschaffen, "A Critical Evaluation of a Total Push Program for Regressed Schizophrenics in a State Hospital," *Psychiat. Quart.,* 28, (1954), 650-67.

7. Ugo Cerletti, "Old and New Information About Electroshock," *Amer. J. Psychiat.,* 107 (1950), pp. 87-94.

8. Robert G. Heath (Chairman, Department of Psychiatry and Neurology, Tulane University), *Studies in Schizophrenia. A Multidisciplinary Approach to Mind-Brain,* published for The Commonwealth Fund (Cambridge: Harvard University Press, 1954), pp. 357-58.

9. August B. Hollingshead and Frederick C. Redlich, *Social Class and Mental Illness. A Community Study* (New York: John Wiley & Sons, Inc., 1958), pp. 155-65.

10. Arthur K. Shapiro, "The Placebo Effect in the History of Medical Treatment. Implications for Psychiatry," *Amer. J. Psychiat.,* 116 (1959), pp. 298-304.

11. Samuel B. Lyerly, Sherman Ross, Arnold D. Krugman, and Dean J. Clyde, "Drugs and Placebos: The Effects of Instructions upon Performance and Mood under Amphetamine Sulfate and Chloral Hydrate," Veterans Administration Center, Martinsburg, West Virginia. (Unpublished manuscript.)

12. Donald R. Gorham and L. J. Sherman, "The Relation of Attitude Toward Medication to Treatment Outcomes in Chemotherapy," *Amer. J. Psychiat.,* 117 (1961), pp. 830-32.

# CHAPTER FIVE

# The Psychological Approach

## I. EARLY ORIGINS OF PSYCHOLOGICAL MANAGEMENT

When first in the history of man was there a deliberate attempt on the part of one person to alleviate the suffering of another by conversation—by question, by instruction, or by suggestion? We do not know. When first in history was it generally recognized that words spoken to another could influence his behavior, his thinking, and his feeling? We do not know, but we may surmise that this latter crude awareness was present in the earliest stages of linguistic man. Zilboorg tells us that among very primitive tribes of Siberia, ancient China, and Malaysia there were shamans and priests who practiced hypnotism as a mode of treatment.[1] Apart from such rare examples of historic anticipation of personal suasion as an avenue of therapy, we find that the earliest civilizations only very slowly came to a recognition of those special forms of disorder which we now label psychological. Having by keen clinical observation and record provided a nosology for manias and melancholias, for fits and for stupors, the earliest observers placed them outside the realm of natural phenomena and looked to supernatural explanation. It was the early Greek philosophers who first brought the disorders of behavior under the canopy of scientific scrutiny and insisted that they must yield to natural explanation. But the early priest-physicians looked for the explanation of aberrant behavior in the terms of their crude knowledge of anatomy and physiology, including the presumed location (and dislocations) of the soul. Even in such dualistic atmosphere, it was possible for a philosopher to anticipate the need for a nonmedical treatment of sickness of the "soul." Cicero wrote, "Assuredly there is an art of healing the soul—I mean philosophy," and "Not all of those who have submitted to treatment [medical] succeed at once in making recovery as well, whereas we see, on the contrary, that souls which *have been ready to be cured* and have obeyed the instructions of *wise men,* are undoubtedly cured." [2] (Italics ours.)

Such insights were not generally appreciated by the earliest physicians even after they had achieved a naturalistic, scientific attitude toward personality disorders and emotional pathology. In their efforts to effect cures consistent with their "physiological" explanations of depressions and excitements they developed a high order of environmental and physical manipulations of the patient that are prototypes of modern psychiatric procedures: removal of the grossly disturbed patient to a protective, stable, and supportive environment, special baths and massage, hygienic diet, prescription of special herbs, exercise and occupational therapy, and, in some instances, soothing music. In contrast to the modern psychiatrist, who has many therapeutic provisions which parallel those of the Greek priest-physicians but who sees them as ancillary to some core therapy, for the followers of the Aesculapian tradition these procedures *were* the therapy.

In the enlightened and naturalistic approaches to mental illness recorded in Greco-Roman history there are no explicit references to psychotherapy—to conversation with therapeutic intent. There could not be psychotherapy as we understand it because psychotherapy rests upon a particular and detailed system of psychopathology, and a theory of the psychological etiology of personality disorders.

Notwithstanding the absence of deliberate psychotherapy in the earliest period of a truly sophisticated understanding of mental illness, it is well to recognize that the procedures of the Greco-Roman physicians were not without psychological impact. Certain *sines qua non* of psychotherapy were present in their ministrations—the patient was perceived and treated as an individual, with respect for his individuality; he was *accepted* nonjudgmentally as an ill person, not a bad person; elements of the treatment were specifically prescribed and involved personal investment of time spent with the patient (*e.g.,* Soranus' prescription that the patient be read to about topics of interest to him).[3]

In the interest of historical perspective it is well to be mindful that the course of enlightenment has not run smoothly and progressively in the direction of increasing factual knowledge about etiology and treatment of mental illness, nor with ever more widely disseminated and consistent humaneness of social programs for the mental patient.

The naturalistic, "medical," and humane propositions and procedures of the golden era of Greco-Roman philosophy and science gave way to the Dark Ages. In the period beginning around A.D. 400, and lasting roughly to A.D. 1400, investigation was suppressed, a religiously oriented dualism held sway, and disorders of behavior became the subject matter of a metascience of demonology. The victim of what we now perceive to have been emotional illness was then an object of suspicion or fear, of ridicule or resentment. The major preoccupation became the protection of society rather than the cure of the ill person. The lunatic or witch was thought to be possessed by, or the active agent of, an evil spirit. Conservative therapy was designed to achieve exorcism, the driving of the evil visitor from the possessed one's body by violent whippings or other scourging. Radical therapy was the stake and fire. In light of modern psychological understanding, we can appreciate that these heroic procedures (when the "patient" lived) may frequently have resulted in dramatic improvements in his behavior. (If he still had hallucinations he may well have learned to keep them to himself!) And after the ignorance and fear of the Middle Ages had given way to a new period of enlightenment, to a renewed spirit of investigation, and to a resurgence of humaneness in attitudes toward the demented, we can understand that some of the physical treatments which had seemed empirically most effective (such as foul-smelling emetics) might persist in the armamentarium of the physician, supported by a naturalistic rationale in terms of psychic trauma and "counter shock," and perhaps giving even better results because they were now administered in an atmosphere of acceptance of the patient and by a physician whose attitude exuded confidence, kindly intent, and therapeutic expectation.

"Kindly and humane though he was, Dr. Rush* accepted without question the necessity of coercion by mechanical restraint and of certain forms of corporal punishment, even advocating whippings in extreme cases. . . . Among the terror-inspiring devices recommended by Rush were his own tranquillizer, a cold shower bath continued for fifteen and twenty minutes. . . . The gyrator consisted of a rotating board to which patients suffering from 'torpid madness' were strapped with the head farthest from the center. It could be rotated at terrific rates of speed, causing the blood to rush to the head. . . . Rush himself recommended the total deprivation of food in some cases of insanity.

* Dr. Benjamin Rush of Philadelphia, called the Father of American Psychiatry, was one of the signers of the Declaration of Independence.

... Kind treatment of mental patients was a major rule in Rush's practice . . . he also taught that the insane should generally be approached with respect and deference that would be accorded them in ordinary social intercourse. . . . He stressed the value of little acts of kindness toward them, such as presents of fruit and sweet-cakes at frequent intervals." [4]

From the vantage point of our current orientation, we look back upon Rush's therapeutics and select those procedures which were in fact kind (and correct) despite his intentions, and those which we feel were in fact cruel (and in error), despite his intentions. In looking back, it is easy to credit those attempts of old which are consistent with current theory and to decry with condescension those procedures of predecessors that appear inimical to contemporary understanding. In this it is somewhat difficult to believe that harsh treatments could be kindly administered or that painful procedures could be in fact therapeutic.

Will tomorrow's reader of today's psychiatric history be able to understand that electroshock therapy was kindly administered by men who really believed that there was some sort of therapeutic physio-chemical effect accomplished by the current? Will they be able to see that there was a consistent, unifying theory of psychopathology and therapy whereby some patients were administered drugs and others were given conversation? Will they perhaps see the present period of history as marking a point at which with the advent of the ataractics and other psychotropic drugs, we were precipitated back into a dualism of therapy from which we were just slowly beginning to emerge?

There have been revolutions in the history of psychiatry.[5] It is reasonable to hope for others. It may well be that the final revolution will come in the future recognition that there is for *every* emotionally disturbed person an *irreducible minimum* requirement for successful treatment, the provision of *a therapeutic relationship with an accepting, understanding, and helping other.*

## II. PSYCHOTHERAPY: EVOLUTION AND PROLIFERATION

The distinctly psychological approach in the treatment of emotional illness is called psychotherapy. A very general definition of psychotherapy is that it is "a form of treatment for problems of an emotional nature in which a trained person deliberately establishes a professional relationship with a patient with the object of removing, modifying, or retarding existing symptoms, of mediating disturbed patterns of behavior, and of promoting positive personality growth and development." [6]* As a specific discipline with an undergirding of theoretical assumptions concerning etiology of neuroses and the dynamics of psychopathology and with a complex of discriminable techniques it is only recently a broadly visible part of our culture. As a method embodying both notions of psychological causation and restricted to psychological intervention of a specified sort, psychotherapy is generally conceded to begin with Freud, with the therapy and technique to which he first applied the term "psychoanalysis" in 1896.[7] The exact origin of the term "psychotherapy" is uncertain, but the term "psychotherapeutics" appears in a publication of 1890.[8]

The evolution of psychotherapy cannot be said to have started with a specific discovery at a given time and place in the same manner as one can document the origin of many scientific "breakthroughs." The origins of modern psychotherapy are to be found in the history of Freud's thought and in this history one finds several periods of dramatic new insights.

But Freud, like all investigators, had the stimulus and challenge of others. Specifically, his was the heritage of the history of hypnosis and the established fact of psychical instigation and relief of physical symptoms. The subject of hypnosis is one of the most fascinating in all the history of psychiatry, illustrating as it does the discovery of startling phenomena that are only slowly appreciated in their full significance.

It begins with Anton Mesmer, physician and friend of Mozart, Gluck, and Haydn, who was stimulated by Father Maximilian Hell, astronomer in the court of Empress Maria Theresa of Austria, to the use of magnets applied to the body to relieve pain or dysfunction. Mesmer found that he could duplicate the success of Father Hell in relieving symptoms through the judicious application of magnets to afflicted portions of the anatomy. He gradually evolved a theory of "animal magnetism" in which the successful physician became the prime focuser of "universal" magnetic currents, the metal magnets apparently potentiated in their curative powers by Mesmer's touch upon the patient's body. His clinical demonstrations were impressive with patients whose symptoms we would now recognize as hysterical and he gained the admiration and gratitude of many who

* Reprinted with permission from Lewis R. Wolberg, *The Technique of Psychotherapy* (New York: Grune & Stratton, Inc., 1954).

sought his treatment, but his theory gained no foothold and, more seriously for his self-esteem, he failed to achieve acceptance by his Viennese medical colleagues.*

Mesmer moved on to Paris where he hoped that scientific audiences would be more receptive. Despite the rapidly growing popularity of his "clinical" salon where he developed what may have been one of the earliest forms of "group therapy," his theories were again discounted and there was disagreement among authorities as to whether the phenomena which Mesmer demonstrated were real or the result of collusion. As a dramatic and somewhat flamboyant personality whose public utterances and demonstrations could not be ignored, he finally achieved the attention of the French Academy of Science which in 1784 appointed a committee to undertake a careful scrutiny of "mesmerism." Included among the members of this special body were Benjamin Franklin, Lavoisier, and Dr. Guillotine. In its formal report, the committee rejected Mesmer's notion of "animal magnetic fluid," remarked upon the significant contribution by the patient's imagination *and* the therapist's touch to the striking behaviors exhibited by the mesmerized subject, and concluded that the procedure was dangerous and not to be condoned for public application. But the trances, seizures, amnesias and paralyses induced by the methods of Mesmer were firmly before the public and had caught the curiosity of many individuals, some of whom were quacks and mountebanks but many of whom were serious scientists who wanted an acceptable explanation for these phenomena.

In time the anesthetic potential of the mesmeric trance was utilized in surgery. English physicians were particularly active in the exploration of the implications of mesmerism for general medical practice. It was a Scottish surgeon, James Braid, who coined the term *hypnotism* in 1843 and thus, with new language, helped to make the study of these strange processes a legitimate part of medical inquiry, avoiding the sensational and unsavory connotations of mesmerism.

Some thirty years later, when hypnosis was introduced to Jean Martin Charcot, the founder of the science of neurology, that master French clinician quickly perceived the remarkable affinity of certain of his "neurological" patients for the hypnotic trance. He determined that certain of his patients with physical symptoms that sug-

---

* For a detailed and readable account of the history of Mesmerism, see Winkler and Bromberg,[9] or Bromberg.[10]

gested a neurologic defect could have those symptoms removed or returned in response to his direction. On this basis he theorized that there was a special relation between the phenomena of hypnosis and the hysterical personality and argued that both were in essence the expression of a neurological pathology. As a dedicated and dramatic teacher, he drew medical students and physicians from all over Europe to his clinic where he domonstrated the joint "pathology" of hysteria and hypnosis. It was in his clinic that many learned for the first time that hysteria was not, contrary to prevailing belief, a disorder limited to females.

In 1885, ten years after he had started his studies with hypnosis, Charcot received Sigmund Freud as a postgraduate scholar. Freud spent a little over four months in Charcot's clinic and was deeply impressed by the man and by the clinical insights he gained from him. ". . . To Charcot must be ascribed the most important influence in turning Freud from a neurologist into a psychopathologist." [11] When Freud returned to Vienna to take up his neurological studies and clinical work, he brought with him both an extended knowledge of the techniques and effects of hypnosis and a much broadened view of hysteria; it was the latter which constituted Charcot's most significant influence on Freud.

In 1889, Freud returned to France, this time to observe in the Nancy hospital of Hippolyte Bernheim and to improve his hypnotic technique.[12] With this visit, Freud's heritage was completed, for it was Bernheim who first clearly understood and communicated the essential truths of hypnotic phenomena: that they were not dependent upon defects of the nervous system but rather were the expression of natural processes which could be elicited in the great majority of normal persons with intact brains, and that the essential factor was *suggestion*. It was Bernheim, first stimulated by observing the technique of A. A. Liebeault, who established the "Nancy school"—a viewpoint, an accumulation of clinical data, and a logical argument which eventually won out over Charcot's Salpêtrière school. Liebeault had dispensed with the hocus-pocus of the old school of hypnotism, had found that special trappings for fixating the patient's attention were unnecessary, and had demonstrated that he could "talk" the patient into a hypnotic state that would be followed by remission of symptoms in accordance with his instructions. In observing this, Bernheim was able to perceive and identify the very heart of the powerful force that had been recruited a hundred years earlier in the magnets of Mesmer—the universal action of suggestion emanating from the word and action of an authoritative person. Over these hundred years, psychotherapy had evolved: from the things of man to the touch of man and, finally, to the word of man. With Bernheim's recognition of the principle of suggestion and his investigation of its forms and potency, we finally arrived at a clear awareness of a thoroughly psychologic therapy. When Freud returned to Vienna from his Nancy trip, he was well oriented to begin his discoveries of psychologic causation. The mode of treatment eventually invented by Freud is only indirectly related to the history of hypnosis, but there have been many schools of psychotherapy, particularly of the directive-instructive and hortatory type which rest heavily on the basic psychology of suggestion.*

Before Freud made his historic visit to Charcot, he had associated with Dr. Josef Breuer, a general practitioner in Vienna. Breuer, a sensitive and painstaking clinician, had shared with Freud the details of his treatment of a 21-year-old maiden who in the final stages of her father's terminal illness had developed a "museum of symptoms." [14] It is not clear how soon Breuer recognized the clearly hysterical character of Anna O's multiple and shifting symptomatology. He was quick to discover that when the patient talked to him of the events surrounding the earliest appearance of a particular symptom such "chimney sweeping" resulted in the almost immediate disappearance of the symptom. Breuer next implemented his "talking cure" by using hypnosis to facilitate Anna's ability to recall the advent of particular symptoms and to "talk out" everything that came to her mind in that connection. Systematically pursuing this procedure, Breuer was able to relieve his patient of much of her distressing symptomatology. Seeing the process of his treatment as involving a sort of emotional purging, he called his technique the "cathartic method."

After his considerably broadened exposure to the phenomena of hysteria in Charcot's clinic, Freud returned to Vienna with enhanced enthusiasm for the possibilities of Breuer's technique; for a period of approximately ten years they collaborated in clinical investigation and in publication, culminating in their classic, *Studies on Hysteria*, 1895.[15] Zilboorg credits Freud and Breuer jointly with "the discovery of the unconscious."

* In his own treatment, Freud was not averse to reliance on strong suggestion. See the account of his treatment of Bruno Walter.[18]

"The discovery was made on a neurotic patient, not on a psychotic; it was made by means of a successful therapeutic test. This was the first time in the history of medical psychology that a therapeutic agent had led to the discovery of the cause of the illness while attacking or attempting to remove this cause. It was the first time in the history of psychopathology that the cause of illness, the symptoms generated by the cause, and the therapeutic agent revealing and removing the cause were combined in one succession of factors. It is doubtful whether the full meaning of this historical fact has as yet been properly appreciated." 16

If Breuer and Freud had together found the unconscious, it was Freud alone who went on to explore this new territory, to map its dimensions, and to discover its relationship to the conscious. Upon returning from his studies with Bernheim, Freud was motivated to dispense with the dramatic features of hypnosis and to treat by suggestion. This he tried in the context of Breuer's cathartic method. It worked, and it could be facilitated by occasional hypnotic sessions, but it was slow and more than occasionally resisted by patients with a negativistic orientation. Finally, as a result of striking episodes of erotic interest in the therapist manifested by the hypnotized patient, Freud abandoned hypnotism entirely and determined to devise a technique that would achieve maximal efficiency for the "talking cure." These efforts led him to the procedure of "free association" which became one of the cornerstones of psychoanalytic therapy. From his systematic analysis of the free-flowing thoughts of his patients and of their dreams, Freud constructed the psychoanalytic theory of personality.

Orthodox psychoanalytic therapy has never had a significant, direct impact per se on the treatment of mental illness. But the discovery within the context of psychoanalytic therapy of the nature and importance of the patient–physician relationship (the central phenomena of transference) has been an influence in nearly every major form of psychotherapy devised since Freud. And psychoanalytic theory has touched nearly every endeavor in the field of psychopathology.

Psychotherapy is 70 years young, is still evolving, as witnessed by very recent innovations in technique, and does not presently show much movement toward a general theory and uniformity of technique. In an exposition of the basic postulates of methods of psychotherapy that have achieved some stability of identification it has been possible to delineate 36 "systems." 17 There has been introduction of significant new rationales and systems of psychotherapeutic technique as recently as 1942,[18] 1958,[19] and 1962.[20]

With appreciation for the recency of the appearance of psychotherapy as a social phenomenon we might wonder at the proliferation of systems. We can date the modern origins of psychological treatment of mental illness at roughly 1900. In the ensuing sixty-odd years we find the development, according to one authority, of thirty-six discriminable approaches. If we restrict ourselves to the individually oriented forms (one patient per one therapist per session), eliminate the group methods, and collapse all the distinctly Freudian derivatives into one "school," we are still provided an outline of at least a dozen different methods of psychotherapy. Does such an apparent multiplicity of approaches mean that we have achieved a refinement of diagnosis and a knowledge of differential therapeutic effect? Does it mean that we can meaningfully assign a particular patient to a particular psychotherapist, knowing that for the former the latter practices the "treatment of choice"? Niceties of evidence aside, this hypothetical possibility is obviated by practical logistics. The clinic or hospital whose staff provides as many as three *distinctly different* forms of psychotherapy is rare, let alone one that would include as many as six or twelve different "kinds" of psychotherapists. Here too, "birds of a feather flock together."

How distinctive are the features which permit differentiation of these approaches? Are the distinctive features of a particular "system" of psychotherapy clearly related to the apparent effectiveness of that approach? Do the different psychotherapies differ significantly in their effectiveness? Is there one "system" of outstanding potency as expressed in the objective measurement of its accomplishments in relieving or curing psychological distress? Is there a differential effectiveness of these several approaches that relates to different forms of psychopathology? Is it possible that we can and should move toward a uniform theory and method of psychotherapy that would incorporate the most valid insights and effective technique from all of the formal therapies? Are there certain basic factors which are common to all methods of psychotherapy and which may account for the successes of each?

### III. THE EFFICACY OF PSYCHOTHERAPY

Apart from specifics of technique and orientation, how effective is psychotherapy? (The proliferation of approaches might be an indication of a yet unfinished search for a method of psychotherapy that would prove in fact to be effective!) Surely in the course of six decades we have accumulated satisfactory evidence that psychotherapy significantly ameliorates (if it does not cure) the symptoms of emotional illness. But what is evidence? Ask those whose professional work is devoted entirely or in large measure to the practice of psychotherapy and they will tell you that there is no doubt *in their minds* that they are able significantly to reduce the suffering of the neurotic, to free him of painful anxiety, to release him from immobilizing phobias, to guide him to emancipating insights and thus to positively adaptive behavior, to acceptance both of himself and of his society.

Does the psychotherapist never have any failures? Yes, he does and this he will readily admit. But he is likely to explain that these are really not failures of therapy so much as failures of diagnosis—the patient was not really a "good" candidate for the treatment.

Such is the nature of the clinical evidence—almost universally positive and enthusiastic. But in no other branch of therapeutics is clinical testimonial accepted as scientific truth, and it cannot be for psychotherapy. We must turn to the research literature.

In 1952, a British psychologist published a summary of the statistics on recovery and improvement of neurotic patients who received psychotherapy of varying degrees of intensity and specificity.[21] The reports which he was able to cull from the published literature covered a period from 1920 to 1950. A total of 24 reports were included in his survey and they provided statistics for a total of over 8,000 patients. Some of these patients had received psychoanalysis, some had received intensive psychoanalytically oriented psychotherapy, a bulk of them had been treated "eclectically"; some of them had been treated as outpatients, a majority of them received their psychotherapy as residents of hospitals or sanitaria.[22] As control groups (samples of patients who presumably received no psychotherapy or very little) reference was made to diagnosed neurotics hospitalized in New York state hospitals in 1925-34, and to a sample of 500 consecutive neurotics who received disability insurance benefits because of their emotional incapacitation and who were treated exclusively by general practitioners.

With such a variety of sources of patients and with such a variety of clinicians and settings for therapy (or nontherapy), it is almost certain that there would be variation in the meaning of neurotic diagnoses and, even more important, sizable variation in the rigor of criteria of "recovery" or "marked improvement." Attempts at comparison of such diverse samples and of the differing treatments they received demand that the surveyor in selecting and combining (or excluding) cases apply his clinical judgment to the descriptive data afforded. For example, should "organ neurosis, psychopathic states, and character disturbances" be lumped with a general sample of "neurotics"? Does the designation of "cured" for a group of patients from one hospital mean the same as "recovered" for patients from another source? The clinical judgments entailed in making such comparisons are subject to all the usual errors of such judgment.

The surveyor of the outcome statistics on psychotherapy was properly mindful of these potential sources of error or distortion, reports that he attempted to hold them to a minimum, and vouchsafes that "another investigator making all these decisions exactly in the opposite direction . . . would hardly alter the final percentage figures by more than 1 or 2 per cent." [23]

Table 2

Response of Psychoneurotic Patients to Psychotherapy[a]

| Form of psychotherapy | Number of cases | Percent cured or improved |
|---|---|---|
| Orthodox psychoanalysis | 760 | 44 |
| Eclectic psychotherapy | 7,293 | 64 |
| Supportive treatment[b] | 500 | 45 |
| Hospitalization (N.Y. State, 1917-34)[c] | 119 | 72 |

[a] Adapted from Table 1, p. 321, Eysenck.[21]

[b] These were the 500 patients with diagnosed psychoneurosis for which they received disability insurance benefits. They were treated as out-patients by general practitioners (not psychotherapy specialists). The 45 percent recovery rate was at the end of one year; at the end of a second year of such management a total of 72 percent were recovered.

[c] Presumably these patients in state hospitals received very little or no intensive psychotherapy. The reported recovery rate is for patients discharged within one year of hospital admission.

On the basis of the data summarized in Table 2, it was suggested (possibly somewhat facetiously) that there "appears to be an inverse correlation between recovery and psychotherapy; the more psychotherapy, the smaller the recovery rate." In a thoroughly serious vein, this investigator concluded that the assembled data (the best then available, for all its limitations and difficulties of categorization) "fail to support the hypothesis that psychotherapy facilitates recovery from neurotic disorder." [24]

This survey constituted the first conscientious and comprehensive attempt at appraisal of psychotherapeutic efficacy (a fact of interest in itself since psychotherapy had been a firmly established and vigorously on-going phenomenon of Western civilization for at least the preceding ten years) and one might have expected the negative findings to have generated massive rationalizations if not violent rejection of their validity, or (more hopefully) intense research efforts to provide cleaner data for a less ambiguous evaluation. That the survey appraisal did not receive more attention is probably in part because of its appearance in a psychological journal rather than in a medical or psychiatric publication. On the average, psychologists (even clinical psychologists) have less intense identification with and investment in psychotherapy than does the psychiatrist.

Within the psychological community, the survey did arouse a fair amount of discussion and controversy. Most typically, and reflective of the distorting effects of an emotional commitment to a theory or practice, many professionals erroneously interpreted the survey to have concluded that the effectiveness of psychotherapy was disproven. Such an inferred conclusion was intolerable and led generally to a rather comfortable assumption that the data which had been amassed were qualitatively so heterogeneous as not to support any generalization. This assumption was frequently enunciated in tandem with the hypothesis that when appropriate and objective data were properly collected from pertinent experimental (treated) and control (untreated) samples of neurotic patients, it would be abundantly clear that psychotherapy was as effective in the relief of neurosis as every therapist "knew" it to be.

Only one psychologist attempted a formal, comprehensive critique of this survey of psychotherapeutic effectiveness.[22] He was particularly critical of the use of the state hospital neurotics and the insurance cases as controls (presumably not receiving therapy), arguing that the general practitioners who treated the latter made use of suggestion and reassurance, as well as medicine, while the former, representing the most hopeful of all hospital admissions were more likely to receive a concentration of such psychotherapeutic resources as were available. From his viewpoint, the survey would justify the generalization that psychoneurotics treated with a range of psychotherapy from intensive psychoanalysis to palliative, supportive reassurance and suggestion may achieve effective results in not less than half and up to three fourths of all treated patients. Even with this somewhat more sanguine interpretation of the survey results, this psychologist accepted the surveyor's restatement of the implications of his findings:[25],[26]

> "When it is realized that these data, poor as they are, are all the evidence available regarding a method of therapy which has been practiced for more than 50 years on hundreds of thousands of patients, then it will, I think, be agreed that the failure of the data to show any degree of therapeutic effectiveness should act as a spur to ensure the initiation of large-scale, properly planned, rigidly controlled, and thoroughly analyzed experimental studies in this important field."

Some ten years after this call we are still awaiting definitive research—we still do not have acceptable *evidence* that psychotherapy accomplishes significant reduction of neurotic symptomatology, let alone evidence that the several different forms of psychotherapy have different levels of efficacy. But opinions remain divided, and convictions remain strong.

Although we still lack the sort of definitive research that would tell us how effective particular forms of psychotherapy are (and whether their respective effectiveness varies according to the types of problems treated), we have experienced an upsurge in the total amount of research in the broad area of psychotherapy.* The bulk of this research divides into three categories: 1) studies of the psychotherapeutic "process"—attempts to discover and portray the natural history of on-going psychotherapy in terms of the shifts in the content and pattern of the therapist-patient interaction, with a view to establishing the existence of certain lawful patterns of evolution in this exchange, at least within the framework of a particular school of therapy; 2) studies of the attitudes, values, predilections, and treatment tactics of therapists of varying theoretical orientations, and appraisal of the effect of increasing clinical experience on intertherapist differences; and 3) exploration of the respective merits and of the *interrelationships* of a host of potential criteria, i.e., measures of the patient's short-term and long-term response to psychotherapy.

* In 1949, the chapter on psychotherapy in the *Annual Review of Psychology* cited only eight research articles; the comparable chapter in 1955 made reference to 40 studies.[27]

Studies of the first type seem somewhat out of order in terms of social utility; it is perhaps premature to invest much energy in the analysis of a therapeutic process before there has been clear demonstration that the process is in fact therapeutic. The studies of process have generally suffered also in that particular methods of analysis have been generated out of and applied only to a particular mode (and theory) of treatment. Quite apart from whatever limitations there may be to the theory and technique of client-centered therapy, Carl Rogers and his students have earned a niche in history by bringing the phenomena of psychotherapy permanently into the realm of research. Increasingly as techniques of process analysis multiply and are rendered more precise, it is likely that any given method of psychotherapy will be examined by a variety of procedures. In this there is hope that truly general laws about the ongoing patient-therapist interactions may be uncovered.

Studies of the psychotherapist, particularly in regard to what features of his therapeutic activity, if any, are apparently related to the specific avenues of his training, his theoretical orientation or "school" membership already show promise of uncovering general factors that cut across professional boundaries. Further elucidation of these common dispositions shared by all psychotherapists should have impact on the training programs. Some of this research will be presented in the following chapter.

Finally, increasing attention to the omnipresent criterion problem is resulting in increasingly sophisticated awareness that no single variable can provide an adequate measure of the over-all response of the patient to therapy. The degree to which his self-concept has become more accepting and positive is a relevant criterion variable. The extent to which he has moved toward a more accepting and positive attitude toward other persons is a pertinent measure. The amount of reduction or elimination of physical and psychic symptoms, as a concrete goal of therapy, must be appraised. Whether or not the patient resumes his full functioning as a responsible social being, or whether he is enabled by therapy to increase his efficiency, productivity, or satisfaction in his varied roles are clearly relevant criteria of therapeutic effectiveness. Finally, the extent to which the patient has gained true and lasting insight into his personality, or the degree to which he has learned how to use the natural equipment of his personality in achieving more effective adaptation to future problems or stresses are vital dimensions in the patient's total response to psychotherapy.

Some of these criterion measures are relatively objective, accessible, and easy to record. Others require the development of particular methods of assessment, direct and indirect. Some are of a nature that demand clinical appraisal and subjective judgment; with these it is necessary to avoid so far as possible the usual sources of error in the fallible human observer-evaluator, especially the bias which operates if the expert responsible for an activity is asked to be a judge of its success.

Through the joint efforts of psychiatrists, psychologists, and social workers there is presently available a sturdy armamentarium of psychometric and sociometric devices that can yield a complex of measures of the patient's level of mental health. There is increasing evidence of readiness to use multiple measures in evaluating the effectiveness of treatment. With all of the above evidences of the vitality of the research endeavor in psychotherapy, it is to be hoped that within the next 25 years we shall have a fair answer to our questions: Does psychotherapy work? Does a particular method of therapy work better with certain patients than another method?

It is probable that, in addition to perfection of research techniques, the answering of these crucial questions will require establishment of special research clinics in order to assure the participation in the evaluation studies of therapists who represent the major schools and who presumably practice different forms of psychotherapy. In this regard, it is interesting to note that the often-voiced opinion that different approaches may be differentially effective with different problems has not led to a general pattern of staffing clinics or hospitals with therapists representing schools of apparently divergent orientation and practice. The homogeneity of the theoretical "climate" in most treatment centers is probably not so much a function of administrative policy (or oversight) as of a "mating" tendency among therapists. To paraphrase the old saw about the birds, "Psychotherapists of a persuasion agglutinate." This tendency toward professional cohabitation of therapists trained in a particular school is probably only a natural response to subtle psychological pressures, and it might be hypothesized that such homogeneous clinics have a higher therapeutic effectiveness on the average than would a group of therapists of diverse persuasion. Obvious differences of conviction interfere with certainty, reduced certainty depresses confidence, and impaired confidence is likely to lower competence!

## IV. THE NATURE OF THE PROCESS: GENERAL FACTORS

The controversial survey of the available statistics on the amount of recovery or significant improvement which is achieved by neurotics under psychotherapy was interpreted by its author as failing to demonstrate that such therapy is effective. He used as control groups neurotics admitted to state hospitals and psychologically disabled patients treated by general physicians, interpreting the recovery rates of those patients as expressive of the base rate of "spontaneous recovery" in the absence of specific psychotherapy. His use of the hospitalized neurotics and the insured disability cases as controls has been criticized on the grounds both that they were atypical of the patients usually seen for outpatient psychotherapy and that they were actually the recipients of psychotherapeutic influences although these might have been casual and seemingly incidental to other aspects of their treatment. Persons taking this position with respect to the control samples, whose recovery and improvement rates were not reliably less than those of the patients who were treated by skilled psychotherapists, could make the interpretation that the data really show that psychotherapy is effective to a certain degree and that its effectiveness is not a function of specifics of method or of setting.

> "Statistical studies of psychotherapy consistently report that about two thirds of neurotic patients . . . are improved immediately after treatment, regardless of the type of psychotherapy they have received, and the same improvement rate has been found for patients who have not received any treatment that was *deliberately* psychotherapeutic." [28] (Italics ours.)

Such interpretations of the limited statistical data are consonant with the frequently offered casual observation, based on the testimonial literature, that all schools of psychotherapy claim a fair number of successes. Together the actuarial interpretation and the clinical overview are consistent with the *thesis of common factors*. This thesis, based upon arm-chair analyses of the irreducible minimum variables in any psychotherapeutic interaction between persons, was stated by psychologists in 1936,[29] and 1952,[30] by an eminent psychiatrist[31] and by still another psychologist,[32] in 1961. Briefly stated, this thesis holds that there are certain basic factors (processes, forces, or dimensions) that occur in every form of psychotherapy and that play essentially the same role in every psychotherapeutic model, that it is the factors common to all types of therapy that account for whatever positive results are obtained by any of them. Separate analyses of the common factors have enumerated as few as three or four to as many as five or six. In recent years there have been some ingenious researches designed to tease out the nature and number of uniformities across "schools"; pertinent findings will be reviewed in the next chapter.

In a psychological analysis of potential common factors in various methods of psychotherapy it is well to start with a clear view of those differences which are explicit. A "school" of psychotherapy is identified by: a) a theory of personality or of psychopathology, and b) a set of techniques and rules for the conduct of therapy. Schools vary in the degree to which their prominence or uniqueness is related to the features of their *theory* or to the nature of their *tactics*. Freud wrote extensively on the theory of psychoanalysis but was relatively silent about treatment technique. The early appeal of Roger's "nondirective" therapy was largely in the explicitness and simplicity of the methods he espoused rather than in his theory of personality. To the extent that each system of psychotherapy has an articulated theory it is easy to point out the differences among them at the level of *theory*. But, the theories do not have direct impact on the patient; patients do not "experience" the theories. Therapists of different theoretical persuasion may be of differing effectiveness because of the differences in their respective theories only in measure as those theoretical differences lead to differences in the way in which they conduct therapy—the actual process by which they interact with, learn about, and influence their patients.

Apparently extensive differences in two theories need not be paralleled by notable differences in therapeutic technique, especially as some theories of therapy specify very little about the tactics of treatment. Even where extensive differences are spelled out in the specific procedures of therapy associated with particular systems, it is not certain that these differences will be clearly manifested in the actual conduct of therapeutic interviews by representatives of the systems. In one survey of orthodox psychoanalysts who were "card carrying" adherents to the Freudian school, it was found that there was striking lack of consistency with respect to a wide range of specific practices.[33]

The differences among systems of psychotherapy either at the level of their personality theory or their prescribed modes of treatment will account for any potentially demonstrated difference in their effectiveness only to the extent that it is demonstrated that the clinicians practicing each system do in fact carry out significantly different processes in their patient contacts. But, as one factor common to all systems there is some theory, some more or less highly explicated theoretical formulation of psychopathology and the therapeutic process. It has been suggested that some sort of "systematic ideology" may be an essential element in successful therapy:

> "Whether the therapist talks in terms of psychoanalysis or Christian Science is from this point of view relatively unimportant as compared with the *formal consistency* with which the doctrine employed is adhered to, for by virtue of this consistency the patient receives a schema for achieving some sort and degree of personality organization." [29]

If we examine the broad outlines of psychotherapy as an interpersonal transaction, certain structural properties emerge which are unavoidably common to all forms of psychotherapy; these common factors do not contribute to differences in the conduct of the treatment and they cannot explain any differences in results which might be demonstrated for the "different" approaches. But these common factors may well be of considerable *potency* and may account for most of the positive results which each of the schools claim.

In essence, psychotherapy is conversation with therapeutic intent. As conversation it entails all of the modes of communication (some facilitant and some deterrent) that are active whenever two persons speak to one another. Language carries the major mediational load and is the primary transmitter of communication in conversation. We have long been aware of the distinctions between connotative and denotative language—words have "agreed upon" meanings as specified by the dictionary, but they also have more or less individualistic meanings for each person who uses them. Communication would be easier (simpler and more accurate) if it were humanly possible for persons to restrict their language to purely denotative words; it is not. While members of a culture may share the same official dictionary, they naturally do not share in identical personal experiences whereby words acquire the personal connotations that individuals unconsciously seek to use in their conversations. Some words make for better communication because they have a scientifically precise definition, or in the nature of the things to which they refer there is a limited range of possible connotations; other words tend to contribute a lot of "static" to communication because they do not permit of objective definition but rather represent certain personal meanings of high frequency in a particular group of persons. The following lists will suggest this aspect of the communication problem:

| *More Denotative Words* | *More Connotative Words* |
|---|---|
| Inch | Good |
| Minute | Strong |
| Black | Liberal |
| Round | Pretty |
| North | Smart |

This is only one of the problem areas receiving intensive investigation in the rapidly evolving technical fields knows as psycholinguistics and communication theory.

Man has long been aware that his oral communications are neither given nor received purely in terms of the words spoken (and their explicit or implicit meanings) but that additional and particular meanings are communicated by the general context of their utterance. The most important part of this contextual communication is undoubtedly the facial expression of the conversants. The particular meaning of a word is frequently signaled by a frown or a smile or a grimace. And responses to questions or assertions may be wordlessly communicated by a nod, by a smile, by "silence freighted with meaning." When communication is emotionally charged, when the topic of conversation is loaded with emotional "meanings" as is frequently the case in psychotherapy, it is imperative that the therapist be skilled in receiving (and sending?) wordless messages or words whose meaning has been silently labeled by the emotional attitude of the sender. In accepting candidates for advanced training in the specialty of psychotherapy, it is generally true that considerable emphasis is given to intellectual ability, with applicants of very superior general intelligence being preferred. There is little in the nature of substantive information or treatment technique to be learned that justifies such emphasis. However, sensitivity to the subtle aspects of the wordless communications in psychotherapy is a most important dimension of therapeutic skill. This skill is not too readily learned but rather reflects native or very early acquired aptitudes that are highly correlated with general intelligence. And a high level of general intelligence is required to meet the scholastic requirements (many of them irrelevant to psychotherapy) that loom large in the formal education of the physician, psychologist, and social worker. (See Chapter Six.)

This nonlinguistic aspect of oral communication is a difficult area for research but it is part of the total domain of psycholinguistics. Any general theory of communication must and will encompass the conversations of psychotherapy and, as a general theory, the researches generated by it must inevitably show those particulars of the communication process which are common to all such conversations. Thus, the essentials of the communication process are identical regardless of the school of psychotherapy under whose aegis a particular therapeutic conversation is being conducted. The participants do not have access to special communication media beyond those of any other conversation—they are limited to words and sentences, to assertions and questions, to the silent "labels" of smiles and frowns, tics and tears, and to silences. Within the frame of the communality of the communication process which is shared by all approaches to psychotherapy is a particular common factor—the therapist. Regardless of his theoretical allegiance, the therapist is an expert conversationalist whose specialized equipment include: sensitivity to the emotional nuances of the patient's communication, an ability to listen selectively, facility in encouraging the patient to start and continue conversation, deftness in leading the patient to particular topics, capacity both to tolerate the patient's silences and to use his own silence in communicating. These are basic common skills of all expert psychotherapists, contributing to their capacity to establish and maintain communication. The presence of these skills in high degree is, unfortunately, not necessarily correlated with the achievement of a valid understanding of the patient (a common goal of most schools) nor with achievement of successful treatment (the ultimate goal of all schools).

Although this section is concerned with the factors common to all psychotherapies, it is well to point out those areas in which explicit differences are clearly possible and even likely. The essential elements and processes of communication are shared alike by all schools, but the selection and emphasis of *topics* for conversation may well differ systematically. In accordance with one theory, the therapist may emphasize certain topics for exploration (and explanation) to the exclusion of others, and in a variety of ways restrict the therapeutic conversation to these topics. Another school will emphasize that the topics for discussion should be arrived at spontaneously and determined primarily by the patient. One theory may emphasize the self-concept as the topic of therapeutic conversation while another may focus on specific symptomatology. A theory which was more "correct" about the topics to be conversed about might achieve some potentially demonstrable margin of success beyond that of other approaches by virtue of this "correctness."

Indirect research evidence suggests that there may be less actual consistent variation in the favored topics of different therapists than their theories would suggest. For example, one would expect psychoanalytically oriented therapists to encourage their patients to reveal their sex attitudes and histories. When a group of such therapists was asked for extended, structured descriptions of patients whom they had been treating for at least 25 hours, it was found that they frequently did not have information about such matters as attitudes toward masturbation, extra-marital relations, and other topics.[34]

There are additional structural aspects of the therapeutic conversation which set it apart from other classes of person-to-person communication but which are common to all forms of psychotherapy. One of these is the status relationships of therapy. The therapist has a certain status of ascendancy, authority, or power. This status is expressed through certain symbols: he has a title (most frequently that of "doctor"), he has certificates and diplomas which imply that he has received special, technical training, he is a member of (or closely affiliated with members of) an established profession from which he derives his visible identification as a "socially sanctioned healer." [35] He may derive additional symbolic identification from his place of business (clinic or hospital), from his professional dress (the white coat), or from his "tools" (*e.g.*, Rorschach cards, tape recorder).

Part of the ascendant status of the therapist is reflective of the fact that his client is supplicant. The patient, suffering and wanting to be helped, seeks out the therapist and comes to him. "Almost all psychotherapy is to some degree disturbing to the patient because it is deflating to the ego to be so maladjusted that it becomes necessary to place oneself in the embarrassing position of having to admit failure and seek help from others." [36] This subjectively experienced lowered status of the client has potential for effecting the therapeutic process positively at the beginning of treatment and negatively in later stages. In the beginning he may be more ready to accept the suggestions of the ascendant therapist while later on, when less acutely distressed, his persisting sensitivity to the status differential can motivate obstinacies that are too luxuriously interpreted as "transference" phenomena.[37]

This status relationship which is common, at least initially, to all psychotherapies generates or supports certain psychological qualities that are universal. In brief, both the therapist and the patient from their respective positions have certain expectancies. The therapist honestly expects to be able to help his client; he knows the dimensions of his status and from these dimensions (training, experience, membership) he expects to be helpful. From this underlying expectation his basic attitude is one of confidence and in a variety of ways his positive expectation and confidence are communicated to the patient.

The patient expects to be helped because in seeking out the therapist he is following the general recommendation of his society as to where he is to expect to be helped. Some patients go reluctantly, even resentfully, to the therapist and without any preformed faith in the process. But even these, since they are never literally forced, cannot be thoroughly convinced that nothing will happen. Increasingly in our society because of the improved education of the public the patient brings to his therapist a readiness to be helped and some faith in the process. Together these initial expectancies of the therapist and the patient provide a positive psychological atmosphere for the powerful healing effects of implicit suggestion. These implicit forces of suggestion are augmented by the social structuring of the on-going therapy as a series of controlled conversations in which, according to some theory that yields "formal consistency," the therapist seeks to persuade the patient (and the patient to be persuaded?) toward new views of himself, and of his problems. These status-derived forces of general suggestion and persuasion are common to all forms of psychotherapy.

Apart from the status roles of the two participants, still another structural factor is common to all approaches. The relationship between the therapist and his patient is not a spontaneous one but rather a controlled, circumscribed, or limited one.[30,35] The frequency of visits, generally regular (and most commonly weekly), their timing and duration, are explicitly determined. What is permissible and desirable for the patient to do during the treatment hour is controlled and what demands he may make of his therapist are very definitely limited. In light of the prolonged nature of the relationship, the intimacy of the material shared, and the qualities of rapport and mutual respect that are engendered, this fact of definite controls on what the patient may do or fail to do, and what he can require of the therapist, constitutes what may be the most distinctive feature of the therapeutic relationship. This feature of controlled relationship is espoused in nearly all methods of psychotherapy.

The quality of the relationship is given specific attention in all formulations of psychotherapy and certain aspects of the relationship are given universal emphasis. There is general agreement that it is the responsibility of the therapist to be accepting of the patient and to communicate his acceptance to the patient. This acceptance of the patient is a complex of therapist attitudes that includes respect for the patient as an individual, positive regard for his personality and his potential, warmth, kindness, and continuing willingness to help no matter what the symptoms or defects of the patient. Most crucially, this attitude of acceptance requires that the therapist relate to his patient in a nonjudgmental, noncritical, nonpunitive way. Of course, failures of conformity, socially inimical attitudes, or even antisocial behavior may not be at the heart of the problem for which the patient seeks help and the therapist may learn of them only incidentally, but he must avoid value assessments which cause him inadvertently to communicate a rejection of the patient. This is a difficult quality of relationship both to describe and to establish effectively. The therapist may share many of his society's values and mores and will not think that it is good for them to be violated or neglected, but it is not his function to condemn or to try to re-create an individual in his own image. This quality of "acceptance" *in our culture at this time* is peculiarly restricted to the psychotherapeutic contract, but it is common to all such contracts. In this sense, psychotherapy provides a very special, perhaps ideal, form of friendship.

It is reasonable to presume that a further reflection of the communality of the quality of acceptance is found in the expectation of the average patient who seeks a therapeutic relationship. The hopeful expectation of "unconditional positive regard" from somebody may well be one of the common factors leading to an increasing demand for psychotherapy and contributing to a positive response when it is available.[38]

Whether or not the impact of the mental health movement and its attendant educational programs has created a general expectation of the therapeutically prescribed acceptance, it seems that a majority of patients have an expectation that their revelation of self and others will be treated with complete confidentiality. Again, in the principle that the patient's communications are "privileged" and protected in principle and by law from release in any form or medium which would cause him or others embarrassment or hurt, we have a structural factor shared by all schools of psychotherapy. As a common factor of the therapy contract, it may significantly contribute to the total therapeutic impact of the relationship. It is, by contrast, a notable characteristic of our general culture that we are gossipy and notoriously indifferent to the ethics of personal confidences!

We have reviewed aspects of psychotherapeutic relationship that are basically of a structural nature, that stem from the universal status factors of supplicant and benefactor and from the general provisions of the psychotherapeutic contract. Are there any aspects of the *process* of psychotherapy that permit of the possibility of being general and not restricted to those therapeutic conversations which eventuate under the aegis of a particular theory? Over fifty years ago, when psychotherapy was aborning, Josef Breuer discovered the principle of catharsis. He observed that patients who were able to recall the origins of a symptom and to give uninhibited expression to the emotions attendant upon the situation in which it evolved were subsequently relieved symptomatically and generally improved in their over-all adjustment. This function of emotional purging or catharsis came gradually to be perceived as but one phase of a more general process in which the patient, under the accepting, encouraging, and supportive friendship of the therapist, was enabled to give expression to his conflicts, his anxiety, his guilts, his resentments, to relieve his previously bottled up feelings without fear of rejection or misunderstanding. To this basic process whereby the suffering supplicant is helped to achieve release from the tormenting burden of his previously suppressed (or repressed) emotions, from the personal isolation stemming from his previously unshared feelings, is given the name ventilation. Catharsis and ventilation are the naturally inevitable first steps in any truly intimate personal relationship, requiring nothing more than an *accepting* (and probably understanding) auditor. It is difficult to imagine any formal psychotherapy which could either in theory or *expert* practice deliberately prevent the occurrence of such ventilation.\* And

---

\* It is possible that full ventilation may be prevented or delayed by the inexperienced, insensitive, or inept therapist who is overly active and insufficiently appreciative of the self-curative forces in nature.

ventilation and catharsis as general factors may prove to account for a sizable portion of the total therapeutic impact of all psychotherapies.

In the prolonged relationships of intensive psychotherapy, it must be recognized that the patient has opportunity for repeated expression of "punishable" ideas and feelings which do not lead in therapy to punishment or rejection. The anxiety originally accompanying the thoughts is gradually extinguished or reduced through repeated expression without pain. Then it is possible for the patient to see his *bêtes noires* differently, to think differently about them, and to plan imaginatively to react differently to their real life representations. Eventually, with the support and positive suggestion of the therapist, he is able to experiment with new modes of response to those persons and situations which are anxiety symbols and, eventually, to extend the process of learning (and extinction of inappropriate, anxious responses) to the "real" world outside of his therapist's office.

Although there are differences in interpretation as to the elements of the process, differences in emphasis as to whether it is mostly an extinction of old, inappropriate responses or an acquisition of new more appropriate responses, differences as to whether there are basic generalities or necessary specifics in the content of neurosis, nearly all psychotherapists agree that psychotherapy is a learning process. In this learning, the therapist serves as guide, tutor, model, and primary source of reward. To the extent that all therapists partake of the role of teacher, self-acknowledged or not, we have yet another common dimension.

Considering the range and basic nature of these dimensions and processes which are common to all forms of conversation with therapeutic intent, it is remarkable that so many have found so much to say about such a variety of apparent diversities in theory and practice. But in our culture it is far more acceptable to present oneself as an expert in some moderately occult and complex professionalized technique than to suggest the more modest (grandiose?) claim to being generally perceptive and intelligent about personal problems. Certainly the average counselor can much sooner be confident that he is technically proficient than he can be assured that he is wise.

In view of the extensive variety and possibly sizable therapeutic power of those factors which do appear to be shared by all schools of psychotherapy, it is suggested that we might do well to concen-

trate our researches on these potential mechanisms of the psychotherapeutic effect, and to emphasize carefully the methods of opti-
mizing their influence when selecting and training psychotherapists,
rather than to pursue almost exclusively the search for differences
in therapeutic practice that *theoretically* should be there and *theoretically* should make a difference.

# References

1. Gregory Zilboorg (with the collaboration of G. W. Henry), *A History of
Medical Psychology* (New York: W. W. Norton Co., Inc., 1941), p. 28.

2. Cicero's *Tusculanes, III,* quoted by Zilboorg, *ibid.,* p. 65.

3. Zilboorg, *ibid.,* p. 83.

4. Albert Deutsch, *The Mentally Ill in America. A History of Their Care
and Treatment from Colonial Times,* 2nd Edition (New York: Columbia Univer-
·sity Press, 1949), Chapter V, pp. 79-85.

5. Zilboorg, *op. cit.,* Chapter 7, pp. 206-35; Chapter 9, pp. 479-510.

6. Lewis R. Wolberg, *The Technique of Psychotherapy* (New York: Grune &
Stratton, 1954), p. 3.

7. Ernest Jones, *The Life and Work of Sigmund Freud. Vol. I., 1856-1900,
The Formative Years and the Great Discoveries* (New York: Basic Books, Inc.,
1953).

8. Zilboorg, *op. cit.,* p. 361.

9. John K. Winkler and Walter Bromberg, *Mind Explorers* (New York:
Reynal & Hitchcock, Inc., 1939). Chapter III.

10. Walter Bromberg, *The Mind of Man. The Story of Man's Conquest of
Mental Illness* (New York: Harper & Row, Publishers, 1937), Chapter VII.

11. Jones, *op. cit.,* p. 185.

12. *Ibid.,* p. 238.

13. Bruno Walter, *Theme and Variations: An Autobiography* (New York:
Alfred A. Knopf, Inc., 1946).

14. Jones, *op. cit.,* p. 223.

15. Josef Breuer and Sigmund Freud, *Studien über Hysterie.* J. Strachey
(translated) (New York: Basic Books, Inc., 1957).

16. Zilboorg, *op. cit.*, pp. 486-87.

17. Robert A. Harper, *Psychoanalysis and Psychotherapy: 36 Systems* (Englewood Cliffs, N.J.: Prentice-Hall, Inc., 1959, A Spectrum Book, S-3).

18. Carl R. Rogers, *Counseling and Psychotherapy* (Boston: Houghton Mifflin Co., 1942).

19. Joseph Wolpe, *Psychotherapy by Reciprocal Inhibition* (Stanford, California: Stanford University Press, 1958).

20. Albert Ellis, *Reason and Emotion in Psychotherapy* (New York: Lyle Stuart, 1962).

21. Hans J. Eysenck, "The Effects of Psychotherapy—An Evaluation," *J. Consult. Psychol.*, 16 (1952), pp. 319-24.

22. Saul Rosenzweig, "A Transvaluation of Psychotherapy—A Reply to Hans Eysenck," *J. abn. soc. Psychol.*, 49 (1954), pp. 298-304.

23. Eysenck, *op. cit.*, p. 322.

24. *Ibid.*, p. 323.

25. Hans J. Eysenck, "The Effects of Psychotherapy: A Reply," *J. abn. soc. Psychol.*, 50 (1955), pp. 147-48.

26. Saul Rosenzweig, "Calumet," *J. abn. soc. Psychol.*, 50 (1955), p. 148.

27. Julius Seeman, "Psychotherapy," in *Annual Review of Psychology*, Vol. 12 (1961), Paul R. Farnsworth, ed. (Palo Alto: Annual Reviews, Inc., 1961).

28. Jerome D. Frank, *Persuasion and Healing: A Comparative Study of Psychotherapy* (Baltimore: Johns Hopkins Press, 1961).

29. Saul Rosenzweig, "Some Implicit Common Factors in Diverse Methods of Psychotherapy," *Amer. J. Orthopsychiat.*, 6 (1936), pp. 412-15.

30. John D. Black, "Common Factors of the Patient-Therapist Relationships in Diverse Psychotherapies," *J. Clin. Psychol.*, 8 (1952), pp. 302-06.

31. Frank, *op. cit.*, pp. 13-14.

32. Nicholas Hobbs, "Sources of Gain in Psychotherapy," *Amer. Psychologist*, 17 (1962), pp. 741-47.

33. Edward Glover, *The Technique of Psycho-Analysis* (New York: International Universities Press, Inc., 1955).

34. Bernard C. Glueck, Paul E. Meehl, and William Schofield, "The Skilled Clinician's Assessment of Personality," Research Project, University of Minnesota, Department of Psychiatry, and Institute of Living, Hartford, Connecticut. Supported by grants from the Ford Foundation and the National Institute for Mental Health.

35. Frank, *op. cit.*, p. 2.

36. Frederick C. Thorne, "A Critique of Non-Directive Methods of Psychotherapy," *J. abn. soc. Psychol.*, 39 (1944), pp. 459-70.

37. Black, *op. cit.*, p. 304.

38. Carl R. Rogers, "The Necessary and Sufficient Conditions of Therapeutic Personality Change," *J. consult. Psychol.*, 21 (1957), pp. 95-103.

# CHAPTER SIX

# The Psychotherapist

Who are the experts to whom the unhappy and maladjusted citizens of our urban communities take their problems for consultations, hopefully for cure? Since the close of World War II it has been increasingly clear that experts in the management of functional mental illness are being drawn from three professions—medicine, psychology, and social work. The medically trained specialist is the psychiatrist. The psychologically trained expert is a *clinical* psychologist. And the specialist from social work is the *psychiatric* social worker. To the extent that all three of these highly trained experts do (in increasing numbers) engage in one-to-one personal conversations with the therapeutic intent to relieve psychological symptoms, modify attitudes, and improve adjustment—and to the extent that their respective efforts must partake of the factors common to all psychotherapeutic exchanges—it follows that there must be certain minimal overlap and similarities in their professional preparation. They do have specific knowledges, skills, values and goals in common. We shall consider the extent and nature of these shared attributes, but it will be helpful to consider first those aspects of their respective professional preparations that most clearly distinguish among them, and to view the pertinence of each unique training experience to the practice of psychotherapy.

## I. THE PSYCHIATRIST

The psychiatrist is a graduate physician. As holder of the M.D. degree he has received basic education in medical sciences (anatomy, bacteriology, pathology, physiology, and so on) and supervised experience with each of the clinical specialties (such as medicine, surgery, neurology, obstetrics). The basic structure of undergraduate medical training is essentially standard in a majority of American

114

medical schools; most commonly there are two years of basic science instruction followed by two years of training and supervised apprenticelike experience in the clinical fields. The basic four years of medical school instruction received by the man who ultimately becomes a psychiatrist (and who may have had this as a goal upon entering medical school) are not different from those of any other M.D. He has spent the same number of class hours as any other physician in the study of chemistry, anatomy, pathology, bacteriology.* The amount of instruction and exposure to general human psychology and particularly to psychopathology and to psychiatric illness which he received during the two preclinical years will depend upon the medical school he attended; it may be as little as 20 hours and rarely exceeds 180 hours. By contrast he is likely to have devoted at least 500 hours to the study of anatomy.

Following medical school, the aspirant psychiatrist must complete a one-year internship in an accredited hospital in which his clinical diagnostic and therapeutic skills are further developed over the full range of medical illnesses. At the end of this internship he has satisfied the basic requirement to qualify for the practice of medicine, and he may then undertake specialized training in the field of psychiatry. This training is known as a "residency" and encompasses a three-year period of instruction and supervision by the staff of an accredited psychiatric hospital. As a psychiatric resident he will be exposed to some formal, didactic instruction on the subjects of psychiatric nosology, psychopathology, techniques of interviewing, special diagnostic procedures, special medical therapies (*e.g.*, electroshock, drugs), and principles of psychotherapy. How much formal instruction he receives will depend upon the particular psychiatric staff responsible for his training. Also, whether his theoretical orientation is "psychobiologic," "psychoanalytic," or "eclectic" will depend upon the setting in which he happens to take his residency.

Apart from these possible particulars of his training he will over the course of the three years be exposed to a wide variety and large number of patients (hospitalized and outpatient) for which, with varying degrees and emphases of supervision, he will be directly responsible and whose treatment, especially when it is psycho-

---

* He may have entered medical school after completing a four-year college degree; more frequently he will have started his medical training at the end of three years of premedical study. His premedical education has to emphasize the sciences (especially chemistry and physics), and depending upon his initiative and ability and upon the quality of his premedical school, he may have studied more or less of psychology, sociology, history, and other subjects.

therapy, he will provide. In essence, the psychiatric residency is an intensive and extensive apprenticeship in the diagnosis and treatment of patients with emotional disorders who are referred to clinics or hospitals. At the end of the three years, some eleven or twelve years after his high school graduation, at an average age of thirty-plus, the physician is fully qualified to begin his professional career as a psychiatrist and, if he chooses (and many do), to specialize in psychotherapy with the ambulatory patient.*

## II. THE CLINICAL PSYCHOLOGIST

The clinical psychologist holds the Ph.D. degree in psychology. This means that he has completed a minimum of three years of graduate instruction in psychology from a major university. Before admission to such graduate study, he has completed a four-year college degree in a liberal arts program with emphasis upon the humanities and the social sciences. His graduate work will encompass study of personality theory, abnormal psychology (psychopathology), methods of psychological measurement, and psychometric theory, statistical methods and research design, clinical diagnostic tests and techniques, principles of interviewing, and theories and techniques of psychotherapy. These constitute his major program; he will probably also complete a program of minor didactic studies in an appropriate related field such as sociology, anthropology, or psychiatry. The psychologist's graduate program includes both didactic instruction and supervised clinical practice in interviewing, testing, and the like. As a major requirement for the doctoral degree, he must design, carry out, and write up an original research investigation in an appropriate problem area. Finally, like the M.D., he must complete a full year's internship in a psychiatric facility having a full complement of professional staff. This total program of instruction, supervised training, and research is completed by the average clinical psychologist in slightly over five years. (The range of years from matriculation to degree completion is from a minimum of four to an upper limit of nine or ten years, this variation being primarily a function of the amount of time required for completion of the doctoral dissertation.) Thus, typically,

---

* If he wishes to specialize in the field of child psychiatry, he must complete two years of residence on a children's service in addition to two years of experience on adult services. Many men take additional spcialized training in psychoanalysis; to qualify as a full-fledged analyst the psychiatrist must complete several additional years of training in an analytic institute.

some nine to ten years following high-school graduation, at an average age of 27-plus years, the psychologist is qualified to begin his professional career as a clinician and, if he chooses (and an increasing number do), to specialize in psychotherapy with outpatient neurotics.*

### III. THE PSYCHIATRIC SOCIAL WORKER

The psychiatric social worker is typically the holder of a Master's degree (commonly the M.S.W., Master of Social Work). This means that in addition to an undergraduate college degree she has completed a two-year course of study in a recognized school of social work. To qualify for admission to such a graduate program she has pursued a college curriculum, especially in her junior and senior years, which has emphasized courses in child and adolescent psychology, sociology, and public health. Her undergraduate major is very likely to be in sociology, entailing the study of community organization, family structure, and political and economic aspects of welfare agencies. As a graduate student she takes didactic instruction in personality development, psychopathology, community organization, social welfare programs and agencies, and principles of social case work. She is required to complete an extended thesis or research project, frequently as a collaborative endeavor with other students. In the first year of her graduate study she enters upon a sequence of intensive field work experience, usually beginning in a general community agency (for example, a family and children's service). Her placement in the second year will be in a psychiatric clinic or hospital where she receives "on-the-job" orientation to the functions of the psychiatric social worker (PSW) and undertakes increasing responsibility for carrying out such functions herself under regular and close case-by-case supervision from an experienced staff member. In total, she will accumulate close to the equivalent of one year of full-time supervised experience in interviewing patients and families, collecting and integrating case material, contacting relevant community agencies, and communicating her findings to other professional staff. In her field work she is required, under very close supervision, to "carry" an increasing

* Both psychiatry and clinical psychology have "specialty boards" which examine and award "certification" in the respective specialty. To be eligible for such examination, the psychiatrist must have two years of appropriate experience after completion of his residency.[2] The psychologist must have at least four years of suitable experience following receipt of the Ph.D.[3]

load of cases, *i.e.*, be the primary source of a patient's therapeutic conversation.* Typically, some six to seven years following graduation from high school, at an average age of 24 years, the PSW is ready to function as one of the sources of therapeutic conversation for the patient of a completely staffed psychiatric clinic or hospital. In areas of heavy population density where the demand for psychotherapy is in great excess to the supply, some social workers (not always trained in the psychiatric specialty) are finding it feasible to offer their services to private clients who consult them directly.[5]

### IV. UNIQUE SKILLS AND FUNCTIONS

There are obvious differences in the patterns and some of the contents of the full professional training of the psychiatrist, clinical psychologist, and social worker. These can be best appreciated if we ask what specific knowledges or skills are unique to each of them, constituting a basis on which each is able to make a contribution to the psychiatric patient that cannot be duplicated by the others. The psychiatrist's unique competence is his medical knowledge and training—he alone is qualified to appraise the medical-physical status of the patient (although any physician can do this as well—possibly better), and he alone is qualified to prescribe and administer medical (physiochemical) treatments; no one else can do this. An additional prerogative of the psychiatrist as a *physician* is a legal authority (existing by virtue of long historical precedent and beginning to show signs of appropriate impress of modern concepts and techniques) to be responsible for certain administrative operations (as contrasted with clearly *medical* procedures), for example, to hospitalize a patient, to discharge a patient, and so on. The long-standing authority of the physician as the final and sole authority on "insanity" or mental disease within the law is beginning to show appropriate decay. The quality of a recent brief filed by the Ameri-

* Historically, intensive individual attention to and frequent contact with a client by a social worker has been a part of "case work." As functions and roles of the social worker have shifted under the increasing burdens of the case load of psychiatric patients and as the *psychiatric* social worker has become more visible, it becomes increasingly clear that she is engaged frequently in an undifferentiated psychotherapeutic endeavor. Largely for purposes of maintaining amicable relationships with her psychiatrist "overseer," she has been content with the professional usage that designates her activity as case work. But attempts to differentiate logically between what should go on in "case work" and what should transpire in psychotherapy have not yielded either numerous or clear distinctions.[4]

can Psychiatric Association speaks eloquently for the inevitable erosion of the physician's role as ultimate arbiter in this area.[6]

The clear responsibility of the hospital psychiatrist for the medical care of patients has historically extended to a quasi-legal responsibility (final authority) for such psychological procedures as prescribing changes in activity programs, giving or withholding passes, allowing or disallowing visitors. But increasingly, partly as a function of the team approach and partly as a function of administrative leadership, such decisions are becoming a group responsibility (in many instances the responsibility of the patient's peers) or transferred to the psychologist.[7,8]

The clinical psychologist's unique contribution to the individual patient comes in his competence to select, administer, score, interpret, and integrate the results of a variety of psychological tests and examination procedures that provide the only truly *standardized* and reliable source of data as to the patient's mental ability and personality. He alone is a skilled diagnostician in the sense of having facility with a set of instruments specifically designed to overcome the errors and inadequacies of notoriously fallible clinical appraisal of complex phenomena. Beyond the application of his diagnostic tools to the individual patient, the psychologist alone has a thorough knowledge of the psychometric theory underlying these instruments and, accordingly, he alone can truly appreciate their limitations. Aside from this contribution to the individual patient, the psychologist's grounding in the methodology of behavioral research, especially measurement of personality and the behavioral correlates of personality types, affords him the capacity to design instruments for appraisal of changes, specifically of changes in major dimensions of personality. Measurement of such changes, and of related criterion variables, lies at the heart of the appraisal of the effectiveness of any psychotherapeutic or other psychiatric therapy. Skill in such personality research at the molar or behavioral level (as contrasted with study of physiological functions) is another capacity unique to the clinical psychologist.*

The social worker has a knowledge of the network of city, county, and state welfare agencies, their personnel, equipment, and services and their administrative patterns and relationships, which is not

---

* There are other psychologists, non-clinicians, who as personality theorists and investigators or as behavioral scientists have these same research competences. "Uniqueness" relative to the clinical pychologist stems from his possession of these skills plus experience in a particular context—the social agency, mental health clinic, or psychiatric hospital.

shared by other members of the psychiatric team. She is sensitive to community structure and to the ways in which that structure can naturally facilitate or impede the recovery of a patient. She is experienced in the relevance of subculture memberships for patterns of psychopathology and for accessibility or resistance to personal intervention. She is skilled in the elicitation and correlation of life history data from relatives and other informants. She is cognizant of the economic problems of various family structures. She is expert in preparation of referrals to particular agencies and in the preparation of the patient to accept and profit from such referrals. These are among the skills of case workers in the old-fashioned sense, and they are not shared by psychiatrist or psychologist.*

The following table highlights certain features of the training of these three professions:

Table 3

A Comparison of the Training of the Three Major Psychotherapists

| Specialist | Total Years of Training Beyond High School | Estimated Cost of Post graduate Specialty Training* | Years of Graduate Training Before Intensive Psychiatric Experience | Estimated Proportion of Graduate Training Years Clearly Relevant to Psychotherapy |
|---|---|---|---|---|
| Psychiatrist | 11-12 | $8,000 | 5 | one third |
| Psychologist | 9-10 | 2,500 | 2 | two thirds |
| Social Worker | 6- 7 | 1,000 | 1/3 | four fifths |

* These are crude estimates of the direct expense to the student of his training and they are very *conservative*. They do not include the sizably greater investment of society in the student's education—the cost of facilities, equipment and teaching staff.[9]

In summary, each of these professionals has some unique areas in the background of general education which he brings to his graduate training and differences in the core emphasis of his specialized

* This comparative review of the skills unique to each profession is relevant, of course, to the typical worker with typical training. A few psychiatrists have also received full graduate training in psychology, some psychologists were previously social workers, and occasionally a social worker successfully pursues the study of medicine or psychology.

graduate preparation. The professions of psychiatry, clinical psychology and social work are presently providing the great bulk of formal psychotherapy in this country. But the members of no one of these three professions are *selected* and *trained primarily* to be skilled psychotherapists. The variation in the cost of training each of these experts and the time required for this training, in light of the proportional relevance of their respective programs as preparation for the specific conduct of psychotherapy, has obvious social implications. It must be recognized that psychotherapy is neither the primary nor unique skill of any one of these professions. The psychiatrist, psychologist, and social worker each does possess specialized and unique competences. Can our society afford a significant reduction in the application of these unique skills in a "shotgun" effort to meet the manpower shortage resulting from the increasing demand for therapeutic conversation?

## V. SHARED THEORETICAL BIAS

It has been remarked that to the degree that all psychotherapy partakes of the beneficial effects of certain common processes the therapeutic functioning of social worker, psychologist, and psychiatrist would manifest these communalities. There are certain shared orientations and attitudes, stemming from common emphases in their respective training, that probably augment the comparability of the therapeutic approaches of these three workers. In essence, this mutuality of implicit response tendencies toward the psychotherapy patient arises from the fact that the theory of neurosis and the theory of therapy is dominated by the massive and ubiquitous doctrine of psychoanalysis. With negligible exceptions, to the extent that the psychiatrist and the social worker are taught anything vaguely psychological (of and about the mind, behavior, motives and emotions) they are taught Freudian psychology. The labels of their formal courses in "Human Development," "Personality and Adjustment," and "Psychopathology" do not directly belie the pervasive psychoanalytic orientation but the doctrine of the content is unmistakable. In some instances, schools of social work import carefully selected psychiatrists to assure that the theoretical indoctrination of their students will be orthodox, in tune with the general climate of psychiatry, and will afford them the "right language" for their ultimate professional collaboration.

The monolithic orientation of most social work schools, and the particular use of psychiatrists or analysts to instruct in personality theory, has contributed to a generally stable *entente cordiale* between social workers and psychiatrists. Certainly the resulting facilitation of communication and coordination is apparently in the best interests of the patient. However, like the peace pacts between nations which successfully avert war, there is no correlated impetus to make discoveries or achieve maximal efforts. At least one voice has expressed concern for the impact of this indoctrination on the specific contribution of the social worker:

"Social problems are social problems, and you cannot psychoanalyze them out of existence. Psychiatric social service . . . is indispensable. But psychiatric social service is increasingly becoming psychoanalytic social service, and more and more even the 'social' is being left out until only psychoanalytic service remains. That doesn't help people with real social and family problems." [10]

The psychologist in his formal training is exposed to a variety of truly psychological conceptualizations of the human mind, personality, and behavior. He studies theories of learning, of perception, of motivation, of communication, of decision making, and so on. He studies scientifically accumulated information (as contrasted with retrospective clinical formulations based upon the pathology of adults) as to how the social, conceptual, and emotional equipment and behavioral dispositions of the human organism unfold, develop, integrate, and disintegrate from earliest infancy through adulthood to senility. He even studies the theory of theories and is provided at least a modest ability to differentiate between "good" theories and "poorer" theories, *qua* theories. The impact of his exposure to methods for investigation of psychological phenomena, within the context of multiple theories that overlap only partially, should fit him with a generally critical orientation toward any univocal explanation of the mysteries of the human personality. And in seminars, in publications, in case conferences it is typically the psychologist, not the social worker or psychiatrist, who is dubious that an orthodox psychoanalytic formulation either truly accounts for the observed pathology or necessarily points to the optimal treatment.*

* This is a generalization about psychologists as students of behavior theory and personality. It must be recognized that there are some graduate departments of psychology in which the training of the clinical psychologist is as theoretically biased, *i.e.*, psychoanalytically oriented, as is that of the average psychiatrist or social worker.

But the clinical psychologist is also exposed didactically (and casually, like any sentient person, through a myriad of cultural media) to the Freudian theory of psychopathology and to Freudian principles of psychoanalysis. He, unlike the social worker and psychiatrist, is more likely to have his Freudian garden sprinkled from the watering cans of the dozen or so recognized variations on the theme,[11] but the exfoliation does not serve to weaken his appreciation of Freud's discoveries or his recognition of the fundamental principles of analytic therapy. And, in the quiet of the consulting room, face-to-face with a candidate for therapeutic conversation, there are multiple reasons (ranging from the sheer pertinence and richness of the psychopathological concepts to the broadly social "prestige" of analytically oriented therapy) that cause the psychologist to tend to think and behave, in that moment of truth, more like a psychiatrist or social worker, and less like a psychologist.

There are a few striking general consequences of the over-arching role of psychoanalytic doctrine in the preparation of current psychotherapists:

—a belief that psychoanalysis is the most powerful of all forms of psychotherapy and that its primary limitation and restriction as the "therapy of choice" for psychoneurosis is a function of its cost and limited supply, not of its general appropriateness.*

—a belief that distinctly psychoanalytically oriented psychotherapy is the next best to psychoanalysis.

—a belief that truly effective psychotherapy must be intensive, *i.e.,* it must entail frequent therapeutic sessions (usually weekly) over a long period of time.

—a belief that the gaining of insight by the patient is a primary goal and result of therapy.

—a belief that the major mechanism of therapy is in the nature of the therapist-patient relationship.

—a belief that the prognosis for psychotherapy rests upon the suitability of the patient which is defined generally in the same terms as the good candidate for psychoanalysis.

These generally accepted orientations, stemming from a shared theoretical bias, lead to common administrative and therapeutic practices on the part of psychiatrist, psychologist, and social worker. There is a common preference to do "intensive" psychotherapy and there are common predilections (leading possibly to subtle therapeutic attitudes and maneuvers of which the therapist may be un-

* *Cf.* the evidence on effectiveness of psychotherapy, Chapter Five.

aware) to keep the patient "in treatment." A fascinating side-effect of this peculiar bias has been a cluster of studies by psychologists which aim to identify *at the outset* just which patients will remain in treatment and which will break off. The purpose of such studies could be to identify the short-term client with a view to providing a specific therapeutic experience for him. Generally, however, the implicit assumption in these studies is that patients who break off after only a few sessions are "failures" and could not possibly have derived any benefit from their limited exposure. The goal appears to be to find ways of selecting "good" patients for therapy, *i.e.,* those who will come back interminably.* If such psychological studies should achieve a high level of predictive accuracy, it would become possible for an increasing portion of psychotherapeutic time to be devoted to a decreasing number of patients! (Perhaps this is a rare example of an instance in which we may be thankful that the accuracy of psychometric prediction is not greater.)

Another result of the common theoretical bias is that all of these expert therapists have a marked preference to provide their services to the same sample (a very small portion of the total population of persons in need of psychological assistance). These "ideal" patients are not prominent among the clients of public clinics and hospitals. By contrast, the typical supplicant to a community psychiatric facility may present a set of attributes (such as level of education and verbal facility) that discourage the "depth-oriented" therapist from feeling that he can either effectively (or usefully?) establish a really therapeutic relationship. As a consequence, they are apt with such patients to effect the sort of brief and "incomplete" therapy of which they are disdainful.

### VI. ORIGINS, EXPERIENCES, AND PREJUDICES

Most of the professional literature on the optimal preparation of psychotherapists has placed major emphasis on the role of training. Relatively little attention has been paid to factors in the selection of candidates for such training; there has been particular neglect of selection factors of a broadly nonintellectual nature and little systematic attention to attitudes, values, and social orientation. There is little quarrel with the notion that careful training and in-

---

* Contrary to what many experts might predict, the sudden administrative termination of "interminable" psychotherapy cases does not appear to precipitate acute disintegration.[12,13]

tensive supervised experience contribute significantly to the preparation of the skilled psychotherapist. We have noted above the nature and extent of similarities and differences in the training of the psychiatrist, psychologist, and social worker. It may be asked if there are factors of life history, personality, and social background that the therapist-to-be brings to his training that may contribute to enhance or to limit his future therapeutic endeavors. Differences in these factors could serve either to increase or reduce the effects of the differences in the formal training of the three professions.

The capacity for and the condition of "understanding" a patient is generally held to be of key importance in the establishment, maintenance, and successful direction of a therapeutic relationship. If it happens that therapist and client have certain identities in their respective social histories there is possible a spontaneous empathy, a preformed rapport that can facilitate the mutual acceptance of each by the other and, more importantly, may serve continuously as a catalyst for the stream of communication, spoken and unspoken, which is the medium of therapy.

With the existence of three apparently different kinds of psychotherapists, we may ask if the different professions provide a range of backgrounds in respect to social class origins sufficient to make possible "natural understanding" across the full range of cultural variables represented in the client population. A second, closely related question is: Does there appear to be evidence of a meaningful division of labor, or assortative mating, such that the differential backgrounds of clients show some degree of appropriate relationship to the differential backgrounds of therapists?

With a view to the possibilities suggested by these questions, this writer investigated the distribution of certain biographical and socio-cultural factors in samples representative of the three major sources of professional psychotherapist; also investigated were the distributions of the same variables in the respective cases of the three samples of therapists.* In this study, the psychotherapist was defined as a worker in the broad area of mental illness who specialized "in intensive personal endeavors of a corrective or therapeutic nature, utilizing the interview as his primary tool." Identification of basic samples from the three professions was provided by the national offices of the American Psychiatric Association, American Psychological Association, and National Association of Social Work-

* This study was supported by a research grant from the Graduate School of the University of Minnesota.[14]

ers, each organization submitting alphabetical lists of those members engaged primarily in intensive individual therapy with emotionally disturbed clients.*

A questionnaire was mailed to a randomly selected subsample of each of the three groups of therapists. Complete returns were obtained from 140 psychiatrists, 149 psychiatric social workers, and 88 clinical psychologists. These subsamples appeared to be reasonably representative of the larger samples from which they were drawn. In accordance with the restriction that they be engaged primarily in individual psychotherapy, it is reasonable to find that less than 2 percent of the social workers were in private practice, in contrast to approximately 55 percent and 70 percent of the psychiatrists and psychologists respectively. Psychiatric social workers have not as yet moved into private practice in large numbers. The psychologist who wants to engage primarily in psychotherapy finds little opportunity for such specialization except in private practice, while the psychiatrist with his medical entrée finds a variety of settings in which he can concentrate on psychotherapy. The findings from this questionnaire study may be examined first with respect to the variables that delineate both similarities and differences among the three types of therapist.

*The Psychotherapist—Personal Characteristics and Background*

—In these samples, the psychologists and psychiatrists were of equal age, an average of 44 years, while the social workers were an average age of 38 years old.

—The social workers were predominantly females, in a ratio of 2 to 1; the psychologists were predominantly males, in a ratio of 2 to 1; 90 percent of the psychiatrists were males.

—The average number of years of experience in psychotherapy ranged from seven for the social workers to 12 and 15 respectively for the psychologists and psychiatrists.

—The largest proportion of single persons (over one third) was found in the sample of social workers, while less than 5 percent of the psychiatrists were single. Ten percent of the psychologists, 6 percent of the social workers, and 1 percent of the psychiatrists were divorced. The divorce rate in the general population of persons 25 years of age and over is 2 percent for males and 3 percent for females. Thus, in two of these three samples of mental health

* The sample of psychologist-therapists was identified primarily through the National Roster of Scientific and Technical Personnel.

experts the divorce rate is clearly in excess of that for the general population.

—The three groups were not different in regard to the proportion of their respective educational costs paid from their own earnings. Essentially half of each sample earned less than half of the total cost of their training (including undergraduate college). Each professional group had at least 10 percent of persons who earned all their expenses.

—The complete range of educational achievement is represented by the fathers and mothers of the three samples of therapists. The proportions of fathers with *less* than an 8th-grade education were 20 percent, 25 percent, and 30 percent for the social workers, psychologists, and psychiatrists respectively. From 40 to 50 percent of the fathers of each of the three therapist groups had not completed high school. The proportion of fathers with a college degree was greatest for the psychiatrists (38 percent), and smallest for the psychologists (15 percent).

—Nearly 40 percent of the fathers of the psychiatrists were occupied in the areas of science, general cultural work, or arts and entertainment; this proportion is twice that for the fathers of the social workers or psychologists. Over half of the fathers in each professional sample are in organizational or technological occupations.*

In summary, both differences and similarities appear in the social backgrounds of the three kinds of psychotherapist. A full range of socio-economic levels is represented in the parental homes of each of the three professions, and while certain variables such as father's education yield a statistically reliable differentiation among the three professions, there is a remarkable overlap of the three groups on all of the background variables. There is a clear evidence of a pressure toward upward social mobility (*i.e.,* improvement of social class status) represented in the professional training of psychiatrist, psychologist, and social worker alike. Correlated with this generalized shift of class identification is a probable homogeneity of social values on the part of all three kinds of therapists and a corresponding reduction of the range of capacity for an empathic or spontaneous understanding derived at least in part from common cultural origins.

Even though the three kinds of psychotherapists do not show

* The fathers' occupations were classified according to the system of Anne Roe.[15]

marked distinctions in regard to their general social background, the possibility of a division of labor might still be seen if the respective clients of the three specialists were different in certain of their demographic characteristics. Each of the participating therapists was asked to describe his case load in terms of variables which were descriptive of his *typical* patient. For example, if his patients fell into a restricted age range he indicated the age range for his typical patient. Similar specifications of the individual therapist's typical patient were obtained for other variables such as education, income, and so on. Age and marital status were the most frequently typifying characteristics of the clientele of all three therapists, with not less than 95 percent of the respondents in any of the three samples indicating a restriction of their respective practices in terms of these attributes of their patients. Less than half of the psychologists and psychiatrists respectively reported their cases to be typically of one sex; by contrast, nearly 75 percent of the social workers worked with a case load predominantly of one sex. No one of the therapist samples was differentiated from the other two by members having markedly homogeneous patients. The distributions of the typifying characteristics of the case loads of the psychotherapists are reported below.

### The Psychotherapy Patient as Seen by the Therapist

—Among social workers and psychologists who see patients of one sex, the male patient was typical for a slightly larger portion of both therapist samples (55-45 percent). By contrast, among psychiatrists who typically see patients of one sex, the female patient was typical for nearly three fourths of such therapists.

—Less than 19 percent of the psychiatrists reported their typical patients to be under age 15; the comparative proportions are 10 percent and 20 percent for social workers and psychologists. At the other end of the age range, while the psychologist rarely "specialized" with cases over age 40, such cases were typical for over 10 percent of social workers and over 25 percent of psychiatrists. Approximately three fourths of each of the therapist samples reported typical patients to be in the 20-40 age range.

—Psychiatrists less frequently than social workers and psychologists have single persons as their typical patient. Only 10 percent of the social workers have divorced clients as typical; the comparable proportions for psychologists and psychiatrists are smaller.

—While over half of the psychiatrists report a typical patient to have a college degree, the comparable proportions of the psychologist and social worker samples are 35 percent and 5 percent respectively. While only 2 percent of psychiatrists "specialize" with clients having less than an 8th grade education, this amount of schooling is typical of the cases seen by 20 percent of the social workers.

—Only one out of 20 social workers does therapy primarily with professional clients, in contrast to 40 percent and 30 percent of psychologists and psychiatrists.

—As follows from the data on education and occupation, the three types of psychotherapist reveal distinctive differences in the income levels of their typical patients. For those therapists reporting a typical income level for clients, the full range from $2,000 to $25,000 (gross annual) is represented in each of the three professions! While the typical patient income is over $15,000 for 16 percent of the psychiatrists, the corresponding proportion of psychologists and social workers with such typical patients is 5 percent and 1 percent.

These findings may be summarized: the distributions of sex, age, marital status, education, occupation, and income of the typical patient are reliably different for the social worker, psychologist, and psychiatrist. But, as was noted with respect to therapist characteristics, the respective clients of the three professions reveal sizable overlap. Predominant characteristics of the respective clients of the three professional samples are directly compared in the following table:

Table 4

Predominant Characteristics of the "Typical" Psychotherapy Case
of the Three Samples of Therapists

|  | *Social Worker's Patient* | *Psychologist's Patient* | *Psychiatrist's Patient* |
|---|---|---|---|
| Sex | Male* | Male* | Female |
| Age | 20-40 | 20-40 | 20-40 |
| Marital status | Married | Single* | Married |
| Education | 8th grade– high school | High school– some college | College-plus |
| Occupation | Unskilled-skilled labor | Professional- Managerial | Professional- Managerial |
| Income | $2,000-$6,000 | $4,000-$8,000 | Over $8,000 |

* Only very slight predominance.

While there appears to be more of a group differential among these broad characteristics of the clients of the three therapists than was found among the therapists themselves, the most distinguishing feature is the level of income of the client. This factor is, of course, reflective of differences in the fees (or absence of fees) involved in the respective services of the three professions, and the difference in fee structure (and also in the relative amount of private practice) is in turn reflective of the differences in the length and cost of their professional training. While the data from this survey bear only indirectly on the possibility of assortative mating, *i.e.*, the tendency for clients and therapists to be of like socio-economic background, and hence to benefit potentially from the empathy stemming from an identity of subcultural experiences and values, the findings are not particularly encouraging to the assumption of such a selective division of labor.

A further reservation on the possibility of a meaningful selective matching of psychotherapist and patient is imposed when the expressed preferences of the representatives of each profession are examined. As part of the questionnaire, each of the psychotherapists was asked to indicate the characteristics of his "ideal" patient, that is, "the kind of patient with whom you feel you are efficient and effective in your therapy." On the average, over half of each of the samples of therapists expressed a distinct preference with respect to each of the variables descriptive of patients. A notable exception is the patient's sex; less than one third of the psychiatrists and less than one fourth of the psychologists expressed a preferred sex in their ideal patient. By contrast, two thirds of social workers and psychologists and three fourths of psychiatrists expressed a distinct preference as regards the ideal patient's educational level. Over 90 percent of the psychiatrists claimed a preferred age range for their patients.

—For those psychotherapists who did express a sex preference, a preference for females was predominant in all three professional samples. The margin of preference for female patients was largest in the sample of psychiatrists, nearly two thirds of this group claiming the female patient as "ideal."

—From 60 to 70 percent of each of the therapist groups place the ideal patient's age in the 20-40 year range.

—Marital status as a factor in response to psychotherapy is viewed differently by the three samples of therapists. A widowed or divorced status is not considered an ideal patient characteristic by any of the three. Both psychiatrists and social workers have a more marked preference for married patients than holds for the sample of psychologists, nearly half of whom expressed a preference for single clients.

—For all three samples of psychotherapists not less than three fourths of the expressed preferences as to the patient's educational level fall in the categories which include not less than high school graduation and not more than an undergraduate college degree. Very rarely do representatives of any of the three disciplines express a preference for their patient to have a graduate degree (*e.g.*, M.A., M.D., Ph.D.).

—The psychotherapy candidate's occupational level is less frequently a basis for common preference than is his education. Nearly three fourths of the psychiatrists and psychologists expressed a preference for patients in professional and managerial occupations. Nearly one fifth of the social workers describe their ideal patient as a skilled laborer.

The following table is a summary of the general characteristics of the ideal patient, the patient most likely to respond well to psychotherapy, as viewed by representatives of the three major psychotherapy professions.

Table 5

The Ideal Patient for Psychotherapy as Viewed by Three Professions

|  | *Social Worker's Patient* | *Psychologist's Patient* | *Psychiatrist's Patient* |
| --- | --- | --- | --- |
| Sex | Female* | Female* | Female |
| Age | 20-40 | 20-40 | 20-40 |
| Marital Status | Married | Married-Single** | Married |
| Education | High school plus | Some college or degree | Some college or degree |
| Occupation | (No clear preference) | Professional-Managerial | Professional-Managerial |

* Slight margin of preference.
** Equally occurring preferences.

*Patient–Therapist Compatibilities*

With data available on the distributions of the actual and preferred characteristics of the patients of each of the professional samples, it is possible to examine the extent to which the social processes that govern therapist–patient matchings afford a natural compatibility out of which effective therapeutic relationships could be expected to grow. How well do the actual characteristics of patients conform to the "idealized" preferences of the therapists?

—The psychiatrists appear to have a satisfactory age representation in their typical patients. With a markedly disproportionate presence of females in their case loads, they would like a more balanced experience with the two sexes. Also, they would prefer to see relatively more married patients than they do. The psychiatrists would like a larger portion of college graduates and a smaller number of patients with advanced degrees. They do not see students as typical patients and they have no preference for such cases.

—The psychologists reveal only minor incompatibility between their experience and their ideal as regards their clients' ages. Unlike the psychiatrists, the psychologists would more frequently prefer to see more females than they typically do. They are essentially content with the distribution of their clients' marital status and educational levels.

—The social workers, like the psychologists, experience little discrepancy between the actual and preferred age representation of their cases. Like the psychologists, they would more frequently prefer to see females predominantly than is actually true in their practice. Like the psychiatrists, they would prefer to work with a higher proportion of married persons than is their experience. They would like a sizable increase in the proportion of college graduates among their clients and a reduction in the number of semi-skilled and unskilled workers.

With the exception of the sex attribute, the other patient variables yield for at least two of the three therapist samples distributions of what is "typical" which are reliably different from the distributions of what is expressed as "ideal," but in no instance are the paired "typical vs. ideal" distributions reflective of very marked incompatibility. In general, it appears that psychotherapy cases with whom the psychologists work present them with least frustration of their conception of the ideal patient. In contrast, the social workers appear to be confronted by case loads deviating considerably from the characteristics which they would ascribe to the ideal patient. The psychiatrist seems to have an experience of "incompatibility" which is less than that of the social worker but greater than that of the psychologist.

It is of particular pertinence to remark on the characteristics of the *non-preferred* candidate for psychotherapy, as revealed by this survey. What is the identification of the emotionally ill person whom the psychotherapists do not expect to be able to reach effectively through therapeutic conversation? Extreme youth (under age 15) or age (over 50) appears to be undesirable. A widowed or divorced status apparently does not contribute to an attractive patient. Limited education (less than high school) or too much education (postgraduate training) is equally rejected by social workers, psychologists, and psychiatrists. Employment in services, agriculture, fishery, forestry, semi-skilled or unskilled labor is not associated with being a "preferred risk."

What is there in the general theory of psychodynamics or psychotherapy to suggest that the neurosis of a 50-year-old commercial fisherman with an eighth-grade education will be more resistant to psychological help than a symptomatically comparable disturbance in a 35-year-old, college-trained artist? Is it simply that feelings of therapeutic potency arise primarily out of accumulated experience —a possibility suggested by the relative concordance of the "actual" and "ideal" patient characteristics? Or do the low frequencies of certain descriptive characteristics in the actual case loads of our therapists imply that these factors are somehow antithetical to the development of neurosis—an improbable conjecture. It seems more likely that there are pressures toward a systematic selection of patients, pressures that are perhaps subtle and unconscious in part and that, in part, reflect theoretical biases common to all psychotherapists. These selective forces tend to restrict the efforts of the bulk of social workers, psychologists, and psychiatrists to clients who present the "Yavis" syndrome—clients who are youthful, attractive, verbal, intelligent, and successful.

Since the medium of psychotherapy is conversation, is the general agreement among all therapists in preferring patients of greater education rather than lesser (and presumably of better than average intelligence) reflective of significant basic restrictions in the verbal ability of individuals who have less than high school education? Is it true that a person with less than a high school diploma probably cannot communicate successfully—cannot make known his confusions, concerns and conflicts and, in turn, cannot understand the questions and suggestions of a *skilled* conversationalist? This is highly improbable—unless in the process of his training the therapist has progressively lost whatever capacity he may have had to communicate effectively with persons whose vocabulary, grammar, and logic is more primitive than his own, or unless the course of his training has provided him with an increasingly restricted set of conversational skills so that he is both comfortable and effective in communicating only with a very restricted sample of patients.

It has been demonstrated that the social-class status of a psychiatric patient is significantly related to whether he will be diagnosed as neurotic or psychotic, whether he will be treated with psychotherapy or organic (strictly medical) procedures, and whether his psychotherapy will be provided by a senior staff psychiatrist, a psychiatrist-in-training (resident), or an undergraduate medical student.[16] In a clinic setting, the patients who are chosen for psychotherapy are most likely to be seen by the staff psychiatrist if they come from the higher social classes, by the psychiatric resident if they are of the middle class, and by the low man on the medical totem pole, the undergraduate medical student, if they are from the lowest levels of the social hierarchy.* It is part of the reality of training that the psychiatrist-to-be must gradually achieve a seniority under which he can select "good" cases for psychotherapy, cases like those seen by his chief, patients from the upper social classes. The less than premium cases may (by default, and under the rationalization of "training" plus the notion that as "poor bets" they are not likely to be seriously injured by not receiving the optimal therapy of the true expert) go to the social worker, psychologist, or medical student.

As pointed out earlier, all three of the professional psychotherapists are influenced by a predominant theoretical orientation that at once specifies the process and goal of therapy and indirectly imposes restrictions on the minimal levels of capacity for introspection, abstract thought, and conceptual vocabulary of patients suitable for therapy. The net effect of this homogeneity in theory-process orientation is the general rejection for psychotherapy of the person with apparent limits on verbal facility, *i.e.,* ability to talk

---

* It is a most thought-provoking finding that undergraduate medical students achieved a higher measured "effectiveness" in outpatient psychotherapy than did staff psychiatric social workers and staff psychiatrists doing psychotherapy in the same clinics! [17]

in the sort of language which is "natural" to the educated (over-educated?) therapist.*

The emphasis on the verbal-intellectual facility of the patient is only one aspect of forces that interfere with an effective division of labor in meeting the total social demand for psychotherapeutic conversation. It has been stated that a very special attitude of "acceptance" of the patient by the therapist seems to be a basic factor in all psychotherapy. Such acceptance is probably more difficult to experience and make manifest when the therapist and patient do not have basic values and attitudes in common. "Optimal conditions prevail when the therapist and the patient belong to the same social class. All too often, psychotherapy runs into difficulties when the therapist and patient belong to different classes. In these instances, the values of the therapist are too divergent from those of the patient and communication becomes difficult between them." † It is not unusual to find a therapist-in-training, who is very firm in his allegiance to the Freudian doctrine of psychopathology, expressing bafflement about the depression of a marginally successful farmer. And his bafflement may be honestly shared by his preceptor who will make no claim to knowing "how to talk to a farmer."

Thus, explicit conformities of theoretical orientation, progressive selectivity of training experience, and implicitly shared values derived in part from the upward social mobility of the recognized therapists mean that potentially diverse sources of therapeutic conversation are available in fact to a very restricted segment of the total number of psychologically distressed persons.

VII. CONCEPTIONS AND PRACTICES: THE EFFECTS OF TRAINING

We have reviewed the social origins of the three most prominent professional psychotherapists in contemporary American culture. We have examined the respective emphases of their professional

* Perhaps the tendency to discomfort or lack of comprehension by the educated therapist seeking to communicate to the "uneducated" patient would be reduced if he could spend some part of his training time observing the communication-teaching processes that go on with grade school children, seeing the arts and techniques of the skilled teacher who must communicate at the level of her pupils. Or, even better, perhaps every psychotherapist should have intensive training with disturbed children even though he may later work exclusively with adults.

† For an excellent discussion of the nature and effects of therapist attitudes toward patients, see Hollingshead and Redlich.[13]

training. We have considered the nature of their theoretical orientations in regard both to the etiology of neurosis and the principles of psychotherapy. We have explored the general characteristics of their respective psychotherapy patients. We have made note of certain characteristics of their preferred patients, those with whom they have greatest expectation of achieving effective therapy. We have noted both differences and similarities among the psychiatrist, clinical psychologist and psychiatric social worker. Their most obvious points of difference, for example, certain aspects of their professional training, seem less obviously certain to make a difference in how they approach the task of psychotherapy. Subtle similarities in attitudes and background seem more likely to be reflected in how they think about psychotherapy. In overview, it appears that these three presumably "specialized" experts in psychotherapy actually are more similar rather than dissimilar in their expertise. The evidence is indirect and does not tell us to what extent the psychiatrist, psychologist, and social worker actually establish and conduct discriminably different therapeutic conversations.

There have been some researches to determine the extent to which therapists trained in different schools (for example, Freudian, Adlerian, Rogerian) reveal differences in their concept of the "ideal therapeutic relationship," differences in their manner of seeking to relate to the patient. The concept of the best therapist–patient relationship seems to be less a function of professional identification (*e.g.,* psychiatry or psychology) and less a function of theoretical orientation (*e.g.,* psychoanalytic, nondirective, or "eclectic") and more a function of amount of experience in being a psychotherapist. Furthermore, a lay person will describe the ideal relationship in much the same way as an experienced therapist. Although the nature of this investigation was such that ordinary sensitivity to what is broadly desirable in any social interaction might have imposed an artificial communality (a shared stereotype), it is pertinent to note that all therapists described the good relationship as one in which the therapist "participate(s) completely in the patient's communication," "is able to understand the patient's feelings," "sees the patient as a co-worker on a common problem," and "treats the patient as an equal." *,[19]

* In respect to the expressed *ideal* of equality of patient-therapist status, note the ubiquity of the authority-supplicant status mentioned in Chapter Five and the problem of social class differences between therapist and patient as remarked on in Section VI of this chapter.

When actual samples of psychotherapeutic interviews conducted by neophyte and expert representatives of the orthodox Freudian, Adlerian, and Rogerian schools were judged for the extent to which the "ideal therapeutic relationship" was demonstrated, it was concluded that expert (*i.e.,* experienced) psychotherapists more closely achieved an optimal relationship than did nonexperts of the same theoretical persuasion.[20] Furthermore, experts from *different* schools were more similar in their therapeutic relationships than were neophyte therapists of the same school. The most important dimensions that differentiated between experts and neophytes, regardless of school, were in the therapist's capacity "to understand, to communicate with, and to maintain rapport with the patient."

In a program of researches designed to tap more directly the extent of comparability in the actual responses made by representative psychotherapists to a standard sample of patient verbalizations, psychologists with a psychoanalytic orientation were compared with psychologists trained in the nondirective approach of Rogers.[21] Marked differences were found between the Rogerians and the non-Rogerians, with the former showing a strong tendency to use "reflective" responses and to avoid the use of exploratory questions. But, when the level of experience was controlled in the two samples, it was found that the Rogerians' preference for "reflective" responses showed a marked decline with increased experience. The patterns of therapist response showed increased diversification with increased experience; heavy reliance on just a few techniques is a characteristic of the inexperienced therapist.

In a study involving the same set of patient verbalizations, therapist responses were obtained and categorized for samples of psychiatrists, psychologists, and social workers all of whom had been trained in a Freudian or neo-Freudian orientation.[22] Apart from a notable tendency for the social workers to make responses of a reassuring nature, the three professional groups showed a high degree of similarity in their pattern of responses. Extensive research comparisons of the therapeutic response patterns of psychiatrists and psychologists, in a close simulation of the actual therapy situation, lead to the conclusion: "As long as the variable of theoretical orientation is held constant, all therapists adhering to psychoanalytic principles employ very similar techniques." [23]

## VIII. THE "INVISIBLE" THERAPISTS

In concluding this survey of who the psychotherapist is, how he gets to be an expert, and how he views the process of therapy, it is well to recognize that our data bear only on the more "visible" healers, that is, on those highly demarcated professions whose members are presently recognized by our society as having some skill in psychotherapy and who are *more or less* sanctioned to provide therapeutic conversation. It is only within very recent time that the psychiatrist has ceased to have unquestioned and sole occupancy of the domain of psychotherapy. The natural lag in cultural evolution presents us still with a prevalence of both professional and journalistic dogma that the psychiatrist is *the* psychotherapist. Official psychiatry has attempted to protect against the inevitable erosion of its "property rights" by an inconsistent combination of authoritative medico-legal pronouncements (the essence of which is that the mind is a "medical" organ) and paternalistic acknowledgments that it is socially useful for psychologists to "counsel" and for social workers to do "intensive case work" provided they are under direct psychiatric supervision. One effect of the struggles of the psychologist to establish his professional prerogatives and his legal status as an expert in the field of mental health and mental illness has been to heighten general social awareness that it is logically fallacious and practically impossible to restrict treatment of mental and emotional disorders to any one profession.

With this awareness has come recognition that there is a host of "invisible" psychotherapists. These are men and women who by virtue of the roles they occupy and the status they hold as exemplars of stability, wisdom, and devotion to service are regularly turned to for help by persons in need of counsel and emotional support.

Most notable among these "invisible" therapists are the clergy. Always the priest, rabbi, and minister have been sought out for help in resolving deeply personal conflicts and anxiety, especially as these arose in the context of family life. Always the more sensitive and thoughtful among them have recognized that they were sometimes called to function in a role other than that of spiritual adviser, at least within the narrow meaning of spiritual. The spiritual leaders of large urban congregations have experienced an increasing call to function as "mental hygienists" and for the most part they have responded with judgment and social conscience. They have offered help and counsel in accordance with their feelings of competence, recognizing that possibly there may be a *spiritual* problem in all neurosis; they have attempted to make appropriate referrals to physicians, psychiatrists, psychologists, and marriage counselors. They have sought to improve their own technical knowledge and skill in personal counseling and they have sought to provide better preparation for this role in the curricula of the theological schools. They have made public the extent to which they find themselves confronted with an inescapable demand to provide therapeutic conversation. It must be recognized that now and in the future a very significant amount of psychotherapy is and must be afforded by the sophisticated clergy.

In like fashion, the teacher occupies a strategic position as a potential source of emotional understanding, acceptance, and counsel for those younger members of our society who become frustrated, fearful, foolish or frenetic. For many persons, it is the opportunity to function in this role which serves as a major attraction to a teaching career. It would be difficult to find a school faculty of any size in which there are not one or more teachers who have earned the respect and gratitude of students and staff alike for their special capacity and willingness to "counsel," to "advise," to give acceptance and understanding. These teachers would blush (or blanch?) to hear themselves called psychotherapists. But a careful analysis of their conversations with students might very well reveal that they were neither different in form from or less effective than those of "experts."

The clergy and teachers are clearly among the more numerous "invisible" psychotherapists. There are others who by virtue of their professional responsibilities are frequently afforded opportunity, sometimes indirectly, to provide therapeutic conversation. Obvious among these are the attorney and the personal physician. Depending upon their individual sensitivities, their values, their capacity to be comfortable about emotional expression, their maturity of judgment, and their ability to give time, and always with the potential effectiveness of the positive suggestive quality of their prestige, they are regularly in positions to converse therapeutically.

The invisibility of these potential psychotherapists is relative. They are not usually considered to function primarily as therapists for ills of the heart or head, but there is general recognition of the frequency with which the essential content of their role relationships to their clients affords the possibility for them to be psychologically helpful.

There are other sources of psychotherapy even more invisible so far as general social recognition is involved. Work supervisors, respected colleagues, "good" *neighbors* and close *friends*. These invisible potential sources of therapeutic conversation are hidden, partly because of an unfortunate artifact of the mental health movement that will be examined in the next chapter.

Because of the established impossibility of meeting the demand for therapeutic conversation within the present and probable future supply of currently sanctioned psychotherapists, it is essential that careful consideration be given to all possible means of increasing the supply and quality of help from these invisible therapists.

# References

1. Group for the Advancement of Psychiatry. Report No. 54, *The Pre-clinical Teaching of Psychiatry* (New York: 1962).

2. American Board of Psychiatry and Neurology, Inc. *General Requirements for Applicants In Directory of Medical Specialists,* Vol. 10. (Chicago: Marquis Publications, Inc., 1961).

3. Noble H. Kelley, Fillmore H. Sanford, and Kenneth E. Clark, "The Meaning of the ABEPP Diploma," *Amer. Psychol.,* 16 (1961), pp. 132-41.

4. Irene M. Josselyn, "The Caseworker as Therapist," *J. soc. Casewk.,* 29 (1948), pp. 351-55.

5. Clara Rabinowitz, "The Caseworker and the Private Practitioner of Psychotherapy," *Jewish Soc. Serv. Quart.,* 30 (1953), pp. 166-78.

6. Erasmus L. Hoch and John G. Darley, "A Case at Law," *Amer. Psychol.,* 17 (1962), pp. 623-54.

7. Warren B. Webb and Hiram L. Gordon, "The Utilization of a Psychologist in Ward Administration," *J. Clin. Psychol.,* XIII (1957), pp. 301-02.

8. Joseph R. Cowen and Lloyd Schwartz, "An Experiment in the Utilization of a Clinical Psychologist as a Ward Clinical Administrator in a State Psychiatric Hospital," *Psychiat. Quart.,* 34 (1960), pp. 472-79.

9. J. Frank Whiting, Lee Powers, and Ward Darley, "The Financial Situation of the American Medical Student," *J. Med. Educ.*, 36 (1961), pp. 745-75.

10. Fredric Wertham, "What to Do Till the Doctor Goes," *The Nation*, 10 (1950), pp. 205-207.

11. Robert A. Harper, *Psychoanalysis and Psychotherapy: 36 Systems* (Englewood Cliffs, N. J.: Prentice-Hall, Inc., 1959).

12. Daniel N. Wiener and Donald R. Stieper, "The Problem of Interminability in Outpatient Psychotherapy," *J. Consult. Psychol.*, 23 (1959), pp. 237-42.

13. Daniel N. Wiener, "The Effect of Arbitrary Termination on Return to Psychotherapy," *J. Clin. Psychol.*, 15 (1959), pp. 335-38.

14. William Schofield, "Psychotherapists and Patients: A Study of Assortative Mating," Unpublished manuscript. University of Minnesota, 1960.

15. Anne Roe, "A New Classification of Occupations," *J. Counsel. Psychol.*, 1 (1954), pp. 215-20.

16. Jerome K. Myers and Leslie Schaffer, "Social Stratification and Psychiatric Practice," *Amer. Sociol. Rev.*, 19 (1954), pp. 307-10.

17. New York City Committee on Mental Hygiene, State Charities Aid Association, *The Functioning of Psychiatric Clinics in New York City, A Study Toward the Prevention of Waste* (New York: 1949).

18. August B. Hollingshead and Frederick C. Redlich, *Social Class and Mental Illness. A Community Study* (New York: John Wiley & Sons, Inc., 1958), pp. 344-57.

19. Fred Fiedler, "The Concept of an Ideal Therapeutic Relationship," *J. Consult. Psychol.*, 14 (1950), pp. 239-45.

20. ———, "A Comparison of Therapeutic Relationships in Psychoanalytic, Non-directive, and Adlerian Therapy," *J. Consult. Psychol.*, 14 (1950), pp. 436-45.

21. Hans H. Strupp, "An Objective Comparison of Rogerian and Psychoanalytic Techniques," *J. Consult. Psychol.*, 19 (1955), pp. 1-7.

22. ———, "Psychotherapeutic Techniques, Professional Affiliation, and Experience Level," *J. Consult. Psychol.*, 19 (1955), pp. 97-102.

23. ———, *Psychotherapists in Action. Explorations of the Therapist's Contribution to the Treatment Process* (New York: Grune & Stratton, 1960).

# CHAPTER SEVEN

# Philosophical Prophylaxis

Mental illness is a cultural universal. Persons who show recognizable patterns of deviant behavior are found in every culture. A pattern is recognized as a set of behaviors that are deviant with respect to the modal behaviors of the individual's group and that are repeated in different members of the group. The level of complexity of social organization or the degree of civilization achieved may vary widely; the society may be urban or rural, industrial or agrarian, nomadic or settled—but in every carefully studied sociocultural group (defined as a collection of persons having functional membership in a community and out of that membership deriving common and interdependent responsibility and shared interests) the sometime occurrence of one or more patterns of deviant behavior has been noted. The specific content and detailed form of the "insanity" reflects peculiarities of the particular culture in which it occurs.[1,2] In respect to content, mental illness can be seen easily to have the quality of cultural relativity. It is in part this fact of the cultural relativity of the content of emotional disorder that leads some authorities to claim that "mental illness" is not a scientific concept but rather a "convenient myth" which "has outlived whatever usefulness it might have had." [3,4] Cultural relativity in the definitions of what is conforming behavior and what is sick (*i.e.*, nonconforming) behavior does not negate the universality of the phenomenon of disordered behavior; as a broad phenomenon which appears repeatedly within all cultures it is accessible to scientific inquiry.

The amount of awareness of emotionally based disturbances in personality has varied over time and varies today from culture to culture. In earliest history apparently only the most deranged behaviors achieved sufficient attention to be recorded. As civilizations have prospered and as the arts of inquiry have become more sensitive, there has been growing recognition of more subtle expressions of psychological disorder. With the extension of the domain of mental illness there has been a parallel increase in the complexity and sophistication of explanations of emotional symptomatology.

Looking back over history it may appear that there has been more change in the perception and explanation of mental illness than there has been in the basic forms of treatment. It is notable, however, that there have been significant changes in the identity of the persons who have assumed major responsibility for the care and management of the emotionally ill. The earliest approach to management of disordered behavior deserving to be called treatment was the responsibility of priests and religious healers. In the enlightened period of the Greco-Roman culture there evolved a special group of therapists who combined the role of religious functionary with the ministrations of early medicine. These were the priest-physicians, and their sanitaria combined the functions of temple and hospital. Because of their dual roles and orientations it is possible that these priest-physicians may have achieved an unusually integrated (and possibly never replicated), truly psychosomatic approach to psychosomatic ailments.

With the growth of medical science and with the final acceptance of a naturalistic explanation of mental phenomena (including disorders of adaptive behavior), the mentally ill became the charge of the physician. The institutional history of medical psychology begins with the establishment of asylums for the insane under the direction of medics. The medical superintendents of these early asylums steeped themselves in the clinical material of their wards and whenever possible made intensive study of associated nervous system pathology. Then the hospital clinic came into existence as a place where less severe symptoms were presented for treatment and from study of this outpatient material came gradual recognition of the neuroses.

Johann Weyer (1515-1588) is credited as being the first psychiatrist: "He was the first physician whose major interest turned toward mental diseases and thereby foreshadowed the formation of psychiatry as a medical specialty. . . . Weyer more than anyone else completed, or at least brought closer to completion the process of divorcing medical psychology from theology. . . ." [5] But the roots of modern psychiatry are seen most clearly in the writings and teachings of the neurologists, the "neuropsychiatrists" led by Charcot, Janet, Liebeault, and Bernheim, who first demonstrated the power of the mind both to cause and to alleviate symptoms, physical and mental. With Freud's discovery of the critical mechanisms of the psychoneuroses and with his establishment of psychoanalysis, we have what has become for many a new religion, a current philosophy for modern man—and with it we have a new "priest."

We have come full circle in assignment of authority in the treatment of mental illness: from priest-physician to physician to psychiatrist and, finally, to the analyst-priest (who frequently is not a physician). And there are signs that we may increasingly recognize the potential therapeutic powers of the spiritual authority. In ancient times the deranged person's wildness was believed due to a possession by evil spirits; today, there is a distinct trend to see the emotional suffering of many persons as stemming from a defect of faith, a lack of meaning.[6,7]

As the definition of neurosis has been gradually broadened so as to encompass symptoms ranging from actual failure of performance to a lack of basic zest for living, and as the optimal treatment of such disorders has increasingly assigned a critical role to therapeutic conversation, it becomes less and less clear that there is any one group of experts in our culture whose background and professional training uniquely equips them to function in the role of psychotherapist—as emotional tutor, as intimate counselor, as master philosopher, or as guide in the quest for self-realization.

## I. THE MENTAL HEALTH MOVEMENT

Tremendous progress has been made in the understanding and treatment of mental illness. Perhaps the most significant component of that progress is contained in the improved education of the public, in the broad dissemination of enlightened attitudes. There have been great inroads on the mass ignorance that caused mental illnesses to be viewed as disgraceful stigmata and the mentally ill to be ostracized. In place of widespread public aversion or apathy toward the mentally ill and their problems, we have broad programs for effective social enlightenment and positive community action to provide more and better treatment. In the efforts to make treatment more accessible there is recognition that earlier treatment is far more effective than later treatment and that early treatment of mild disturbances may interrupt and divert a process that might otherwise eventuate in total personality disruption.

Much remains to be done. There are still people who have feelings of shame or guilt about mentally ill relatives. There are still people who think "insanity" is "inherited," like blue eyes. There are still people who are afraid of former mental hospital patients. There are still employers who would avoid hiring persons with histories of psychiatric treatment. But all media of public communication are being used almost daily to mount a massive offensive of information against these uninformed or unthinking purveyors of archaic attitudes.

Credit for these significant educational accomplishments to date cannot be given to psychiatrists, psychologists, or social workers. Rather, these accomplishments represent the impact of the "mental hygiene movement." This is a crusade which was announced with publication in 1908, of the autobiography of Clifford W. Beers, *A Mind That Found Itself,* and officially launched with the founding in the next year of the National Committee for Mental Hygiene.[8] In the formal statement of its objectives, the National Committee included as a goal "the protection of the mental health of the public." [9] While the burning instigation to the crusade was aroused in its leader, Clifford Beers, by his experiences as a hospitalized mental patient, the goal of the movement was never restricted to correction and improvement of hospital treatment of the severely ill. From the beginning, continuously and increasingly, the mental hygiene movement has placed major emphasis on education and prevention—on programs designed to teach positive methods of achieving and maintaining mental health. In working toward these goals, the movement has benefited from the active participation and contributions of psychiatric social workers, psychiatrists, psychologists, teachers, physicians, the clergy and, most particularly, from a host of lay persons who have consistently volunteered their time and energies in a variety of projects, ranging from assisting in recreational programs in state hospitals to lobbying for improved legislative provisions for care of the mentally ill.*

In pursuing its preventive and therapeutic aims, and especially in arousing the interest and support of the public, the mental hygiene movement (which has become the mental health movement)† has of necessity communicated in overly simplified terms about

---

* For an excellent history of the mental hygiene movement, see Chapter XV, of Albert Deutsch.[10] For a review of the current nature and programs of public and private mental health agencies, see Chapter 15, of James C. Coleman.[11]

† The National Association for Mental Health amalgamates the former National Committee for Mental Hygiene, the National Mental Health Foundation, and the Psychiatric Foundation.

mental illness and mental health. The ways of seeking mental health are not always clearly distinguished from the ways to avoid mental illness. Mental health is most readily (though not most helpfully) defined as the absence of mental illness. Mental illness is defined in terms of certain symptoms, and the specifications of those symptoms has been a primary responsibility of psychiatrists. As the mental health movement has gained momentum the psychiatrist has found himself increasingly on call to speak out to the public about mental health (rather than illness) and it is only human of him to react to his enhanced prestige by relinquishing the smaller role of expert pathologist–therapist for the larger role of arbiter of social values. In this role, the psychiatrist has frequently expanded the domain of mental illness to include all degrees and kinds of psychological distress, failing to appreciate that the human suffers some pains not because he is sick but because he is human. Invitation to the role of "expert" in an area in which society has suddenly developed intense interest is always a seductive one. (Note the number of chemists and physicists who have become "social" scientists since World War II!) The psychiatrist well may be forgiven if he has occasionally failed to note that as an authority on values, the meaning of existence, and how to live he is *at best* on a par with other learned and thoughtful men. The psychologists and social workers have not been noticeably less susceptible to the sacerdotal appeal, but have been called less frequently to the altar than have the psychiatrists.

The mental health movement together with psychiatry suffers from imprecision in the definition and delineation of psychopathology. The subjectivity of diagnosis, especially where neurotic behavior is in question, coupled with expansive or inclusive trends in the diagnostician, creates particular problems when by broadcast methods the public is being encouraged to self-examination and to the seeking of "preventive" therapy. The insufficiency of therapeutic resources to meet the legitimate needs of truly neurotic patients is seriously exacerbated when uncritical enthusiasms encourage persons with the non-neurotic frustrations common to all inhabitants of a less-than-perfect world to seek expert therapy, and when ambiguous nosology encourages the therapist to a nondiscriminating investment of his expensively acquired skills. There is a historical parallel to this problem which has been noted in the earlier period of the mental hygiene movement:

"Indeed, so great was the enthusiasm over mental hygiene, that it led for a long time to a dangerous overemphasis on the mental factors in problems of social work. The important sociological factors were lost sight of while psychological factors were given almost exclusive attention. Mental Hygiene was being 'oversold' by over-enthusiastic adherents." [12]

The mental hygiene movement has had a very significant positive impact on the problem of mental illness. There can be little doubt that it has contributed to an enhanced general level of mental health in our country. Certainly it has achieved marked improvement in public attitudes toward mental illness. As a perhaps unavoidable consequence of its educational effort it has created new and greater demands for psychotherapy and not all of the increased demand is fully appropriate.

"The pattern of psychotherapeutic practice in America is seriously unbalanced in that too many of the ablest, most experienced psychiatrists spend most of their time with patients who need them least. This has been the unfortunate, though probably inevitable, consequence of the concept of mental illness as personal malfunctioning which in itself represents a gain in understanding. The trouble is that this view makes it impossible to draw the line, so that many persons who are showing essentially normal responses to the wear and tear of life or who are unhappy for reasons other than personal malfunctioning see themselves —and are seen by others—as proper candidates for psychotherapy." [13]

A favorite colleague and renowned philosopher is fond of the observation, "Philosophy is that disease for which it should be the cure." * The mental hygiene movement has inadvertently added to the problem which it intended to reduce. It is time for the leaders of the mental health movement to put their minds to a tough philosophical analysis of problems which psychiatry and psychology have tended to neglect: to criteria of mental health, to delimitation of the meanings and forms of mental illness, to specification of precisely what are and what are not *psychiatric* problems. It would be a positive contribution for mental health educators to develop ways of communicating to the public on such questions as: "When not to go to the psychiatrist," or "What to do before you see a psychiatrist"; "What psychotherapy cannot do for you"; "Ten sources of helpful conversation"; "Problems which do not make you a 'Mental Case.'"

* Professor Herbert Feigl, Director of the Center for the Philosophy of Science, University of Minnesota.

148

## II. THE PHILOSOPHICAL NEUROSIS

It is a painful paradox of civilization that so many of our major discoveries seem to contribute almost equally to the solution of one problem and the creation of another. Dynamite is perhaps the most often noted example, but there are many others. Our discoveries seem to extricate us from an old set of limitations only to burden us with new frustrations. Happily, there seems to be a period of relatively unadulterated enjoyment of each new technological advance. But, sooner or later, its "fringe" handicaps come to equal or even surpass its benefits.

Thanks to the invention of the automobile we have had a marvelous mobility and a great expansion of our "living space," and now we have an increasingly serious problem of what to do with our cars when they are not in use. Discovery of nuclear fission may have helped to end one war, but now we are threatened by a war of total annihilation. The industrial revolution which enormously increased the supply of goods has been augmented by scientific advances in the twentieth century that threaten to poison the air we breathe, pollute the water we drink and the food we eat. Automation of industry has made possible better control of processes and more efficient production with fewer workers, and it is as yet uncertain whether we shall be able successfully to absorb the displaced and unneeded labor force as our industries become increasingly places of autofacture rather than manufacture.

Medical science and modern technology have added significantly to longevity. Each year our population receives a sizable increment of persons who have been retired from the productive community and who may live another five or ten years; we find we must cope directly with the problem of supplying meaning to these "golden years." In light of the ageless struggle to maintain and extend biological life against the assaults of famine and pestilence, in light of the individual struggle to protect health and preserve life, it is a poignant paradox that we must search out ways to help the retired warrior to cope with a life that is now secure, comfortable, and certain. It is an important fact to which all psychotherapists should be fully sensitive that for very many persons when the steadily recurrent daily problems of work—of earning, of building, of planning, of saving—are over, the problem of meaning comes promptly, pressingly to the fore. Enjoyment of existence does not come naturally to the person whose earlier life has given neither time nor stimulus to question ultimate purpose or to explore for meanings that superscribe the orientation provided by inescapable basic demands for effort.

Thus, paradoxically, each new freedom brings the possibility of new entrapments. We may wonder whether the pace of discovery may soon achieve so many solutions that the problems created by those solutions will surpass our problem-solving capacities!

By focusing national attention on the numbers and needs of the thousands of patients who suffer incapacitating emotional illness, the mental health movement has served to arouse attention and to mobilize efforts in their behalf. It has won increased expenditures to provide better facilities, more personnel, more and better treatment for the hospitalized patient. It has stimulated the founding of clinics so that milder disturbances may come to early diagnosis and it has encouraged the provision of resources for early outpatient therapy so that developing symptoms can be halted in their first stages and prevented from progression into complete disruption of the personality.

The mental health movement has achieved a significant increase in public enlightenment in regard to mental illness. There has been a reduction in the older attitudes of fear and distrust of the mentally ill. Each year fewer and fewer persons remain who hold to an archaic attitude of shame toward any implication of mental illness in themselves or their families. The public has been effectively educated to recognize symptoms of personality disorder and has been encouraged to seek professional consultation for emotional problems.

But the mental health movement has inevitably created problems as it has offered solutions. As was suggested in Chapter One, the nature of neurosis as presently defined is such as to encourage over-interpretation of the significance of a host of idiosyncrasies and eccentricities. The mental health educator has understandably, in the first phase of the movement, operated within the pathological framework afforded by essentially gross medical definitions of emotional illness. Emphasis has been upon detection and prevention of illness, rather than upon modes of achieving and maintaining positive mental health. The meaning of neurosis, ambiguous to begin with, has been subtly extended to cover a variety of cultural delusions, perhaps the most prominent of which is the Western myth that a state of happiness is both a primary and achievable goal of life. One effect of the mental health movement has been to encourage many people to see their unhappiness as a sign of mental illness and to believe that there are experts who can treat their unhappiness.

Psychotherapists, both visible and "invisible," are increasingly confronted by would-be patients who do not manifest any of the more objective hallmarks of a neurotic problem (Chapter Three), who do not complain of failures of productivity or achievement, who do not suffer from serious interpersonal conflicts, who are free of functional somatic complaints, who are not incapacitated by anxiety, or tormented by obsessions, whose objective life circumstances they confess are close to optimal. These seekers for help *suffer* a freedom from complaint. The absence of conflicts, frustrations, and symptoms brings a painful awareness: of absence—the absence of faith, of commitment, of meaning, of the need to search out personal, ultimate values, or of the need to live comfortably and meaningfully each day in the face of final uncertainty. For increasing numbers of rational, educated, and thoughtful men the central struggle becomes one of finding and keeping an emotional and psychological balance between the pain of doubt and the luxury of faith. A distaste for this struggle, or an insistence on its resolution as a necessary condition for continued existence is at the heart of the *philosophical neuroses*. In contrast to the psychoneuroses, we have no established knowledge or technique to bring to bear on this form of dis-ease. We do not have a scientifically confirmable matrix of ideas concerning how or what to teach those who suffer philosophical neuroses. The philosophical neurotic suffers in his struggle to be both reasonable and hopeful, and he can be helped in his struggle by access to human wisdom and by encouragement to expose himself to it. But in this seeking for counsel and for opportunity to test doubt against faith or faith against doubt, he must not be misled to think that any group of experts has a corner on some specialized wisdom about the meaning of life or how to live it. It is an unfortunate side-effect of the mental health movement that a large portion of the limited psychotherapeutic resources afforded by psychiatrists and psychologists is being consumed by persons who suffer a philosophical anomie for which neither psychiatrist nor psychologist can offer specific therapy. The person with a philosophical neurosis deserves care and can be helped; it would be in his own interests and in the interests of social economy for him to be encouraged to seek guidance from those who are most practiced and equipped to think with him in the domain of values, meaning, ethics, and eschatology. Recognition of the philosophical neurosis and of the special problems it presents has been delayed on the part of psychotherapists because the well-bred, well-fed, well-read qualities typical of this patient appeal to the intellectual and social prejudices of the therapist and make for spontaneous rapport and empathy.

In combating the general ignorance and superstition of the public about mental illness, the mental health movement has necessarily attacked the idea that emotional and mental problems should be a source of shame. The public has been taught that mental symptoms are natural, that they do not reflect simply defective heredity or sinful practices. The public has been taught that everyone has a basic susceptibility to psychological maladjustment and, furthermore, that a very large number of people in fact suffer from some degree of "nervousness." All of this teaching is true and was most necessary in ending the shameful connotations that formerly prevailed. But, as an unfortunate consequence of these positive changes neurosis has achieved respectability. In some sophisticated segments of our society it has become expected and accepted for the individual to acknowledge his "neurosis"—and to have all manner of immature, selfish, irresponsible behaviors explained by him (and accepted by his companions) as "symptoms" of his "sickness." Among persons whose work demands some degree of creative imagination there is a popular stereotype which equates genius with neurosis. It becomes a tempting apology to substitute symptoms for effort; to manifest the temperament of an artist may be an easier road to achieving an artistic identity than to be truly creative.

When individuals are volubly proud that they are "in therapy," although they remain silent on the content and course of that self-discovering endeavor, with discussion of the causes and treatment reserved by a socially sanctioned conspiracy of silence between therapist and client (or with normal social respect for the individual's privacy), it may be wondered if the continuation of therapy is required at least in part because the patient is reluctant to lose the dramatic appeal of his mysterious status. And when the patient does speak freely of the content of his therapeutic conversations to any and all willing listeners, it may be wondered if he suffers from lack of any other mental content with which he would hope to hold an audience.

To be proud of an illness or a defect is a separate illness, and perhaps needs to be treated first. Man's capacity to feel shame is not pathological in itself; pathology arises from what he does or fails to do about shame. Shame can be hidden by repression and denial, but the massive effort required to hide one's shame results in symptoms. Or, shame can yield a sense of responsibility and this can power a search for self-understanding, for self-acceptance, and for better behavior. The mental health movement has lifted the pathological shame previously associated with emotional illness. Now it must be attentive to combat the tendency for the unashamed to have pathological pride in their maladjustment.

### III. ANXIETY: NORMAL AND OTHERWISE

It has been said that we live in the Age of Anxiety. Certainly we have much about which to be anxious and worried. Uncertainty is perhaps the greatest stimulus to anxiety, and at the present time we are confronted by a universal uncertainty as to the future of our world that has an urgency and immediacy surpassing that of any previous period of history. We are faced with the imminent possibility of cataclysmic destruction of the world through nuclear war. Insofar as all peoples of the world know this uncertainty they share for the first time in a universal anxiety. But the fact of a common and heavy anxiety does not mean obviously that ours is a more anxious world than ever before. As suggested in Chapter Two, uncertainty is a condition of life; anxiety has been experienced by all men in all periods. Civilization is the process whereby men change what it is they fear. But ultimate uncertainties have always been coupled with immediate dangers to make men anxious.

If this is the Age of Anxiety it is not so simply as a function of absolute increase in the things about which man is fearful. Rather it is so because *we have taught man to be anxious about his anxiety.* We have created a distorted image of anxiety. We have attributed to anxiety and to the efforts to escape anxiety all of man's neurotic ills. We have sensitized ourselves to recognize the signs of anxiety, and we have been taught that the signs of anxiety are *symptoms.* We have been encouraged to the fallacious value of a total avoidance of anxiety as a goal of life; we have been led to believe that a complete freedom from anxiety would be the distinguishing characteristic of an adjusted life.*

Much of what we have learned about psychopathology, and especially about the etiology of the neuroses, has come through an

* Many persons are unaware that the psychopathology of a significant portion of psychiatric patients (the so-called psychopaths and character disorders) is attributed by some authorities to a pathological incapacity to experience anxiety.

understanding of the effects of severe anxiety and of the mechanisms by which the individual copes with anxiety. It is essential to the aims of mental health education that the importance and role of anxiety be understood by everyone. But in this endeavor, there has been a failure to distinguish between normal and pathological anxiety.

If a person were totally incapable of experiencing pain his life would be seriously jeopardized. The experiencing of continual pain is abnormal and signals the need for efforts to correct the cause of the pain. But, it would be inimical to the welfare of a normal person to drug him so that his pain sensitivity was continuously reduced or absent.* The capacity to experience pain is normal, and the sensation of pain is normal under certain conditions.

Likewise, anxiety is a normal experience when present in certain degrees in appropriate situations. It is normal to be anxious when taking an examination, when applying for a job, when getting married, when being prepared for surgery, when making a speech, and so forth. It is normal to experience some anxiety when facing any new situation or demand for which there is an uncertain outcome. The signs of anxiety (such as increased heart rate, dry throat, perspiring hands) are indications that one's physiological apparatus is in state of readiness for special effort. One could interpret these experiences as signs that one is keyed up and "ready to go."

Or, one can interpret these as *symptoms* of anxiety, and become anxious about them—and this may have a disrupting effect on performance. It is an unfortunate result of the massive attention which has been given to anxiety that people have been led to view all experiences of the signs of "nervousness" as *symptoms* of pathological anxiety. Once they arrive at this orientation they are potential candidates for psychotherapy, and in presenting their complaints of incapacitating anxiety, it may not be immediately clear to the therapist that their symptoms represent the circular, autocatalytic effects of being "anxious about anxiety."

Again, the limited resources for expert psychotherapy should not be dissipated upon individuals who have made a faulty self-diagnosis or who have inappropriate attitudes and expectations. Mental health educators must make a concerted effort to teach the public about normal anxiety and its necessary role in adjustment. In particular, they must teach that physiological changes under stress are

* The medical literature contains fascinating accounts of the injuries and illnesses (and abnormal complications thereof) of persons apparently suffering a congenital defect in their neurological system for the sensation of pain.

signs of normal functioning, not symptoms of pathology. The adult public must be helped to correct its currently predominant and unhealthy tendency to overinterpret and be fearful of normal anxiety. In the instruction and rearing of children we have opportunity both to teach them the biological utility of anxiety and to assist them in the progressive development of tolerance for it.

## IV. THE STUDY OF PSYCHOLOGY

In programs of education aimed at the prevention of mental illness it would be well to recognize the secondary school as an institution providing an excellent opportunity to reach large numbers of students with instruction in the positive principles of mental hygiene. At the early school age it is more important that they be given sound suggestions as to how to maintain healthy attitudes, how to manage conflicts, and how to deal with strong emotions than it is that they be informed about mental illness. But thoughtful courses in mental hygiene are not enough.

Not later than high school every student should receive a solid course of instruction in general psychology. Such a course should enable the student to see that the behavior of people is a proper, indeed a crucial, area for the application of scientific method. He should be introduced to the general principles that have been uncovered through careful study of how people learn, how they perceive their world, how they acquire attitudes and how those attitudes influence their modes of adjustment. The aim of such a general psychology course taught at the secondary school level would be not simply to provide the student with an awareness of the substantive content of psychology as a field of human inquiry but, more importantly, to instill in him attitudes toward behavior, his own and that of other persons, likely to encourage and maintain hygienic personal relationships. The study of psychology encourages an attitude of objectivity and of persisting examination of *reasons* for behavior; it provides a foundation and stimulus for the student to seek to understand himself and others. With a scientifically psychological orientation toward the understanding both of self and others the individual is less likely to be victimized either by his own emotions or by the irrationalities of others. An adequate general psychology would introduce the student to the "psychopathology of everyday life," would sensitize him to the meaning of errors, oversights, and momentary distortions in his perceptions and thought. With this instruction he would have at least the equipment, if not the motivation, for the life-long exploration of his own developing personality—for the continual challenge to self-realization and self-understanding.

As the frontiers of geography have been progressively pushed back and exhausted, it becomes increasingly difficult for the average man to be an explorer, to make discoveries. For the average man, the last frontier challenging his urge to search and to uncover new lands is provided by the complex vastness of his own mind, by the boundaries of his own spirit. It is a sorry epiphenomenon of the mental health movement that many persons who are admirably equipped to embark on this voyage and who long for insight for the sheer sake of discovery and not out of any pressing need, have been persuaded that they require the services of an expert guide. While it is true that the psychotherapist may shorten the trip to the island of insight it is not certain that the seeker cannot find it on his own, or that he will be significantly discommoded by the longer journey. Sound courses in psychology and inspired instruction can afford possibly a reduction in the susceptibility to neurosis. Certainly it can reduce the number of sentient persons who relinquish the responsibility and privilege (and the exquisite rewards) of a personal, life-long exploration of their existence, and who in so doing waste the time and energies of the therapists whose skills are required by those voyagers who are truly lost.

Until very recently courses in psychology have been almost totally restricted to colleges and universities, and in these settings they have frequently been unavailable before the sophomore year. While the proportion of the college-age population attending institutions of higher learning is steadily rising, it is still very small. Consequently, it is good to find increasing signs of thoughtful planning for the introduction of psychology as a basic subject in high school, and experience with such instruction is being carefully recorded.[14] In this context, the study of psychology is *not* provided by courses in how to be successful, how to be popular, how to be socially proper, and the like. There is a need for research to determine at what minimal age levels a formal course in psychology can be effectively introduced. In light of the central role of psychological phenomena in the entire life of the individual it seems incredible that we have been so slow to find a place for the study of psychology in our secondary school curricula. The mental health movement should lend its resources and energies to supporting those teachers and educational leaders who are seeking to find a stable and adequate place for the study of psychology in our secondary schools.

### V. PASTORAL COUNSELING

The survey of attitudes of the American public toward their personal adjustment and toward mental illness, which was referred to in Chapter Three, also collected data on where individuals turn for help when faced with perplexing problems.[15] Of those persons with acknowledged problems who sought consultation and advice beyond the family circle, *the largest proportion (42 percent) turned to clergymen.* Another approximately 30 percent sought counsel from a general physician. Only 18 percent reported seeking assistance initially from a psychologist or psychiatrist.

Of those persons who went for help to psychiatrists, psychologists, or marriage counselors nearly one third had been referred either by their physicians or by their clergymen, although a very small proportion of these referrals came from clergymen. Of those persons who received assistance from their clergymen or physicians, over three fourths reported that they had received some help, and nearly two thirds reported having been "helped a lot." Significantly smaller proportions of those who saw marriage counselors, psychologists, or psychiatrists (25 to 46 percent) reported having been definitely helped. Of those persons who claimed to have been helped much by their consultation, the largest single proportion (73 percent) was contributed by those with a "personal problem with defect in self."

> "We are left with an apparent inconsistency that should, somehow, be accounted for: individuals who recognize personal adjustment problems caused by some personal defect claim to be helped by therapeutic treatment more often than individuals with other kinds of problems; psychiatrists are consulted more often about just these kinds of problems; yet psychiatrists are not perceived to be the most effective source of help." [16]

In view of the general disdain for, if not outright counter-prescription of, advice-giving as a part of formal psychotherapy, it is interesting to note that not fewer than 15 percent of those who were helped definitely by psychiatrists attributed their relief to the receipt of advice; the comparable figures of helpful advice are 24 percent and 34 percent for the physicians and clergymen respectively. By contrast, 23 percent of persons helped by the clergymen credited the receipt of "comfort" and an "ability to endure"; of those who were helped by physicians and psychiatrists only 9 percent and 7 percent respectively claimed that this was the way in which therapy had helped them.

The data from this survey do not permit a comparison of the relative efficiency of the clergyman as a psychotherapist with the psychiatrist or other experts. It may be that the clergymen "treat" a very different group of "patients," and that the medical and psychological experts receive the more difficult cases. It is important to note, however, that they tend to seek to help all those who come to them with personal problems, making fewer referrals than do the physicians. Nevertheless, their effectiveness as evaluated in subjective appraisals of helpfulness by those who consult them is equal to that of the physicians, and both of these "nonexperts" are credited with giving more "help" than are the psychiatrists, psychologists, and marriage counselors.

It seems obvious that the clergy constitute a great potential resource in helping to meet the psychotherapy needs of our society. It is not known to what extent this potential is being fully realized. In the past there have been pseudo-antagonisms (based upon presumed conflicts of values and philosophy) between religion and psychiatry. Some psychotherapists have feared that the clergy were doing harm through failure to distinguish neurosis from spiritual discontent and through slowness to make referrals to experts. Concern for the possible usurpation of a role for which they were inadequately prepared has been based partly on a recognition that the older spiritual adviser had rarely received intensive instruction in scientific psychology or orientation to the nature of neurotic illness. In the face of some of these antipathies and with growing recognition for the extent to which the clergyman is turned to for help with emotional and mental problems, both the church and psychiatry are moving toward a rapprochement. Seminaries are showing increasing attention to provision of some background in pastoral counseling as a necessary part of the training of future churchmen; in providing sophistication in the techniques of counseling there is also attention to the problem of recognition of psychiatric illness.[17,18] Priests, rabbis, and ministers in increasing numbers are being encouraged to pursue graduate study in psychology.*

* Through the cooperation of the Wheat Ridge Foundation of the Lutheran Church and the graduate department of psychology of the University of Minnesota, a small and highly select group of ordained pastors are studying for the Ph.D. in clinical psychology. These men will later be key resource persons in providing mental health consultation to other pastors and to church programs of mental health education.

Psychiatrists and psychologists are showing a growing willingness to participate in special seminars and short courses designed to provide clergymen with a basic understanding of psychiatric illness and treatment.*

The increased education of clergy in the field of mental illness should have a positive effect. It should bring this important source of therapeutic conversation to increasingly direct and effective expression. It should mean that more and more clergy will come to do more and better personal counseling. It should have this effect, but it may not! The net effect of the increased "psychiatric sophistication" of the clergy may be simply that they will reveal a new tendency toward making increasingly frequent referrals to the already overburdened "experts."

It is of the utmost importance that clergymen be sensitized not only to the presence of serious psychological disturbance, which may be occasionally masked by a plea for spiritual guidance, but that they be made equally aware that they have within themselves the potential to render significant help and relief to many of the persons who seek their counsel with strictly secular problems. It would be unfortunate if the tuition of clergymen in the field of mental hygiene were to be so diagnosis-and-pathology oriented that they were simply rendered over-ready to make referrals rather than to accept a basic, appropriate responsibility to render aid.

It is obvious that religious leaders should be among the first to recognize a "philosophical neurosis" and should know that they may have a special expertise in the treatment of this form of pseudo-neurotic disturbance. They should prepare themselves to receive the referrals which, hopefully, psychiatrists and psychologists may be making in increasing numbers. Beyond this, the mental health movement must seek to give the clergy an increasing feeling for the strategic advantage of their special status as suppliers of therapeutic conversation, an increasing sense of the legitimacy of their functioning in this role, and an increasing awareness of their need to take responsibility for their distinctly psychotherapeutic skills over and above their qualities as spiritual leaders.

### VI. THE NEW REPRESSION

In the Victorian Age, we are taught, man was a victim of repression. He was raised and lived in an atmosphere heavy with censor-

* A notable example are the summer courses conducted under the auspices of St. John's University, Collegeville, Minnesota.

ship. Proper behavior was very formally prescribed; the domain of the improper was large and its contents were determined by the silent agreements of parents, of teachers, of preachers, of friends. That which was improper was not talked about and that which was not talked about was improper. Since to speak of certain things was *verboten,* it was difficult to understand (and prohibited to try to understand) why these things were proscribed. Those matters not admitted to discussion were naturally not proper to think upon. But it is a far easier chore to restrain the tongue than to inhibit the thought. And though impulses can be denied labels, or even falsely labeled, as impulses they permit of only one natural translation. Lust may become poetry and prurience may become scholarship, but only so much of libido is translatable. Always there is an irreducible minimum which demands expression (and recognition?)—else a man will be very nervous.

So discovered Freud and so taught Freud. And in his searching examination of the nervous man (and woman) he learned of the tricks and failures of repression. He demonstrated that certain neurotic symptoms represented the partial failures of repression. He helped society to see that sex was what was being repressed in the Victorian culture.

It was Freud's intention to give man a greater freedom (if only by reducing the number of forces and constraints determining his behavior) by enhancing his knowledge of himself as a biological organism.* And the impact of Freudian psychology has been to bring a very perceptible degree of new freedom into at least one aspect of man's functioning. Now it is not only acceptable to have sexual impulses, recognized and labeled as such, but it is allowed to talk about those impulses. We are an unrepressed and liberated culture—at least as regards sex, apparently. We seem to have publicly guiltless freedom of expression concerning sexual matters and even when there are frustrations or malfunctions of sex these are not stringently reserved for the physician's consulting room. Paradoxically, the individual who may by nature be reserved and believe that sex should be a private matter (without necessarily having any unhealthy attitudes toward it) may suffer from the repression of her "prudery"! Is there something repressive about our Freudian liberation?

* While there is much in Freud's biography that reflects tendencies to autocracy and authoritarianism, his argument for the training of lay psychoanalysts bespeaks his greater concern for society than for the welfare of a professional union.[19]

Repression is in essence a *biological* phenomenon—it is psychological only with respect to the content of what is repressed and this is determined largely by the values peculiar to a culture at a particular time. Freud's discovery of the sexual basis of some neuroses and of the techniques for alleviating repression, together with the science of contraception, have served largely to solve the problems of the sex-life of modern man, only to leave him with the problems of his love-life—problems possibly more difficult of solution because they are inaccessible to our technology. It would seem that the sexual freedom which resulted from Freud's lifting of the forces of repression may now be recruited in the repression of our acquired drives to love and to be loved.

It is a further paradox that Freud's efforts to liberate man and to free him from repression should have resulted in the cult of the expert psychotherapist. We have learned to appreciate the pathological effects of repression and to be sensitive to the benefits of emotional ventilation; we have learned that when we are troubled it is good to talk to someone. But the forces of repression have been served by the cultural fallacy that it is good to talk only to a very select group of persons. Now we are confronted by a cultural neurosis so that people who would speak freely of their sex life to even casual acquaintances feel that less "intimate" personal problems, their anxieties, frustrations, conflicts, and confusions must be revealed only in the magic privacy of the psychotherapist's office. The person with a painful and perplexing personal problem is loath to ask a friend to share the knowledge of it, and his friend is loath to encourage him to talk it out.

Reluctance to share one's problems with even a very close friend can be traced not simply to the rise of modern psychiatry and the enhanced public awareness of psychotherapy. The mental health movement has had a definite impact on dissuading individuals from looking to "non-experts" for even passively supportive roles. By emphasizing the activities of mental health specialists and by attributing to the psychiatrist, psychologist or other "expert" a specificity of therapeutic effect (which has thus far not been demonstrated) it has encouraged the notion that the non-expert cannot be truly helpful and, hence, that it is useless to talk with him. Furthermore, the sensitive and help-oriented individual has been led to believe that either by failure to do something specific or, more likely, by virtue of making an inappropriate response he can do serious psychological injury to the friend who "consults" him.*

The long-standing, mutually oriented and mutually respectful friendship provides a relationship with definite potential for the provision of therapeutic conversation. If, as has been suggested in Chapter Five, there are basic processes that are natural to all conversations with therapeutic intent, and if certain of these processes (such as ventilation) may account for a significant portion of the benefits derived, then certainly the benefits of such conversation could be expected from communication with close and respected friends. Everyone could be encouraged to recognize those qualities that contribute to the character of the very special form of "friendship" that exists between psychotherapist and client. If, as there is much reason to believe, it is the character of the relationship that affords much if not most of the therapeutic effect (as distinguished from specifics of the content or management of the conversations) then all thoughtful and sensitive persons could be supported in the effort to provide this kind of relationship, when needed in the context of their natural friendships.

It is pertinent to note that friendships as psychological phenomena have received very little attention as the subject of research. Some investigations have been made of certain of the more obvious demographic and situational determinants of the formation of friendships. There has been remarkably little probing research into the manner in which friendship relationships function in the total psychological economy of the individual.

Perhaps in twentieth-century Western culture there is a general absence of the kind of friendship that could readily provide the relationship required for therapeutic conversation. Certainly there is much evidence of an activity focus rather than relationship focus in our friendships. We have bowling friends, golfing friends, hunting and fishing friends, and drinking friends. Shared interests, cultural or political, athletic or aesthetic, provide the medium of friendship rather than the interdependencies that fostered the close, sharing friendships of older, less urbanized communities. It is possible that the cult of the psychotherapy expert may in itself have

---

* There appears to be a difference between the sexes in degree of reluctance to share worries and anxieties, with women generally more ready than men to ventilate their concerns. With the greater proneness of women to introspection, self-doubt, and conflict, the injunction against "casual therapy" may have more impact on their tendency to seek professional help.[15] This may partly account for the fact that two thirds of psychiatric clinic patients are females.[21]

contributed to the deterioration of the "best friend" and "confidant" relationships.

In any case, it would be well for mental health experts to examine carefully their attitudes toward friendships as potential resources of therapy for the mildly maladjusted. It is a proper part of mental hygiene for the individual to understand the necessity for and functions of friendship, and to be encouraged to look to friends for something more than playful companionship. It may be argued that some neurotics are in the very nature of their illness persons without friends, without effective or satisfying personal relationships, and with a reduced or absent capacity to form sound relationships. This is frequently the case, but it does not alter the need for the therapist to seek as rapidly and effectively as possible to move the patient in the direction of achieving his supplies of affectionate acceptance from the natural reservoir of spontaneous relationships. It seems equally probable that there are many disturbed, conflicted, and unhappy persons who, neither finding nor affording a professional therapist, would experience significant relief by sharing their problems with a trusted friend. It is unfortunate if this avenue of help has been doubly closed by the impact of an injudicious public campaign that has denied the potential therapy of friendships and dissuaded the more thoughtful and sophisticated members of the public from offering the therapy of friendship, while at the same time over-selling the therapeutic power of experts who are in very short supply.

It is not dangerous for people to talk to each other about their problems. The person who shares his perplexities with one close and respected friend is more likely to be helped rather than harmed. If his needs exceed what can be afforded by the therapy of friendship the experience is more likely rather than less likely to encourage him toward expert counsel. The net result of a careful effort to educate the public to the proper and potential role of friendship as a source of therapeutic conversation should be to reduce that part of the case load of the skilled psychotherapists composed of individuals with good natural supplies who are responding to the paradoxically repressive effect of the "cult of the expert."

It is a well accepted part of the operation of many psychiatric clinics that a sizable number of clients are carried in what is commonly designated as *"supportive therapy."* On any scale of evaluation of the potency or value of various types of psychotherapy, most therapists would rate supportive therapy at or close to the bottom; among experts it is not a prestigeful form of therapy. Yet all recognize it as a type of therapist-patient relationship that must be offered and developed with certain patients. In essence, this form of therapy is emotionally supportive. It affords an anchor, a stabilizing, personal point of reference for the patient whose history, symptoms, or attitudes are blocking him from achieving mature and satisfying personal relationships in his natural environment.

Sometimes supportive therapy is undertaken when a patient appears to have achieved maximum response to earlier more intensive treatment procedures (including insight therapy, drugs, and, possibly, hospitalization) but has a residual discomfort that warrants continued contact with the therapist. Sometimes supportive therapy is indicated for the essentially healthy personality that has been disrupted by a sudden situational stress or emotional trauma. Supportive therapy may yield significant benefits to the distressed person who is not motivated (or lacks aptitude) for an intensive, uncovering, interpretive form of therapy.

It is unfortunate that too few therapists seem to be adequately oriented toward supportive psychotherapy as a distinctive type of *therapy*, with specific goals and of reasonably limited duration. For many therapists, supportive therapy is approached as a "continuing relationship therapy" without critical examination of either the appropriateness or necessity of their continuing indefinitely as the patient's sole "support." This uncritical acceptance of a long-term surrogate role may partly reflect the instruction to the supportive therapist to attempt "to win the patient over to a conviction that the therapist is a *helpful friend*." [20] (Italics ours.) It undoubtedly reflects also an implicit assumption that the patient either has no other accessible friendships or is *neurotically* prevented from realizing the emotional support they could afford (rather than simply inhibited by current cultural proscriptions against use of the friendship relationship for anything other than recreational purpose).

Each passive acceptance of a role as long-term surrogate friend seriously reduces the availability of the therapist to contribute his unique professional knowledge or his specific psychotherapeutic talents toward the care of persons with a real need for skilled treatment. It is a particularly serious defect for the supportive therapist to fail to see his responsibility and opportunity to teach and encourage his patient continuously to generalize the "emotional learning" of the therapy relationship to his extra-therapy life, to seek and to find the satisfaction of his emotional needs in the natural supplies of his social world. The passive continuation of a supportive relationship has potential to defeat its very own purpose by encouraging the patient's delusional, derogatory self-concept: "only a therapist could love me!"

It would be hygienic for all therapists and clinics to make an audit at not less than six-month intervals of all patients being carried in supportive therapy to determine: whether there is in fact a therapeutic process entailing more than an emotionally supportive substitute friendship, and whether it is a fact that the patient has no extra-therapy resources for friendship that are psychologically accessible to him. All therapists should be critically sensitive to the recognition of those cases in which they are in essence functioning as no more than culturally accepted "professional friends."

If prostitution be the oldest of professions, is there any pride to be taken in the fact that the sale of friendship may be the commerce of the newest?

# References

1. Ralph Linton, *Culture and Mental Disorder* (Springfield, Illinois: Charles C Thomas, 1956).

2. N. J. Dererath, "Schizophrenia among Primitives," *Amer. J. Psychiat.*, 98 (1942), pp. 703-07.

3. Thomas S. Sasz, "The Myth of Mental Illness," *Amer. Psychol.*, 15 (1960), pp. 113-18.

4. David Ausubel, "Personality Disorder Is Disease," *Amer. Psychol.*, 16 (1961), pp. 69-74.

5. Gregory Zilboorg (with the collaboration of G. W. Henry), *A History of Medical Psychology* (New York: W. W. Norton Co., Inc., 1941), p. 228.

6. Viktor Frankl, *Man's Search for Meaning. An Introduction to Logotherapy* (Boston: Beacon Press, 1962).

7. Rollo May, *The Meaning of Anxiety* (New York: Ronald Press, Co. 1950).

8. Clifford W. Beers, *The Mind That Found Itself* (rev. ed.) (New York: Doubleday & Co., Inc., 1948).

9. The National Committee for Mental Hygiene, *Origin, Objects, and Plans of the National Committee for Mental Hygiene* (New York: 1912).

10. Albert Deutsch, *The Mentally Ill in America. A History of Their Care and*

*Treatment from Colonial Times,* 2nd Edition (New York: Columbia University Press, 1949), Chapter XV.

11. James C. Coleman, *Abnormal Psychology and Modern Life,* 2nd Edition (Chicago: Scott, Foresman and Company, 1956), Chapter 15.

12. Albert Deutsch, *op. cit.,* p. 323.

13. Jerome Frank, *Persuasion and Healing. A Comparative Study of Psychotherapy* (Baltimore: The Johns Hopkins Press, 1961), p. 231.

14. T. L. Engle, "Annual Report of Committee on Communication with High School Teachers," *Agenda and Reports of the Annual Meeting of the American Psychological Association,* New York City, August 28-September 5, 1961 (Washington, D.C.: American Psychological Association, 1961).

15. Gerald Gurin, Joseph Veroff, and Sheila Feld, *Americans View Their Mental Health,* Monograph Series No. 4., Joint Commission on Mental Illness and Health (New York: Basic Books, Inc., 1960) Chapters 9, 10.

16. *Ibid.,* p. 320.

17. Wayne E. Oates, *An Introduction to Pastoral Counseling* (Nashville, Tennessee: Broadman Press, 1959).

18. Richard V. McCann, *The Churches and Mental Health,* Monograph Series No. 8, Joint Commission on Mental Illness and Health (New York: Basic Books, Inc., 1962).

19. Sigmund Freud, *The Problem of Lay-Analysis* (Translated by James Strachey) (New York: Brentano, 1927).

20. Lewis R. Wolberg, *The Technique of Psychotherapy* (New York: Grune & Stratton, Inc., 1954), p. 525.

21. *Outpatient Psychiatric Clinics, Special Statistical Report, 1961. State and Total United States, Demographic and Psychiatric Characteristics of Patients* (Bethesda, Maryland: United States Department of Health, Education, and Welfare; Public Health Service, 1963).

# CHAPTER EIGHT

# Conclusion: A Modest Proposal

## I. SERVICE VERSUS RESEARCH: A CRITICAL CONFLICT

The most visible and acute part of the mental health problem resides in those patients with major psychiatric disorders who require hospitalization. These are the patients who must have the intensive and coordinated services of the most highly trained members of the mental health team—especially of the psychiatrist. If there were no limitations of money or personnel for the treatment of the major forms of psychiatric illness, the effectiveness of the treatment of the psychotic patient would still be sorely restricted by our lack of knowledge about etiology, pathology, and specific avenues of therapeutic action. There is an urgent need for a greatly expanded research endeavor. The design and execution of research into the causes and treatment of major mental illness requires the full-time effort of psychiatrists, psychologists, psychiatric social workers and other mental health personnel. But these highly trained experts are in critically short supply and their potential contribution to research is seriously reduced and in many instances totally blocked by the demand that they provide those clinical services presently thought to be therapeutic. To the extent that circumstances force them into purely service roles they are prevented from generating investigations that could lead to significant changes in the quality or effectiveness of their services. At the present level of our specific technical knowledge it is well to make explicit distinction between programs of custodial management and programs of active treatment. It is totally unjustifiable and a serious social waste of critically restricted resources for the most highly trained of our mental health experts to be encouraged to assign higher priority to their clinical services and a lower priority to their responsibilities as investigators.

As was pointed out in Chapter Five and Chapter Six, a significant (and possibly major) part of the care afforded by the usual psychotherapist is neither specific to nor dependent upon his technical, professional training. Ways must be found to maximize the contribution of the psychiatrist when he is using precisely those skills and knowledges which are unique to his medical training. We must come to recognize the social inefficiency and anachronism represented whenever the psychiatrist spends any sizable portion of his time in therapeutic conversation with individual patients—unless such individual psychotherapy is imbedded in a *true* research endeavor. The same waste is present when the clinical psychologist functions as individual therapist.

The shortage of psychiatrists, psychologists, and social workers in our institutions for severely disturbed personalities (and these include not only mental hospitals but reformatories and prisons as well) is the most easily documented of the mental health manpower problems, but it is possibly exceeded by the critical shortage of these experts in the community where their coordinated efforts have a potential for prevention or effective early treatment that may far exceed the impact of their institutional work. In the setting of the community and an outpatient clientele, the most obvious pressure on the psychiatrist, psychologist, and social worker is to function as individual psychotherapists. But their greatest potential impact would come if they could be freed to function as researchers and consultants, and if there were a reduction of the pressure on them to do psychotherapy.

What are the possible avenues of action whereby we might hope to achieve a more effective utilization of the special skills of the psychiatrist, psychologist, and social worker and broaden their contribution to solution of the mental health problem? Any procedures or developments which would enable them to make greater use of their special aptitudes and lesser use of their nonspecific, shared or common abilities would be helpful. Programs which would reduce the demand upon them to furnish individual psychotherapy and which would diminish their attraction toward this activity would be beneficial.

## II. EXTENDING THE SUPPLY

The principles and practice of group psychotherapy (several patients having a simultaneous session with a single group leader-therapist) have been in existence for some time.[1] This approach to psychological treatment of emotional illness has been continually assigned a secondary role. It has been considered by many authorities to be a desirable adjunct to individual psychotherapy but it has not generally achieved the status and prestige in the eyes either of the professionals or of patients which has been accorded to individual psychotherapy.[2] The general preference for and greater effectiveness presumed for individual therapy is not founded on any rigorous research that has properly compared the relative efficacy of the two approaches. It is quite plausible that such study might demonstrate group methods to be of at least equal potency to individual therapy. Until this is adequately disproved, if it is absolutely incumbent upon psychiatrists and psychologists to do therapy, they would do better to extend their skills to the larger numbers treatable in a group setting. Experts who have had extended experience in individual psychotherapy will have acquired some sensitivities, skills, and insights that can be usefully applied in group therapy. Those persons administratively responsible for the treatment programs of clinics and hospitals should provide increasingly for group approaches to psychotherapy, with a corresponding de-emphasis of the one-to-one therapeutic conversation. Where both forms of treatment are to be offered there should always be provision for careful evaluation of their relative effectiveness in producing significant changes in the patient.

### III. REDUCING THE DEMAND

The problem of critical shortage of expert mental health personnel must be attacked simultaneously on *two* fronts: there must be enhanced effort to recruit and train for the mental health professions, and there must be careful efforts to reduce the demand for their services. In the past it would appear that there has been too exclusive an emphasis upon efforts simply to produce more psychiatrists, more psychologists, and more social workers. There has been a relative inattention to factors which may inflate artificially the demand for the services of these specialists, and too little attention has been paid to the difficult problem of defining a *valid* psychiatric case, *i.e.*, one needing and probably responsive only to the services of a psychiatrist and his professional colleagues.

The data reviewed in Chapter One indicate very little promise for a significant reduction of the shortage in terms of increasing the rate with which our society produces psychiatrists, psychologists, and social workers. Consequently we must be very concerned with the efficiency with which we utilize the talents of these specialists, and we must seek to rectify any influence leading to an inappropriate demand for their services.

Reduction of the demand for the direct services of the mental health professions is possible through at least three channels: education directed toward mental hygiene; public education toward limited and enlightened expectations of these professions; and increased use of "peripheral" resources, such as teachers, clergy, and others.

All of those efforts which are made to develop and maintain the mental hygiene practices of our citizens help to restrain what would otherwise be an ever growing demand for psychiatric services. The role of the family in contributing to emotional stability is a most crucial one and the programs in parent education which are offered under a variety of auspices play a vital role in contributing to sound psychological environments in the home. We would do well to give all possible support to programs in parent education and to resources for parent consultation; we should be particularly concerned to provide programs of parental guidance in those areas and communities in which they are presently lacking. The psychiatrist and psychologist can find especially effective avenues for their services as consultants in clinics or other programs for parent education.

Next to the home, the school provides a universal setting with potential for teaching and demonstrating sound mental hygiene principles. If the schools have been less than optimally effective in this responsibility in the past it is partly because they have been uncertain of the relative priorities of the provision of subject-matter instruction versus the stimulation of the pupil's total personal growth. While the contribution of the individual teacher can occur in a variety of ways, ranging from early detection of emotional distress and referral to provision of "emergency" tension relief and even relationship therapy, the optimal participation of teachers in mental hygiene activities is greatly enhanced in those schools that have provided for formal integration of mental health services, with the consultative assistance of professional workers.[3] Better preparation of teachers for their opportunities, responsibilities, and limitations as mental hygienists can help much to reduce the demand for specifically psychiatric or psychological treatment. Such resources for expert treatment of childhood problems are even more severely restricted than are those for adult patients, and there must be increasing attention to the development of consultative skills—on the part both of teachers and experts.[4]

The potential of the church and the clergy in helping to promote mental health and to render assistance in cases of milder personal maladjustments is presently only partially realized. On the basis of a questionnaire survey it was found that the average clergyman devotes only about two hours per week to personal counseling. Fewer than one out of ten spend as much as ten hours a week in this activity. There is, in light of the readiness of the distressed person to turn to his clergyman, a clear need to augment the preparation of the minister for this activity and to support him in his endeavors to render assistance, especially by giving him access to consultation.

Increasing the effectiveness of our public education toward positive mental health and working toward more effective utilization of the front-line troops in early recognition and treatment of emotional upsets constitute two ways of holding down the always excessive demand for psychiatric help. A third avenue deserving of careful consideration would consist of efforts to educate the public more specifically as to the precise nature of psychiatric treatment, specifically of psychotherapy, to try to lower the public's presently naïve and immodest expectations of what occurs in and what can happen as a result of psychotherapy, and to encourage a proper appreciation for therapeutic conversation. As an important part of this effort, *both* psychotherapists and potential patients should be helped to recognize that there is neither magical cure nor specific expert treatment for the philosophical neuroses.

If all of these methods of reducing the demand for the psychotherapeutic services of psychiatrist, psychologist, and social worker are vigorously pursued, the problem of manpower shortage will be alleviated but not solved. There will still be a fully "legitimate" call for individual psychotherapy exceeding the supply available through the present and future supply of the acknowledged specialists. Is there a rational and socially conscionable answer to this problem?

## IV. BROADENING THE BASE

In 1955, the United States Congress passed the Mental Health Study Act which provided for the establishment of a Joint Commission on Mental Illness and Health. This commission was charged to make a thoroughgoing appraisal of the extent of mental illness, the availability of resources for treatment and research, and the needs for the future. The following statement appears in the commission's final report:[5]

> "Persons who are emotionally disturbed—that is to say, under psychological stress that they cannot tolerate—should have skilled attention and helpful counseling available to them in their community if the development of more serious mental breakdowns is to be prevented. This is known as secondary prevention, and is concerned with the detection of beginning signs and symptoms of mental illness and their relief; in other words, the earliest possible treatment. *In the absence of fully trained psychiatrists, clinical psychologists, psychiatric social workers, and psychiatric nurses, such counseling should be done by persons with some psychological orientation and mental health training and access to expert consultation as needed*" [italics ours].

The Joint Commission recognizes the vital preventive and treatment potential of persons other than the acknowledged "experts." The above statement seems to suggest that it is as an unfortunate artifact of the "absence" of the psychiatrist and his colleagues that the important task of secondary prevention "should" be done by others. It would be more positive and realistic to emphasize that preventive counseling *can be* and *is done* efficiently by the non-experts, that it *must* be done by persons with something other than a stereotyped "full training," and that it is the effectiveness of these invisible therapists that keeps the experts from being completely swamped. It is time to recruit actively the assistance of these people, to encourage positively their important contribution rather than to acknowledge it reluctantly as better than nothing, and to provide reasonable avenues whereby their skills and sophistication may be enhanced.

Exciting empirical support for the feasibility of the Joint Commission's proposal has been generated by an experimental project at the National Institute for Mental Health. Under the direction of an experienced clinical psychologist, a group of mature housewives without previous professional training but with serious interest in mental health work was selected for a two-year program of part-time study and practice of psychotherapy under close supervision. Careful evaluation by three experts of the recorded therapy sessions of these women led to the conclusion that their skills were equal to those of psychiatric residents, analytic institute candidates, and graduate students in clinical psychology. On an objective, written examination in psychiatry prepared by the American Board of Psychiatry and Neurology these women scored above the national average. Upon completion of their training, all were employed in local mental health agencies.[11]

### V. TOWARD MORE EFFICIENT TRAINING

The explicit psychotherapy needs of our population are currently being served primarily by the members of three major professions. No one of these professions trains primarily and emphatically for the practice of psychotherapy. The training of the members of each of these professions is lengthy, expensive, and provides them respectively with unique skills and knowledge which are either irrelevant or at best tangential to the practice of psychotherapy. While there are a variety of schools of psychotherapy, diverse techniques and approaches to therapy, and different theories as to how it works, there is no evidence that the differences in these academic properties are significantly related to differences in the actual effectiveness of the psychotherapies carried out within them. As a matter of fact, the sheer amount of experience in doing therapy appears to be a major determinant of how the therapists think about or conduct therapy. Major differences are found among the least experienced therapists; experienced therapists are more alike in their conceptualizations and practices than they are different.

As yet a very limited amount of practical research has been conducted into this phenomenon. It has not yet been demonstrated to the general satisfaction of behavioral scientists that psychotherapy is in fact effective in relieving neurotic symptoms or achieving major and lasting re-orientation of disturbed personalities. The need for research is great and, in terms of the numbers of persons participating in therapeutic conversations, the opportunities are equally great. But, the highly trained experts who should be devoting major portions of their time to collaborative research are prevented (or dissuaded) from investigation by virtue of the pressure they feel to render those services whose efficacy is as yet uncertain!

If we are going to do more and better research, we have to provide more therapy and at the same time permit our most highly skilled experts to do less direct therapy. Obviously, we need more therapists—and the only logical way we can hope to get them is to develop a more efficient program for training therapists.

In its final report, the Joint Commission makes a half-step toward the recognition of the ideal solution:

> "A host of persons untrained or partially trained in mental health principles and practices—clergymen, family physicians, teachers, probation officers, public health nurses, sheriffs, judges, public welfare workers, scout masters, county farm agents, and others—are already trying to help and to treat the mentally ill in the absence of professional resources. . . . *With a moderate amount of training through short courses and consultation on the job, such persons can be fully equipped with an additional skill as mental health counselors . . ."* [italics ours].[6]

This is a reasonable proposal but it does not make explicit whether it is believed that such "short course" training superimposed on a different basic vocation would make a *psychotherapist.* While the *mental health counselor* could undoubtedly make a valuable contribution in meeting our society's mental health needs, he would not represent an optimal answer to the pressing demand for psychotherapy. The only thoroughly logical answer to that demand, in view of the utter impossibility of its being supplied by the present professions, is to create *a new profession*—to train properly selected persons to function specifically and exclusively as *psychotherapists.*

What would constitute the ideal program of training for the psychotherapist? How should candidates for this training be selected? What personal characteristics should they manifest? No one can say with certainty.[7,8] And it would be a mistake to propose a highly restrictive set of specifications for this new profession, for this would constitute a premature attempt at authoritative rigidification of standards of a kind that is already proving embarrassing to the existing mental health professions. In thinking about selection and training of members for this new profession it would be well to hold clearly in mind what their ultimate function and setting would be: they would work in hospitals, in mental health centers, in child guidance clinics, and in various social agencies where they would be under the general direction of and have continuous consultation with the senior professional staff in psychiatry, psychology, and social work; their primary and exclusive responsibility (except for special work entailed in research collaboration) would be to provide therapeutic conversation.

It is perhaps easier to specify those properties which would *not* be pertinent to their recruitment and training than to list those which would with certainty be applicable. A high level of academic performance would be less critical than substantial evidence of sound general intelligence. Modest intellectual endowment would perhaps prove a more positive qualification than extremely high intelligence. A balanced record of good scholastic achievement coupled with extracurricular interests and a reasonable number of effective social pursuits, including group participations, would probably make for a better candidate than would an outstanding academic record in the absence of nonscholarly interests and pursuits. Evidence of measured social interests and welfare motivations rather than of strong scientific interests and material motives would be pertinent. The young person who had revealed both interests and aptitudes for working effectively with others in personal settings would probably be a good bet. Thus, the person with a record of leadership in school activities, in camping, scouting, boys' clubs or girls' clubs, settlement house or other volunteer service activities would reveal some promise for effective response to training toward a personal service career.

Ideally, in the interests of a total educational program that would prepare for early entry and effective functioning in a professional role, the recruitment process should begin in high school. Potential psychotherapists should be encouraged as junior and senior high school students to become familiar with the field of mental health, the problems of mental illness, and the nature of the resources used in combating emotional disorder. They should have opportunity for field trips to hospitals and mental health clinics. They should be able to hear at first hand about the work of the psychiatrist, psychologist, and social worker, and they should be given an overview of the problems and challenges of psychotherapy. Ideally, as seniors, they should be able to elect introductory courses in general human psychology and in sociology.

Their undergraduate college work (perhaps leading to a bachelor's degree in psychology, sociology, social work, educational psychology, or possibly anthropology) should provide them with an orientation to the range and variety of individual differences in mental ability, personality, and subcultural memberships. They should study developmental and child psychology. They should be exposed to the general facts concerning the physiology and psychology of emotion. They should learn about attitudes, their determinants, and their effects. They should study the laws of habit forming and habit breaking. They should learn something about the forms of mental illness and the theories of etiology and psychopathology. They should be introduced to the principles and techniques of interviewing, and the problems of person-to-person communication. During their first two years they should be encouraged and assisted in finding opportunity to function as volunteer-workers in some community social agency; hopefully in this context, they would have opportunity to observe experienced workers in a variety of therapeutic conversations. Not later than their senior year they should have a formal course in psychotherapy which should include opportunity to hear taped interviews by skilled therapists.*

If their undergraduate record was sound and they showed general aptitude for the field, they could then be screened for admission to an intensive one-to-two year graduate course in psychotherapy. Not over half of this graduate curriculum should be didactic. Assigned readings in a tutorial context and seminars could be designed to broaden their knowledge of psychodynamic theory, current psychiatric nosology and therapeutics, and patterns of state and federal programs in the mental health area. Through these media they would become acquainted with the general professional practices and contributions of psychiatrist, psychologist, and social worker.

At least half of their graduate training should entail closely supervised field-work experiences in a variety of in-patient and out-patient settings. Much of this would be devoted to direct observation of the total therapeutic program, including individual and group psychotherapy, as conducted by experienced professional staff. At the end of their formal training, they would receive degrees as graduate specialists in personal counseling and be ready for full-time employment in a fully staffed clinic or hospital.†

The Joint Commission has recommended that the mental health professions "launch a national manpower recruitment and training program." [9] Such a recruitment endeavor would be more likely to

* With this much concentration on psychological subjects there would naturally be reduced time for study in other liberal arts and sciences; specifically the undergraduate student preparing for a career as a psychotherapist would take fewer courses in mathematics, history, and foreign languages.

† Again, it is pertinent to ask what the psychotherapist will not have studied. He is likely to have dispensed with courses in statistics, research methodology, community organization, social pathology, psychoanalytic theory (per se), psychometric theory, anatomy, and comparable "core" courses in the curricula of the three professional therapists we now recognize.

meet with success if it were directed toward high school students, who could be encouraged to consider a service career in the field of mental health for which graduate preparation would not be excessively long. Many persons who entered upon professional work as psychotherapists might subsequently be attracted toward further study and preparation in one of the existing mental health professions. Thus, the specialty of psychotherapy, as a new profession, would provide an "entry" occupation for the established professions and contribute positively to the recruitment endeavor.

The successful planning and instrumentation of a new curriculum toward the specific training of psychotherapist-specialists would demand the wholehearted sympathies, energies, and integrated collaboration of medicine, education, and the community. Obviously psychiatry, psychology, and social work should contribute to the training program. The assistance of community agencies would be required in providing not only the critical field experiences of the graduate program but in offering suitable appointments to the graduates. With respect for the recent and continuing professional antagonisms, especially those between psychiatry and psychology, the proposal that they might see fit to join forces in the creation of a new (and potentially threatening?) profession may seem to be the kind of romantic nonsense that only an impractical, idealistic professor could dream up. But the course of history suggests that social needs are inexorable, in spite of the slowness with which they are met.

In the absence of certain knowledge of what may prove to be the best possible programs for selection and training of psychotherapists, it is fortunate that throughout the country there are a number of universities and medical schools so situated with respect to each other and to large metropolitan complexes of ideal field training resources that it is possible for a variety of professional curricula to be evolved. There is opportunity for imaginative exploration of a variety of training patterns. The results of such programs, measured in terms of the efficiency of recruitment of trainees and of their effectiveness as therapists, would have to be carefully evaluated. Such evaluation might lead to an eventual relative standardization of training for psychotherapists (as it has for the present mental health professions); it might also lead to the finding of a real social need for a variety of therapists having different emphases in their preparation.

The thesis of this volume has been that there is a great and growing social need which is presently being inadequately and inefficiently met by the limited resources of three quite different professions. As psychiatry, psychology, and social work have tried to contribute directly to the demand for psychotherapy they have suffered serious dilution of their basic and unique contributions. When prolonged individual psychotherapy is involved, the psychiatrist is perjuring medicine, the psychologist is failing what should be his basic commitment to research, and the social worker is being asocial.[10]

If these disciplines will take joint initiative toward the creation of a new, socially efficient and socially responsive profession they will maintain proper consultative authority for that profession, they will help to meet the social need, and they will create the means whereby they may be freed for intensified, specialized efforts in accordance with their respective, unique and interdependent skills —to the end that we may gain better understanding, better treatment, and better prevention of mental suffering.

# References

1. S. R. Slavson, *The Practice of Group Therapy* (New York: International Universities Press, 1947).

2. Lewis R. Wolberg, *The Technique of Psychotherapy* (New York: Grune & Stratton, Inc., 1954).

3. W. Allinsmith and G. W. Goethals, *The Role of Schools in Mental Health*. Monograph Series No. 7. Joint Commission on Mental Illness and Health (New York: Basic Books, Inc., 1954).

4. R. Robinson, D. F. De Marche, and M. K. Wagle, *Community Resources in Mental Health* (New York: Basic Books, Inc., 1960).

5. Final Report of the Joint Commission on Mental Illness and Health, *Action for Mental Health* (New York: Basic Books, Inc., 1961), p. 256.

6. *Ibid.*, p. xii.

7. Robert R. Holt and Lester Luborsky, *Personality Patterns of Psychiatrists*. Vol. I. Menninger Clinic Monograph Series No. 13 (New York: Basic Books, Inc., 1958), Chapter 15.

8. Nicholas P. Dallis and Herbert K. Stone (editors), *The Training of Psychotherapists—A Multidisciplinary Approach* (Baton Rouge: Louisiana State University Press, 1960).

9. Final Report of the Joint Commission on Mental Illness and Health, *Action for Mental Health* (New York: Basic Books, Inc., 1961), p. 252.

10. William Schofield, "Logistics in Professional Psychology," In *Manpower and Psychology: Proceedings of a Workshop.* Sponsored by Northeast States Governments Conference on Mental Health, New Jersey Department of Institutions and Agencies and National Institute of Mental Health (U.S. Dept. of Health, Education and Welfare, August, 1963).

11. Margaret J. Rioch, Charmian Elkes, Arden A. Flint, Blanche S. Usdansky, Ruth G. Newman, and Earle Silber, "National Institute of Mental Health Pilot Study in Training Mental Health Counselors," *Amer. J. Orthopsychiat.*, 1963, XXXIII, 4, pp. 678-689.

# Appendix

In addition to psychiatry, two other professions play major roles in meeting the demands for mental health services: clinical psychology and psychiatric social work. With both of these professions, also, demand considerably exceeds supply. In 1957, it was estimated that there was a national need for 10,000 psychologists in addition to those already employed.[1] In that year, there were 15,545 members of the American Psychological Association; in the ensuing five years, membership in the Association has increased by slightly over 1,500 members. In 1962, of the total membership only 2,577 were in the Division of Clinical Psychology, which encompasses a majority of the members who are in activities (teaching, research, or clinical work) related to mental health.[2] In 1953, the Veterans Administration estimated that it had a shortage of 800 psychologists; in the following year, 100 trainees completed their graduate programs and accepted V. A. appointments.[3] At the present time, only about 1,000 doctoral (Ph.D.) degrees are awarded annually in *all* fields of psychology.[4,5]

As of 1957, there were less than 3,000 fully trained psychiatric social workers in the United States. On a state basis, these yielded ratios of worker to population ranging from at best 1/78,000 and, at worst, 1/318,000.[6] A survey of the needs of public mental hospitals in 1957 indicated a shortage of nearly 3,000 social workers for these institutions alone.[7] A total of less than 3,000 students each year are completing graduate study in schools of social work.[8]

# References

1. G. W. Albee and Marguerite Dickey, "Manpower Trends in Three Mental Health Professions," *Amer. Psychol.*, 12 (1957), pp. 57-70.

2. *1962 Directory*. American Psychological Association (Washington, D.C.: 1962).

3. Report by the Health Resources Advisory Committee, *Mobilization and Health Manpower II* (Washington, D.C.: U.S. Government Printing Office, January, 1956).

4. D. Wolfle, *America's Resources of Specialized Talent* (New York: Harper & Row, Publishers, 1954).

5. W. Schofield, *"Logistics in Professional Psychology." Manpower and Psychology: Proceedings of a Workshop.* Sponsored by Northeast States Governments Conference on Mental Health, New Jersey Department of Institutions and Agencies, and National Institute for Mental Health. (U.S. Dept. of Health, Education and Welfare, August, 1963).

6. George W. Albee, *Mental Health Manpower Trends*, Monograph Series No. 3, Joint Commission on Mental Illness and Health (New York: Basic Books, Inc., 1959).

7. Changes in Number of Personnel, Public Mental Hospitals, 1956-59. *Fact Sheet*, No. 16. Joint Information Service, American Psychiatric Association and National Association for Mental Health, September, 1961.

8. George W. Albee, *op. cit.*, p. 335.

# Index